ASPECTS OF ACCOUNT
IN THE
BRITISH SYSTEM OF GOVERNMENT

ASPECTS OF ACCOUNTABILITY
IN THE
BRITISH SYSTEM OF GOVERNMENT

Edited by

ROBERT PYPER

TUDOR

© R. Pyper 1996

This version first published in Great Britain by Tudor Business
Publishing Limited.

A CIP catalogue record for this book is available from the British Library

ISBN 1 872807 66 6

Typeset by Deltatype Ltd, Ellesmere Port, Cheshire
Printed and bound by Athenaeum Press, Ltd.,
Gateshead, Tyne & Wear.

Contents

Notes on Contributors

ALLAN BRUCE is a Lecturer in Public Administration at Glasgow Caledonian University. His research interests are in the funding and delivery of health care, and he has written a number of articles focusing upon key aspects of the NHS.

PETER FALCONER is a Lecturer in Public Administration at Glasgow Caledonian University. He is co-author of *Local Government Charges: Policy and Practice* and has published articles on aspects of United States politics. He is currently conducting research into charging for public services, and is writing a book on Congressional Oversight in the United States.

ALLAN McCONNELL is a Lecturer in Public Administration at Glasgow Caledonian University. He is the author of *State Policy Formation and the Origins of the Poll Tax* and is currently working on a book entitled *The Politics and Policy of Local Taxation in Britain*. He has also published numerous articles on aspects of central and local government in the UK.

AIDAN ODONNELL is a Lecturer in Law at Glasgow Caledonian University. He is the co-author of *Scottish Business Law: Text, Cases and Materials*, co-author of *Employment Contracts: Managing the New Agenda* and of *Sale and Supply of Goods*. He is joint editor of *Green's Business Law Bulletin* and has contributed to *The Laws of Scotland: Stair Memorial Encyclopaedia*.

ROBERT PYPER is Reader in Public Administration at Glasgow Caledonian University. He is the author of *The Evolving Civil Service*, and *The British Civil Service*, joint editor of *Britain's Changing Party System* and *Governing the UK in the 1990s*, and he has written numerous articles on aspects of UK government.

Preface

The issues and debates surrounding accountability in the British system of government have been of interest to me for a considerable period of time. My Ph D thesis concerned the doctrine of individual ministerial responsibility with particular reference to changing aspects of Parliamentary accountability. In the years since completion of my doctoral research, I have been given the opportunity to develop this interest in accountability, both in the context of research projects and publications, and in relation to my teaching.

Accountability at all levels of the British polity now looms larger and larger as an issue in its own right. Fundamental questions are asked, with increasing frequency, about the relative responsibility of ministers and civil servants in central government, the adequacy of Parliament as a means of securing accountability and redress of grievances, and the efficacy of "popular" extra-Parliamentary channels of accountability. Further questions are raised with regard to the place of legal and quasi-legal methods in the system of accountability, the appropriateness of charters as guarantors of citizens' rights, and the problems associated with securing accountability in the NHS, local government and the former public utilities.

This book represents an attempt to provide those whose teaching and research impinges upon such themes and issues with an insight into the functioning of, and debates surrounding, accountability in Britain today. The idea for the book stemmed from my own interests, and from the frustration I felt when attempting, unsuccessfully, to find a single text which might serve as a point of departure for my Honours students who were studying systems of accountability and control in the British public sector. Neil Fuller, of Tudor Business Publishing, showed great faith in the project from the outset, and I was able to persuade a number of my colleagues in the Department of Law and Public Administration at Glasgow Caledonian University to contribute chapters within their own specialist fields.

I am grateful to Neil Fuller for the patience he has shown in waiting for the book to take shape. Thanks are also due to the contributors, who stuck to their respective remits, and delivered on schedule. Naturally, I must be held fully accountable for any perceived failings in this enterprise. A final word of thanks is due to my wife, Elinor, and my children, Emma and Michael, who continue to put up with an irritable and distracted member of the household, apparently (but not really!) more interested in the word-processor in the study than in the pleasures of family life.

Introduction

THE PARAMETERS OF ACCOUNTABILITY

Robert Pyper

> Accountability is an enduring value not only in government but in society generally. Indeed, accountability is often treated as an ethical principle, that is, as a rule which provides a guide for ethical behaviour. Individuals have a deep personal interest in ensuring that those persons who exercise authority over them, whether they be corporate leaders, union leaders, medical professionals, or public servants, are held to account for the exercise of that authority. Those who exercise such authority are well advised to consider the importance of accountability from behind a "veil of ignorance." If they didn't know what their position in life was going to be, what measure of accountability would they deem appropriate? (Kernaghan and Langford, 1990: 160).

Kenneth Kernaghan and John Langford identify the virtually intangible, and strongly ethical, flavour of accountability which lies at the heart of the concept's attraction. They also uncover the implicit desire for effective and functioning lines of accountability on the part of those who are the recipients of services, the clients and customers, and those who work at the lower levels of administrative hierarchies.

In its very broadest sense, the concept of accountability is often used as a basic benchmark against which systems of government can be judged. Accountable government is deemed to be good government, and carries with it connotations of advanced democracy. Governments which can be characterised as unaccountable or not properly accountable are likely to provide fertile ground for the cultivation of authoritarianism, totalitarianism and every type of abuse of power.

However, to describe accountability in these terms takes us only so far (and not very far at that!) along the path to understanding. Accountability is a complex, elusive and multi-faceted concept. It does not lend itself to neat, self-contained definitions, although this has not prevented the proliferation of these.

To a considerable extent, our understanding of accountability may be affected by the initial perspective we adopt. Thus, for example, we might choose to view accountability in terms of the nature of the tasks and duties undertaken by those in government. In broad terms, these could encompass policy work, administrative or managerial duties, and service delivery or implementation of policy. This type of "top-down" perspective may lead us to a particular interpretation of the meaning and functioning of accountability. Alternatively, we might view accountability, utilising a kind of "bottom-up" approach, in terms of the work carried out by various agents or agencies of accountability. Here, the starting point for analysis would be the functioning of *inter alia* Parliament, the courts, regulatory bodies, professional organisations, and the inchoate generality of "the public" as consumers and clients of services. A further possible perspective might be gained through viewing accountability in terms of process: the provision of information, answering of questions, acceptance of blame in cases of error, and the imposition of sanctions of various types.

Arguably, the adoption of one of these perspectives without paying due recognition to the others is likely to produce a partial, and perhaps misleading, picture of accountability. If we are to come to terms with the concept we must be prepared to adopt a wide, all-encompassing perspective. One way in which this might be done is to consider a series of key questions.

It can already be seen that, when utilising the word accountability in the context of government, we raise a series of general questions which must be answered (at least in part) if we are to discern the parameters of the concept:

- accountable for what?
- accountable to whom?
- accountable through which mechanisms?
- is accountability synonymous with answerability?
- is there a tension or a contradiction between accountability and other imperatives, such as efficiency or state security?

Let us attempt to shed some light on the concept of accountability by looking in turn at these key questions.

Accountable for What?

Andrew Gray and William Jenkins link the concept of accountability with responsibilities (of the type we will later define as "role responsibilities") and stewardship.

> To be accountable is to be liable to present an account of, and answer for, the execution of responsibilities to those entrusting those responsibilities. Thus accountability is intrinsically linked to *stewardship*.
> (Gray and Jenkins, 1985: 138).

Stewardship involves the delegation by a principal (who may be an individual, or a collective entity) of a set of duties or functions, perhaps accompanied by material and financial resources, to a steward.

In the context of British government, it is possible to view stewardship in a broad, all-encompassing manner. Thus, Dawn Oliver argues that the liberal-democratic tradition in this country is for the institutions of the state to be entrusted with, and held accountable for, " . . . their stewardship of the public interest" (Oliver, 1991: 23). This raises a number of questions, not the least important of which is: what, precisely, is the nature of this stewardship – beyond the vague notion of "the public interest", for what are the stewards held accountable?

Let us take a step back, to look again at the "responsibilities" to which Gray and Jenkins refer. Stewards are said to be accountable for the discharge of their responsibilities. This theme can be discerned in the writings of numerous authors. For example, Ian Thynne and John Goldring describe the responsibility of ministers and civil servants for " . . . doing certain things, or performing certain acts, which attach to the positions they occupy within the governmental system." (Thynne and Goldring, 1981: 199). In the same vein, H. L. A. Hart set out the concept of "role responsibility":

> . . . whenever a person occupies a distinctive place or office in a social organisation to which specific duties are attached . . . he is properly said to be responsible for the performance of these duties or for doing what is necessary to fulfil them. Such duties are a person's responsibilities.
> (Hart, 1968: 212).

Rather confusingly, Thynne, Goldring and Hart conflate two distinct meanings of "responsibility": the first meaning (" . . . to be responsible for . . .") corresponds with the concept of accountability. However, the second meaning, which refers to the specific duties associated with an individual's post or office, is suitably described, by Hart, as "role responsibility".

What is the nature of this role responsibility in the context of British government? Let us take the examples of ministers of the Crown, and their departmental civil servants. In the broadest terms, we can say that government ministers have basic role responsibilities for:

- policy leadership within their departments
- managing departments
- piloting legislation through its successive parliamentary stages.
- representing departmental interests in Cabinet, with pressure groups, and with departmental clients.

Taken together, these are the areas of responsibility generally associated with the role of a government minister. (For a full discussion, see Pyper, 1987: 51–57). These are the matters for which ministers can be said to be accountable. The precise nature and extent of this accountability are moot points, which will be discussed at appropriate points in the course of this book.

Depending upon their precise location within government departments or executive agencies, the fundamental role responsibilities of civil servants could be said to cover:

- providing policy advice to ministers;
- the administration or implementation of policy;
- departmental or agency management.

Again, these are the broad spheres of work for which civil servants are accountable (for a full discussion, see Pyper, 1987: 60–63).

It can be argued that elected office-holders and officials are accountable not only for the performance of certain functions which are connected with specific duties but also for conducting themselves in accordance with the laws of the land, and with respect for the quasi-legal, or even moral, codes of their peers (Pyper, 1987: 48–51; 58–60). These can be considered to be personal responsibilities, which are reasonably distinct from role responsibilities. This can be illustrated with reference to our previous exemplars, government ministers and civil servants.

Ministers share with their fellow citizens the need to obey the law in their personal lives. It might be argued that this responsibility is likely to come under greater scrutiny in the case of ministers, as a consequence of their high public profile: any misdemeanour will be sure to attract considerable publicity. Beyond this, ministers share with their fellow MPs the need to abide by the rules and conventions of Parliament. Finally, as ministers, they are subject to a further set of rules of conduct, most of which are now published as "Questions of Procedure for Ministers". Less tangibly, and beyond the realms of statute and codified rules, ministers are expected to act in accordance with an unwritten, moral code. There is no shortage of examples of ministers coming unstuck, not because they have broken the law, or parliamentary or ministerial rules, but because their personal behaviour offended against this unwritten code.

Civil servants' personal responsibilities can also be said to begin with the need to obey the laws of the land as private citizens. Beyond this, they are extended through the rules set out in the Civil Service Management Code and departmental and agency handbooks. These documents delineate the restrictions which apply to civil servants in relation to political activities; the acceptance of gifts, rewards, awards and prizes; the procedures for reporting bankruptcy, insolvency, arrests or convictions; and the holding of shares or directorships.

In brief, our argument is that basic information about the matters for which the relevant political and official actors are accountable – their role and personal responsibilities – is a vital key to understanding accountability in the British system of government.

Accountable to Whom?
One way of looking at this question is to consider the numerous agents and agencies to which, or through which, political and official actors might be considered to be accountable. Thus, government ministers can be said to be accountable to:

- their ministerial colleagues in general, and the prime minister in particular;
- the wider party, both at Westminster and out in the country;
- "the people", via their Parliamentary representatives.

Short catalogues of this kind can be compiled in relation to civil servants, local government members and officers, and the members and officers of Health Boards and Trusts. While this sort of information may be useful, it often produces a need for further classification. However, it should be recognized that attempts to move beyond a fundamentally descriptive approach do not necessarily lead to comprehensive analytical models or watertight categorizations.

A common first step, taken by those who wish to move beyond the simple listing of sources of accountability, is to identify dual, internal and external lines of accountability, as a means of differentiating between two broad categories of agents of accountability. External accountability is in evidence when individuals or bodies beyond the confines of the governmental organization play a part in securing accountability. Ministers are accountable for the work of their departments, beyond the confines of the government machine itself, to Parliament. The financial accountability of local authorities and the National Health Service is secured through the work of external auditors, under the auspices of the Audit Commission and the Accounts Commission in Scotland. Internal accountability operates concurrently with external. This form can be illustrated with reference to the civil servant's accountability to departmental or agency line managers, up to the permanent secretary and/or agency chief executive, and to ministers.

Beyond these broad categories, some observers attempt to construct slightly more sophisticated models, designed to further classify the various sources of accountability. Howard Elcock posits a directional model, which speaks of accountability upwards, outwards, and downwards (Elcock, 1991: 162). Superficially attractive, the limitations of Elcock's model become clear on detailed examination. Elcock makes it clear that he intends the model to apply primarily to the accountability of officials, who may be "simultaneously accountable *upwards*, ultimately to politicians, *outwards* to professional colleagues and *downwards* to citizens." (Elcock, 1991: 162).

By leaving politicians out of the analysis, Elcock simplifies matters (apart from anything else, would the accountability of government ministers to Parliament best be characterized as *upward*, *outward*, or *downward?*) but he also omits a key element of public sector accountability. However, even in the limited context of official accountability, there must be serious doubt about the extent to which this type of directional model is helpful. To say that officials are, or even may be, accountable "*downwards* to citizens" can only be taken to be an aspiration, since such a statement flies in the face of formal constitutional practice in Britain. The conditions of service which apply to civil servants specifically preclude the concept of accountability to Parliament (except in limited, and very carefully defined circumstances) or the people.

A more conventional approach to the problem of developing a typology of accountability is adopted by Lawton and Rose (1991; 23). They cite five strains of accountability: political, managerial, legal, consumer, and professional. For example, political accountability, often referred to as Parliamentary accountability, encompasses the twin doctrines of ministerial responsibility (individual and collective). Lists of this kind, although useful up to a point, tend to suffer from two flaws. First, by carefully differentiating types of accountability, it can be tempting to minimise the possibility of conflict and overlap between types. At any given time, a local government officer might experience the conflicting pull of accountability to customers and clients for the effective delivery of a particular service, and to senior managers for tight budgetary control. If the two strands are viewed in isolation, this kind of conflict may be ignored. Second, each list is open to the criticism that something has been omitted. In the case of Lawton and Rose, the omission of an explicitly ethical or moral dimension has been noted by subsequent commentators (Hinton and Wilson, 1993: 129).

In brief, it can be said that the question of accountability *to whom* is rarely susceptible to a clear and straightforward answer. The simplest approach runs the risk of being narrowly descriptive, while attempts to construct analytical models of varying degrees of complexity tend to be dashed on the rock of exclusivity. This is not to deny the need for the question to be asked in relation to all of the key actors in each element of the British polity.

Accountability Through Which Mechanisms?
Closely associated with the question of accountable *to whom*, is the matter of channels or mechanisms of accountability. Through which mechanisms can accountability be secured? In the real world of British government, an extremely diverse range of devices operate at different points in the system. Three broad categories can be established in order to bring some kind of order to this issue.

The first category relates to an array of mechanisms which are specifically focused on the need to secure the accountability of officials (including civil servants and local government officers) to their administrative superiors. These mechanisms would include systems of performance appraisal and review, which identify key indicators, against which the general and specific performance of officials can be judged. Such systems conventionally function as elements of line management processes and procedures. Mechanisms which are clearly tailored to the requirements of internal financial accountability and control include delegated budgetary systems, which combine the decentralization of financial authority to designated cost centres with specified reporting and control procedures.

The second category comprises mechanisms which relate primarily to politicians, although in some respects officials may be indirectly affected by their operation. The most attenuated of these mechanisms are elections, in theory the purest form of democratic accountability, but in practical terms often susceptible to such a range of party-political considerations that the true strength of accountability becomes substantially diluted. Questions directed to political office-holders, debates designed to elicit ministerial (and equivalent) responses and the scrutiny exerted by both legislative and investigatory committees, all come within the ambit of this category. There are some significant differences between the manner in which such mechanisms function in the worlds of central and local government, which should be briefly noted. For example, the partial executive nature of local authority committees serves to blur the distinction between the policy-making and scrutineering functions, and there are no direct local government equivalents of Parliamentary standing and select committees.

Finally, there are intermediate mechanisms of accountability, which are likely to be focused on the ultimate accountability of political office-holders, while bringing scrutiny to bear on the day-to-day activities of officials. Such mechanisms would include the Parliamentary, health service and local government ombudsmen, the agencies of external financial audit (the Audit and Accounts Commissions), and the plethora of regulatory agencies covering the activities of public utilities.

Is Accountability Synonymous With Answerability?

In the process of mapping out the broad parameters of accountability, we must be prepared to address the often confusing issue of terminology. As we have already seen, there are certain benefits to be derived from drawing distinctions between "responsibility" and "accountability", if only in order to be able to identify the matters for which politicians and officials are to be held accountable. However, there is a further, potentially knotty, definitional problem to be addressed. Is it possible to differentiate between the usage of "accountability" and "answerability" in the context of British government?

Some social scientists, including H. L. A. Hart (1968; 264–265) and Avery Leiserson (1964), have based their arguments on etymology. Since the original meaning of the word "answer" was not limited to the mere answering of questions, but also conveyed the concept of "answering" or rebutting accusations which, if established in fact, carried liability to sanctions, it is possible to argue that "answerability" is synonymous with "accountability". However, other observers favour drawing a distinction between the two concepts. David Butler (1973) has argued that "answerability" involves nothing more than a commitment to answer questions. Thus, office-holders (political and official) have a commitment to answer questions in connection with their duties, without admitting to any liability for matters which may have gone wrong. Geoffrey Marshall has used the phrase "explanatory accountability" in this context (Marshall, 1986: 78). According to these interpretations, "accountability" is a stronger concept, the practical manifestation of which goes beyond a mere duty to provide answers, and connotes the possibility of sanctions being invoked in cases where the answers are unsatisfactory or problematic.

As we shall see in due course, when we come to examine the parliamentary dimension of accountability, this distinction between "answerability" or "explanatory accountability", and "accountability" *per se* is a feature (and, it might be argued, an increasingly prominent feature) of the operation of British government. A further point worth making at this stage is that "accountability", unlike "answerability" or "explanatory accountability" would seem to imply, at least in theory, a preparedness to deliver redress of grievances in cases of proven error.

If we accept that accountability implies the existence of sanctions, we must take into account the role of the controlling agent or sanctions-holder. It is important to stress that not all agents or agencies of accountability are effective sanctions-holders. Thus, although government ministers are accountable to Parliament, and may be faced with the prospect of sanctions being imposed upon them if they fail to properly discharge their responsibilities to Parliament, this is not to say that Parliament will normally be in a position to invoke the sanctions. For ministers, the effective sanctions-holder is the Prime Minister, in whose power it lies to displace, demote or dismiss ministerial miscreants. Similarly, although civil servants are ultimately accountable to their ministers, the effective sanctions-holders are their own civil service superiors, who may impose formal reprimands, financial penalties, demotion or dismissal.

Accountability Versus Other Imperatives

Lauded though it may be in democratic theory, the concept of accountability frequently raises practical and political problems when other imperatives enter the scene. This can be illustrated in a very basic fashion with reference to the practice of government departments refusing to supply answers to Members of Parliament on the grounds that disproportionate financial costs would be incurred, or state security imperilled.

At every level of the system of government, there may be tensions or contradictions between the demands of accountability on the one hand, and efficiency, economy or security on the other. As local councils transform themselves from service providers on a wide scale, to enabling authorities which effectively sub-contract many service delivery functions to voluntary agencies or private enterprises, fundamental questions arise regarding accountability. Are the new service providers directly accountable to the customers, clients, and/or tax-payers? Alternatively, do the lines of accountability run via the local authorities? If the latter, what mechanisms are being put in place in order to secure effective and rigorous accountability? In specific terms, for what are the new service-providers to be held accountable? These, and other questions can equally be posed in relation to the new regimes of contract and market in the health service, and the plethora of executive agencies within the civil service. The fundamental point is that the relative importance (relative to "Value for Money", for example) attached to accountability within elements of the new public management is occasionally less than clear.

The marked, and increasing, tendency for government in Britain to resort to quangos as mechanisms of policy formation and execution, raises the same issue in a slightly different form. What price accountability when political convenience is at stake?

There may be greater room for optimism in relation to matters of security. At the national level, the Major Government has certainly taken steps to open up the security services to greater scrutiny, and it may be possible at some future stage to say with confidence that the security services are accountable to Parliament, in general and specific terms. We are not yet at that stage, however, and while the Official Secrets Acts still hover above the system of government, some degree of tension between accountability and security is likely to remain.

We shall return to these themes in the concluding part of the book, when the question of the limits of accountability in the British system of government will be addressed.

The Book

From the foregoing, it will be clear that the concept of accountability does not lend itself to simple answers and broad generalizations. Notwithstanding this, an attempt has been made to sketch out the rough parameters of accountability, in terms of the fundamental questions it raises in a governing context. Many of these questions and themes will recur, in different forms, throughout the book.

The purpose of this book is to offer an analysis of aspects of accountability within the British system of government. The chapter topics have been selected in order to provide wide coverage of areas of government and forms of accountability. The contributors have not been whipped into line behind a particular definition of accountability. They have been invited to develop their own perspectives, and apply these to their own topics while utilising apposite case studies and illustrative examples.

The book begins with Allan McConnell's analysis of the strengths and limitations of popular accountability in the British polity. Robert Pyper examines parliamentary accountability in its traditional and more modern forms in Chapter Two, before Aidan ODonnell provides an exploration of legal and quasi-legal forms of accountability. The operation of internal and external systems of accountability in local government and the National Health Service is charted and analysed by Allan Bruce and Allan McConnell in Chapter Four. The problems and challenges associated with accountability in the public utilities are examined by Robert Pyper in Chapter Five. Peter Falconer turns his attention to the increasingly topical issues of charterism and consumerism, and investigates the links between these and true accountability. In the concluding chapter, Robert Pyper discusses the various limits on effective accountability in Britain.

References

Butler, David (1973), "Ministerial Responsibility in Australia and Britain", *Parliamentary Affairs*, Volume 26, Number 4, 1973.

Elcock, Howard (1991), *Change and Decay? Public Administration in the 1990s*, Harlow: Longman.

Gray, Andrew and Jenkins, William I. (1985), *Administrative Politics in British Government*, Brighton: Wheatsheaf.

Hart, H. L. A. (1968), *Punishment and Responsibility*, Oxford: Clarendon.

Hinton, Peter and Wilson, Elisabeth (1993), "Accountability" in Wilson, John and Hinton, Peter, *Public Services in the 1990s*, Sevenoaks: Tudor.

Kernaghan, Kenneth and Langford, John W. (1990), *The Responsible Public Servant*, Halifax, Nova Scotia: The Institute for Research on Public Policy and the Institute of Public Administration of Canada.

Lawton, Alan and Rose, Aidan (1991), *Organisation and Management in the Public Sector*, London: Pitman.

Leiserson, Avery (1964), "Responsibility", in Gould, J. and Kolb, W. L. (eds), *A Dictionary of the Social Sciences*, London: Tavistock.

Marshall, Geoffrey (1986), *Constitutional Conventions. The Rules and Forms of Political Accountability*, Oxford: Clarendon.

Oliver, Dawn (1991), *Government in the United Kingdom. The Search for Accountability, Effectiveness and Citizenship*, Buckingham: Open University Press.

Pyper, Robert (1987), *The Doctrine of Individual Ministerial Responsibility in British Government: Theory and Practice in a New Regime of Parliamentary Accountability*, Leicester: University of Leicester Ph D Thesis.

Thynne, Ian and Goldring, John (1981), "Government 'Responsibility' and Responsible Government", *Politics (Australia)*, Volume 16, Number 2.

1

POPULAR ACCOUNTABILITY

Allan McConnell

Introduction

Subsequent chapters in this book will deal with a number of specific means by which different branches of the British system of government may be held accountable to the people. These encompass the range of devices at the parliamentary level, including Questions, debates standing and select committees (Chapter Two), through to the contemporary emergence of the Citizen's Charter and its attempt to ensure that consumers of public services are able to hold to account the providers of these services (Chapter Six). We must complement our study of all this, however, by recognising that there is a wider "democratic" context. This can be linked to accountability via the suggestion of Dahl (1971: 4) that the term "democracy" be reserved for "a political system one of the characteristics of which is the quality of being completely or almost completely responsive to all its citizens." This means that the capacity of the people to hold government to account is also possible through wider mechanisms which are intrinsic to the liberal democratic nature of the British political system and the spreading of political power therein. Logically, therefore, we are led to considering the roles of elections, competing political parties, pressure groups and the media, and the way in which these allow (and do not allow) the people to hold government to account.

The purpose of this chapter is to explore such matters in greater depth, but in order to do so we need to be quite clear what we mean when we talk of "accountability" in this context. Notwithstanding the comments contained in the Introduction to this book, and whilst recognising that many consider it to be an intriguing and complex term (Hinton and Wilson, 1993: 123; Lawton and Rose, 1991: 17), we need not become over cautious in our approach. John Stewart (1993: 4) provides us with a very succinct definition, when he suggests that accountability involves two key elements. First, it involves giving an account for actions taken (sometimes known as answerability or explanatory accountability). Second, it involves being held to account for those actions (sometimes known as accountability *per se*). The corollary of this, therefore, is that an "accountable" government is one where government reports back to the people by giving an account of its actions, and where government is then held to account for these actions because people have a means of restraining it.

This chapter will deal essentially with two main matters. The bulk of the chapter will be taken up by examining in turn the "popular" mechanisms of elections, parties, pressure groups and the media. Throughout, a series of arguments and associated evidence will be deployed to illustrate that there is a persistent theme, namely that these mechanisms both promote and hinder the "popular" accountability of government. The remainder of the chapter will then attempt to take an overview of this tension by relating it to principles which are central to the British parliamentary state – namely representation, consent and legitimation.

Popular Mechanisms: A Dual Role
Knowledge by the people of the activities of government is vital in a liberal democracy. As Bealey (1988: 263) suggests:

> without knowledge democracy is flawed. Not only participation in institutional decision-making but also popular discussion and controversy is hampered when certain information is not known.

In addition, the ability of the people to restrain government and hold it accountable is one of the hallmarks of liberal democracy. Just as surely as these are true, however, it is also true, as MacPherson (1972: 39) suggests, that even "the most liberal of democrats recognise that the liberal-democratic state . . . is a system of power." The implication of this, it can be suggested, is two-fold. On the one hand, the popular mechanisms of elections, parties, pressure groups and the media are genuine and meaningful in that they *do* assist the dissemination of information and act as vehicles for promoting the accountability of government. On the other hand, however, they also perform a countervailing role by acting as powerful barriers to the accountability of government. It is this dual role which we must now explore in greater depth, looking in turn at each of these mechanisms.

Elections

If "consent" is the first priority of government (Rose, 1984: 235) then, at least from the time of the 1832 Reform Act, the franchise has become a key factor in conferring legitimacy on the British political system and its policy outputs. Yet this confluence of consent and legitimation is fused with a third factor – representation – to form the hallmarks of the British parliamentary state (Judge, 1993). In practice, this representation operates through an amalgam of the Burkean and delegate traditions of representation (Bealey, 1988: 40), with the common denominator (in contemporary terms) being the ability of the people to chose between representatives competing for political office. It is this link between elector and elected which is central not only to "democracy" in Britain, but also to the accountability of government. This can be expanded upon by viewing elections from *one* angle and seeing that they do indeed promote accountable government. There are two main reasons for this.

First, elections provide a periodic opportunity for the governing party to parade and disseminate information on its record of "achievement". Such activities as the publication of manifestos, daily press conferences and a constant succession of interviews may have their problems (as we will see), but at least they are there, and this fact promotes a quasi-pluralist dissemination of knowledge. Second, this in turn assists the promotion of accountable government because of the very nature of elections themselves. Anthony Downs' (1957: 295) seminal work *An Economic Theory of Democracy* encapsulates in very general terms the implicit constitutional assumptions of elections when he states that politicians "formulate whatever policies they believe will gain the most votes, just as entrepreneurs produce whatever products they believe will gain the most profits." The corollary of this is that elections constrain politicians, because the sanction of removal or non-election to office ensures that they must pay some modicum of attention to the wishes of voters. Mrs Thatcher (1993: 571), for example, drew back from committing the Conservative Party to fundamentally reforming the NHS in the 1987 manifesto, stating that apart from the fact that not enough detailed work had been done on it, "[t]he NHS was seen by many as a touchstone for our commitment to the welfare state and there were obvious dangers of coming out with proposals out of the blue."

When we view elections from another angle, however, they are very far from this apparently ideal vehicle for the promotion of accountable government. This is because governments may not have the resources or the desire to disseminate information, whilst the timing of elections, partisan voting preferences, the vagaries of the electoral system and the nature of representative democracy, all impede the ability of the people to restrain government. Let us now consider each of these factors.

In the first instance, it must be recognized that elections act as barriers to the flow of information. One prohibitive factor is the cost of electioneering within a minimalist system of state funding for political parties where there is a propensity for a "fiscal crisis" of the parties, and where the demands to spend are often greater than the ability to raise the necessary finances (McConnell, 1994). Perhaps more contentiously, however, governments may not *want* to disseminate information. At election time, tactics to win votes are crucial. Putting this at its crudest level, political advantage (or the avoidance of disadvantage) may be obtained by withholding information. For example, Mrs Thatcher ordered the 1987 Ibbs Report on the introduction of "Next Steps" agencies to be kept secret until after the general election in June (Pyper, 1991: 123–4). Another barrier to the free flow of information is that government may distort the reporting back process, by giving a misleading impression for the purposes of obtaining political advantage, or in order to protect what it perceives to be the national interest. The very nature of electoral competition ensures that governing parties will, if they possibly can, avoid saying anything which is liable to damage their electoral prospects. The rise and rise of "spin doctors" and public relations advisors simply exacerbates this. Furthermore, there is an increasing tendency towards negative rather than positive campaigning. For example, Butler and Kavanagh (1992: 264) note that during the 1992 General Election campaign, "Conservative ministers were regularly criticised at their press conferences for 'going on about taxation again' and spending more time attacking Labour proposals than presenting their own."

If the ability of elections to promote the free flow of information is somewhat problematic, therefore, accountability is doubly hindered by the fact that elections in many respects are less than useful in terms of being able to hold government to account. There are a host of reasons for this. The people are unable to call a general election. Only the prime minister has the power to do so, and even then he or she may do so within the context of a Parliament nearing the end of its life, the absence of a working majority, and a number of other constraining factors (Kavanagh, 1989). The fact that roughly 20–25% of the electorate do not vote also means that the government remains unchecked by *all* those eligible to vote. There are, it must be said, theorists such as Dahl (1961) who would see this as relatively unproblematic. The argument implies that such individuals effectively act as watchdogs. They are seen to have the sanction of the vote at their disposal, they have broad beliefs in democracy and political equality, and this then prevents government from breaching these conventions. More realistically, however, we should perhaps see non-voting as a partial manifestation of powerlessness whereby those with poor "life chances" perceive that the impact of their vote will change little – if anything at all.

The choice made by electors in the ballot box may also have very little to do with holding government to account. It is worth quoting at length the findings of Rose and McAllister (1990: 152–3), in their work on the "lifetime learning" of the loyalties of voters:

> To paraphrase Walter Bagehot's comment about the Cabinet, values are the buckle that joins an ordinary person's early family experiences and socio-economic interests with the problems that face government. Given political values, an individual does not need to take much interest in politics, in the current issues of the day, or even in the personalities projected through the media. Bits and pieces of information about current events can be interpreted in the light of what a person already believes. Because political values reflect family loyalties and social structural influences formed in a lifetime of learning, they are central to an individual's experiences and are thus of first importance in determining voting.

Rose and McAllister (1990: 154) found that only 10.5% of the variance of voting in the 1987 election could be accounted for by the current performance of the parties. The impact of this on accountability is clear. It means that governments are to a large extent not judged simply on their record, because many people still vote for them – irrespective of what that record actually is.

A further problem is that the signals sent to government by electors are not as clear as might be assumed. The nature of the first-past-the-post system and its propensity to favour the two main parties and squeeze out others whose votes are insufficient to win large numbers of seats outright, means the existence of "an essentially unrepresentative Commons . . . which produces a caricature of political feeling in the country" (Walkland, 1983: 43). Thus, the voice of the people "in Parliament" as they attempt to hold government to account, is not the same as the voice of the people at the ballot box. It should also be noted that some of the signals sent by the regions of the UK may be swamped by the unitary nature of British government. Thus, for example, the people of Scotland are disadvantaged when trying to use the electoral system in order to hold government to account. They have (for better or worse) no constitutional right to have an electoral voice which is independent of the UK electorate.

Finally, a crucial factor which contributes to the ability of government to partially distance itself from the views of electors and their attempts to hold it to account is the very nature of representation, and its indispensability in terms of the smooth functioning of Parliamentary democracy. Miliband (1982: 38–9) suggests that the

> essence of parliamentarism is that it provides a buffer between government and people. It accords to the people the right to elect their representatives and to engage in many forms of political activity; but it also bids the people to let their representatives bear the burden of sustaining or opposing the government of the day.

This distance between elector and elected is heightened by the multiplicity of factors (such as the strong party system, the whip system, the careerism of MPs and the *Realpolitik* of Westminster), which have led to the dominance of the executive within the Parliamentary structure. Indeed some commentators have taken this further and emphasised the monarchical or presidential nature of prime ministerial power (Lenman, 1992; Foley, 1993). Whatever the merits of these arguments, it is difficult to escape the fact that the broader picture in terms of elections is a distinctly ambivalent role in promoting the accountability of British government. On the one hand, they do play an important role in the dissemination of information and no government can operate without paying attention to public opinion from time to time. On the other hand, however, the structure and operation of the British system gives substantial autonomy for governments to partially insulate themselves from popular pressures, and in effect to de-popularise the activities of government.

Political Parties

Elections in 20th century Britain are linked inexorably with parties. As Katz (1980: 1) suggests:

> Modern democracy is party democracy; the political institutions and

practices of democratic government in the Western view were the creations of political parties and would be unthinkable without them.

If we want to comprehend the roles of British political parties with regard to promoting accountable government, however, we can only do so by comprehending the particular type of parliament which they inhabit and attempt to influence. In this regard, few would disagree with Brand (1992: 341) who describes the British Parliament as a "reactive legislature . . . [where] the main mode of policy activity is reaction to the proposals of the government." This statement is particularly useful because it contains within it the very essence of the dual role of parties in promoting and impeding popular accountability within Parliament. On the one hand, it implies a degree of power on the part of parties, reacting to and attempting to hold to account a government with substantial powers at its disposal. On the other hand, it implies largely impotent parties, relegated to a reactive and marginal role in the executive-dominated power structure. In the same manner as elections, therefore, we can view parties from two different angles and obtain two different perspectives on their role with in relation to the popular accountability of government. In this regard, parties can of course use a variety of devices within Parliament (such as Parliamentary Questions and select committees), and these will be dealt with in Chapter Two. We can nevertheless avoid overlap by concentrating on the general roles of parties within Parliament, and taking a view from each of these vantage points in terms of their ability to promote or hinder the accountability of government.

When viewed from one angle, the parties do indeed assist in extracting information from government and also in restraining it. The reasons for this lie with the nature of adversary politics, the need to maintain the legitimacy of government, the existence of "outer circle" MPs, and the matter of intra-party accountability. Each of these can be considered in turn.

First, the adversarial nature of the House of Commons – the clear division between the governing party and opposition parties – places enormous pressure on the opposition parties, particularly the main opposition party, to unite against the government. Bernard Crick (1968: 246) encapsulates this well when he describes Parliament as "a continuous election campaign" where the primary function of the opposition is to *oppose*. Just because opposition parties are in a minority, however, does not mean that they are powerless in attempting to hold the government to account. Apart from the fact that they have access to the fruits of media investigations into government activities, opposition parties have at their disposal a vast range of Parliamentary devices which allow them to extract information from government (see Chapter Two for further details). More generally, parties are members of policy networks which include think tanks and pressure groups (Brand, 1992). Thus, they are one of a number of sets of actors attempting to place and keep items regarding government activities on the public agenda. This is assisted when there is a focusing event such as a "crisis" (Hogwood, 1987: 36–7) and in some areas, such as new tax proposals, political parties are easily the most important force in placing such matters on the political agenda (Robinson and Sandford, 1983). Overall, therefore, the fact that the opposition is denied access to state power beyond election time forces it into the situation where one of its main activities is to use the resources and information at its disposal in order to constantly call into question the activities of government.

Second, it must be recognised that the role of Parliament is not confined to the normally understood function of legitimating legislation. It includes the role of "latent legitimation" where it legitimates government itself (Packenham, 1970: 527–29). This is important because leaving aside "crisis" issues and taxation, parties *do* often attempt to raise issues and set the agenda in matters which are of particular concern to them. It is not always easy for government to constantly ignore such calls. At times (and depending on the particular context) the legitimacy of government depends on it *appearing* to be accountable and answerable to wider public concerns as raised by opposition parties. In the summer of 1992, for example, the Government conceded to Labour's demands for the recall of Parliament in order to discuss the sterling crisis and policy towards the conflict in the former Yugoslavia. As Norton (1994: 136) suggests, the outcome of the debate may be predictable, but "for government to take any fundamental decision without some parliamentary debate . . . is to convey the impression of acting improperly."

Third, Brand (1992: 343) suggests that "the process whereby an opposition raises matters which are uncomfortable for the government has the result that a small proportion of these are seen as valid points, even by the government side." This is particularly the case because of the existence of a group of MPs who do not fit the mould of archetypal careerist members. Rose (1982) calls this the "outer circle" of MPs, who are expressive enthusiasts for causes and interests, publicity seekers, extra-Parliamentary careerists, and constituency representatives.

Fourth, governing parties within Parliament are not monolithic blocs, and there exists within them some form of two-way relationship between leadership and backbenchers. This is facilitated by informal communications, the "sounding out" role of the whips, and the existence of various backbench committees which ministers regularly attend. In terms of the Conservative Party, for example, these range from the regular weekly meeting of the 1992 Committee for all Tory backbenchers (usually but not always confined to announcing Parliamentary business for the forthcoming week), through to committees covering specific policy areas. These meetings involve ministers giving an account of their policies and activities, and backbenchers attempting to extract information and restrain the minister when they feel it necessary to do so. If such actions are motivated even partly by constituency concerns, electoral repercussions and other such matters, then to some degree they are indicative of popular concerns holding government to account.

All of this illustrates that political parties do indeed perform a major role in facilitating popular accountability of government. However, this is true only when viewed from one particular perspective, and so we must move swiftly to our second vantage point. From here, we can see the stark realities of political life. John Garrett (1992: 16) encapsulates this with his contention that "in every function of Parliament, government throws its weight, not only against any opposition to its will, but against enquiry, scrutiny and discussion." Or, to adapt a phrase used by Austin Mitchell MP, we can see the opposition parties "heckling the steamroller" of government (quoted in Garrett, 1992: 16). What, might we ask, are the factors which inhibit the abilities of parties to hold government to account? There are four main matters to be considered here.

First, the "winner-take-all" nature of the electoral system has tended to squeeze out third parties, thus ensuring that the Commons is dominated by the two main parties. One of these is typically installed in government whilst commanding less than 50% of the popular vote. In this adversary system, therefore, there are pressures for the governing party to unite in order to govern, and for the opposition to unite in order to oppose. As indicated previously, this does facilitate a climate of enquiry and scrutiny on the part of the opposition. The other face of this, however, is that it may also weaken the accountability of government, because it tends to make the governing party more cohesive in being able to deflect opposition attempts to hold it to account.

Second, once a government is installed within Parliament, then like any organization "the normative system of the House . . . reflects the predilections of the most powerful actors and so supports the existing distribution of power." (Judge, 1983: 190). These norms are considered to be ones of generalism, where independent and specialist scrutiny come a distant second to careerism and a general allegiance to the party. As William Waldegrave (quoted in Riddell, 1993: 17) argues: "Any politician who tells you he isn't [ambitious] is only telling you he isn't for some tactical reason; or more bluntly, telling you a lie."

Thus, the careerism of government backbenchers tends to militate against rigorous scrutiny of government. Backbenchers are of course extremely wary of being explicit about this, since independence of mind has a value in the eyes of many constituency supporters. Yet as Radice *et al* (1987: 9) suggest, "Experts may be admired for their specialist contribution, but this is still not normally the way to make a political name." This is certainly evident in the select committee system, whereby an element of independence is nevertheless often accompanied by some form of deference to government activities. A case study of the Select Committee on Scottish Affairs, for example, plots clearly the "pull" of partisanship when backbenchers are involved in scrutinising their own party in government (McConnell and Pyper, 1994).

Third, and linked to this, the Executive is in a unique position to perpetuate its own dominance by maintaining party unity. On the one hand, ministers are at the apex of the departmental hierarchy and have access to the specialist knowledge of the civil service, allowing them to frame legislation and justify government policy. On the other hand, whilst approximately one-third of the Parliamentary party of government are kept in line because they hold positions in government and are bound by the doctrine of collective responsibility, the remaining two-thirds are kept in line because the prime minister holds the power of patronage. Again, therefore, the norms are of generalism and allegiance to the party (as opposed to genuinely independent scrutiny) if, as is generally the case, a ministerial post is desired.

Fourth, when we add to all this the discipline of the whip system and that fact that each party tends to exhibit a broad and shared ideology, then as Brand (1992: 20) suggests, "the party will normally stand behind its chosen leader and his or her team to reject virtually any criticisms from the other side." When viewed from this angle, therefore, the functioning of political parties hardly bodes well for ensuring the accountability of government.

It must be emphasised, of course, that whilst the dominant tendency of political life is of highly partisan parties entrenched within an adversary Parliamentary system, we must be wary of a one-dimensional approach.

The true realities of political life are that there is a counter tendency which can undermine this cohesion and so facilitate the popular accountability of government. As we have seen, important factors in this regard range from a straightforward inability of government to secure the requisite level of support from its backbenchers (as happened in 1994 over the forced abandonment of plans to privatise the Royal Mail), through to a "crisis" pushing the government into a corner where its legitimacy is called into question unless it is seen to act in some way (as happened again in 1994 where allegations of "sleaze" prompted the Government to set up the Nolan enquiry into standards in public life). Like elections, therefore, parties are both promoters of and barriers to accountable government.

Pressure Groups

Unlike parties, whose aim is to hold political office, pressure groups attempt to influence those who hold public power. It is difficult to deny their growing importance in the governing of 20th century Britain. At the end of the 1970s, for example, Richardson and Jordan (1979) made the now famous pronouncement that we live in a "post-Parliamentary" democracy where policy communities of civil servants and pressure group interests marginalise Parliament and parties from policy-making. Still, in the 1990s, this view continues to be adhered to by Richardson (1993), who chooses to interpret Judge's (1990) thoroughgoing critique as merely a "qualification". More generally, the study of "generic" policy networks (Rhodes and Marsh, 1992: 186) has become a burgeoning field of activity, although some writers such as Smith (1993: 1) suggest that an inordinate amount of attention has been paid to the role of groups, at the expense of neglecting the broader context within which the groups operate.

Whatever their wider role in the policy process, our focus here is on their contribution to the promotion of accountable government. In this regard, it seems appropriate to reflect on the usefulness of David Easton's (1965) *A Systems Analysis of Political Life*. In this, he conceptualises political life as an open system, in which a variety of demands and supports impact on the authorities (i. e. the governmental system), creating a variety of outputs which then have the potential to feed back into the political system. Pressure groups can be conceived as one element of this, reacting to the outputs of government and attempting to feed back into the system to restrain government when this seems necessary. As Easton observes, however, this is not a "neutral" process.

The way in which the authorities will react to feedback response will in part hinge on the kinds of sanctions that the politically relevant members might be able to exercise in pressing their points of view upon the authorities. These sanctions will be heavily dependent upon the nature of the regime. Control of votes, wealth prestige, or other values of the society, or the ability to threaten physical coercion will serve as sources of influence for impelling the authorities in the direction sought by those who hold such power.
(Easton, 1965: 435).

In the same manner as elections and political parties, therefore, pressure groups can be viewed from different angles as both facilitators of, and obstacles to, the popular accountability of government. Let us now consider each of these possibilities in turn.

When viewed from one angle, groups do indeed promote the accountability of government. What, might we ask, enables a group to have the power to extract information from and restrain government at times? The distinction made between "insider" and "outsider" groups (Grant, 1989) provides a useful means of considering this. An insider group is one which is perceived by government as legitimate, and which it consults on a regular basis. The most extreme example would be the groups found within a "policy community". Here, there is a high degree of consensus among the participants, who as Pross (1992: 119) observes, have

acquired a dominant voice in determining government decisions in a field of public activity. This is by virtue of . . . [their] functional responsibilities . . . vested interests, and . . . specialized knowledge.

According to Jordan and Richardson, this is typical of government in Britain. More specifically, the normal policy style is seen to be one of "bureaucratic accommodation", in which "the prominent actors are groups and government departments and the mode is bargaining rather than imposition" (Jordan and Richardson, 1982: 81). Thus, this "institutionalization and regularisation of compromise" facilitates reciprocity and accountability (Jordan and Richardson, 1981: 92). As a consequence, government is restrained because

no longer do the assets of government markedly outweigh the assets of any given group or set of groups in a particular bargaining structure. Increasingly, pressure groups and governments have come to recognise that they need each other in order to achieve their respective objectives. (Richardson and Jordan, 1979: 172).

Within the broad "insider" category, relationships may be much looser and less consensual, and hence veer toward the issue network end of the policy network spectrum. Even here, however, it is still possible for groups to hold government to account. For example, Richardson, Maloney and Rudig's (1992) study of water privatization notes how the government's failure to produce an unproblematic consensus for its initial proposals resulted in more extended consultation in a loose issue network. This backfired, however, because it brought in groups which were to play an important role in the government withdrawing its original proposals.

In addition to "insider" groups, there are "outsider" groups. Grant (1989: 15) defines these as groups which "either do not wish to become enmeshed in a consultative relationship with officials, or are unable to gain recognition." Within this category, and nearest to insider status, are groups which are attempting to become insiders. At the farthest reaches of this category are those groups adopting tactics regarded as outside "the normal spectrum of political activity" (Grant, 1989: 18). Even here, restraining government is possible. One of the most obvious examples of this in recent years is the role of the Anti-Poll Tax Federation and all the various groups campaigning for non-payment of, and abolition of, the Poll Tax (see Tonge, 1994). These groups, as part of a wider pressure movement, undoubtedly helped impede the Government's desire to proceed with implementation of its policy in this area. In so restraining government, therefore, they were able to facilitate a strong measure of popular accountability.

In general, all groups which are in a position to hold government to account have one common characteristic: they possess something which is of use to government. Kingdom (1991: 402) summarises this as expertise, a role in policy implementation, and the ability to communicate with certain sections of the populace. In simple terms, therefore, within the system of political life, and when viewed from one angle, government will tend to be held accountable by those groups strategically placed to exercise some hold over it through the positive contributions they can make to government.

Again, however, we must avoid one-sided perspectives and be prepared to view pressure groups from another angle. A useful framework is provided here by Lukes (1974) and his critique of the pluralist "one-dimensional" concept of power. He points to power in the "second" and "third" dimensions. We can utilise these to see how feedback within the political system may be suppressed, or may not even exist at all, thus detracting from the ability of groups to hold government to account.

Power in the second dimension is put forward most directly in the work of Bachrach and Baratz (1970), and their study of poverty, race and politics in Baltimore. They argue that

> Political systems tend consistently to develop a mobilization of bias, a set
> of values, beliefs, rituals and procedures which can be exploited by
> beneficiaries of the unequal value-allocation to defend and promote their
> preferred position.
> (Bachrach and Baratz, 1970: 105).

They do not argue that this is power is entrenched, however, and indeed they do recognise a large degree of dynamism and the possibility of change through a strengthening or weakening of the resources available to the various groupings involved. Nevertheless

> those in a position of dominance lay particularly heavy stress upon
> preventing the disaffected from raising issues that are threatening to the
> former's preferred position.
> (Bachrach and Baratz, 1970: 105).

We can apply this to pressure groups, and provide illustrations of three main ways in which they may be thwarted in their attempts to hold government to account. First, dominant political values are part of the mobilization of bias. They can be a powerful force in suppressing or minimising a challenge to government from pressure groups. A range of writers from neo-pluralists such as Lindblom (1977) through to Marxists such as Miliband (1973), note that the political consensus is biased in favour of big business. This implies, of course, that other groups are less strategically placed to restrain government. Offe (1984: 55–6) provides a more sophisticated version of such thinking when he suggests that the process of policy formation gives

> preferential treatment to the functional problems of the capitalist
> economy – a commitment guaranteed by objective, political-organiza-
> tional channels and mechanisms – imply[ing] material, social and
> temporal "'biases'", i. e. privilege granting rules whose effect in turn play
> an essential role in "delegitimating" political conflicts.

There are areas, therefore, where pressure groups are severely limited in their ability to restrain government because their demands are delegitimated by dominant political values. For example, ever since the Thatcher Government came to power in 1979, the ideas (not to mention legislation) emanating from government have hardly been sympathetic to trades unions. Marsh (1992: 111) suggests in his study of trades unions that the Thatcher Government saw the unions as responsible for the failures of the Heath and Wilson/Callaghan Governments, and that "to negotiate with the unions would have been to sup with the devil". More subtle than political values such as these, however, is the very existence of policy communities. These can help mobilize against groups outside this closed world by confirming their outsider status. More subtly still, however, as one commentator states bluntly with regard to her case study of Women's Aid in Scotland – "to be in on the act one has to be invited, and to be invited one may have to compromise" (Jordan and Richardson, 1987: 230). Overall, therefore, whether it is delegitimation of ideas or simply pressures to water down input, there can be an erosion of accountability because such factors partially insulate government from those seeking to restrain it.

Second, another element of British government which can be mobilized against groups is the very flexibility of policy formation. For present purposes, we can say that it is flexible in two main senses. In the first instance, government has the potential to manage "indicators" of problems in an attempt to downplay their seriousness (Stringer and Richardson, 1980: 27). In 1978, for example, a dispute between the Housebuilders' Federation and the DoE led to the sides trying to prove, respectively, that there was, or was not, a land shortage.

A further type of flexibility can be seen via Hogwood's (1987) observation that issues can be processed in a variety of ways, once they reach the policy-making agenda. These can be categorised as:

- imposition;
- internalised within government;
- processable through consultation;
- policy emerges from practice;
- non-internalisable.

One of these – consultation – epitomises the potential for a mobilization of bias against groups. The reason for this is that government consultation papers, like the bulk of the British constitution, can be moulded with considerable ease. In effect, they allow a "trial" opposition to policies and, if the government still feels that it is able to proceed, it can (quite legitimately in constitutional terms) interpret the consultation exercise in any way that it wants in order to arrive at its final decision. A good example of this is the Scottish Office's consultation process on the introduction of School Boards in Scotland. An EIS survey of the unprecedented 7600 responses, found 88% expressing condemnation, disagreement or dissent, whilst only 1% gave unconditional endorsement (SLGIU, 1988: 1). Despite all this, the government argued that the deficiencies of the existing system of local authority control were so strong that it was necessary to proceed with the reforms regardless. In total, therefore, the very flexibility that government has in managing indicators of problems and in processing policies, imbues it with the potential to dampen attempts to restrain and hold it to account.

Third, the procedures of British government also allow for mobilization against groups seeking to hold government to account. A central element of these procedures is the very nature of the legislative process, in which governments theoretically have a majority for every vote on the Floor and in Standing Committee. Unless a government seeks to make changes which will improve a bill in terms of practicality, or unless there are internal or external pressures which effectively force it into making concessions, then the cards are stacked overwhelmingly against pressure groups. For example, in 1986–87 when Parliament considered a poll tax for Scotland in the form of the Abolition of Domestic Rates Etc. (Scotland) Bill (see McConnell, 1995 for a full study), the Federation of Scottish Ratepayers was the only group lobbying in favour of the tax. In contrast, there was substantial lobbying against it by over twenty groups ranging from the Convention of Scottish Local Authorities and the Association of Metropolitan Authorities, through to the Scottish Council for Single Homeless and Strathclyde Poverty Alliance. Yet this massive lobbying exercise was to no avail. As the then Labour MP Dick Douglas suggested, the Bill was "dragooned through because the Government have an overwhelming majority" (quoted in McConnell, 1995: 172), and the Bill passed with considerable ease – without a single Conservative MP voting against the Government. In these circumstances, Parliament is indeed largely a "rubber stamp" on executive-initiated legislation, and the effective exclusion of the opposition from holding government accountable also extends to pressure groups and their articulation of broadly popular concerns.

If this is power in the second dimension, where the values and procedures of British government ease the pathway for governments to avoid being restrained by pressure groups, then this can be taken further in the terms of Lukes' three-dimensional view of power. He offers an "explanation of how political systems prevent demands from becoming political issues or even from being made" (Lukes, 1974: 38). It is this latter element which is crucial, because the three-dimensional view suggests that a power relationship can exist when

- there is inaction in terms of an absence of demands;
- those exercising power may do so unconsciously;
- this exercise of power may be attributed to collectivities, such as groups, classes and institutions.

Lukes rightly recognises the methodological problems of studying such matters, although one tentative but necessarily complex example will perhaps illustrate that it does not require a gigantic leap of faith or the adoption of perverse logic to support the existence of power in the third dimension.

If government policy in the 1990s is predicated broadly on free market principles and therefore helps cause unemployment, then why are there no major contemporary demands from groups (trades unions, welfare groups) trying to hold government to account and demanding full employment and the right to work? The answer would seem to lie partly with the exercise of power in the third dimension. Taking each component of the third dimension of power as highlighted in the previous paragraph, it can be suggested that there is an absence of demands for full employment and the right to work; that government ministers are exercising power unconsciously because there is no need to reflect on demands which do not exist and that government has been able to exercise power and prevent such demands arising, because it has managed to shift the political agenda towards suppressing inflation and emphasising the interdependence of Britain with a complex and dynamic world economic system. As a consequence, major calls for full employment and the right to work do not even arise in the first place, because they would automatically be perceived as anachronistic and illegitimate – even by the opposition parties. These three factors combined lead us to the conclusion that the conditions for the existence of the third dimension of power have been satisfied. Thus, this example allows us to add the third dimension of power to our global picture of the limitations of popular accountability.

To sum up, therefore, we must remember that a true reflection of political reality requires us to consider not only how pressure groups are able to assist the accountability of government, but also how they unable to do so. In the system of political life pressure groups provide feedback which may restrain government, yet at the same time this feedback can be mobilised out of the system or may not even exist at all. Yet again there is a paradoxical tension running directly through the popular mechanisms of accountability.

Media

Karl Deutsch (1966) recognised the importance of information communication within a political system. More recently, Christopher Hood (1983) conceptualised information as an "effector" (one component of government's "tool kit" for having an impact upon citizens), and as something received by "detectors" (instruments which government uses to receive information). The media is central in this use and dissemination of information. Curran and Seaton (1991: 315) suggest that "[t]o inform, to discuss, to mirror, to bind, to campaign, to challenge, to entertain, and to judge – these are the important functions of the media in any free country." We cannot say unequivocally that the media reflects popular concerns in doing this. Nevertheless, if people utilise (by purchase or otherwise) the outputs of the media, and if people have a general interest in the maintenance of media freedom, we can say on a very basic level that the media's role in promoting the accountability of government approximates with that of popular accountability.

If liberal democracy is a system of power, however, it is evident that the role of the media in attempting to ensure accountable government can be viewed from very different perspectives. On the one hand, it may be considered as a quasi-pluralist disseminator of information and power, by providing a counterbalance to government views, and in this sense it facilitates the popular accountability of government. On other hand, however, it may be unable to perform these roles, for a variety of reasons, including censorship. Once again, therefore, we can view another key vehicle for popular accountability from two distinct vantage points.

From one perspective, the media may promote the accountability of government. In Stewart's definition of accountability, there were the requirements that government "gives an account" and provides information. Quite simply, government *needs* the media to do this. The business of governing requires that government communicates its policies and its views to the public at large, in the hope of obtaining support and letting "citizens know what is expected of them" (Rose, 1989: 196). Cockerell *et al* (1985) paint a picture of the vastness of Whitehall's publicity role, describing it as a pyramid-like "machine", with public relations "troops". Coupled with the vast amount of information published though the Central Statistical Office, HMSO and others, there is an enormous amount of publicity available. As Hood (1983) recognises, government may target information in different ways. There may be group-targeted messages, these being particularly important because of the existence of "powerful pressure groups seeking to act as 'opinion leaders' " (Hood, 1983: 27). There are also more general "broadcast" messages which are aimed at the population and the world at large. Certainly, these may be conveyed through lobby journalists, but in other respects the media is crucial in the collection, interpreting and conveying of information. As Hood suggests, the information may be "privished" i. e. freely available but still relatively private – such as a government publication selling at a high price. Alternatively, it may be a "packaged self-serve message", where some initiative is required to extract the required information from the range of materials that are on offer. Whether it is government consultation papers, White Papers or government statistics, however, it is a function of the media to gain access to these (in a crude sense, on behalf of the people) in order to perform wider roles.

These matters relate to the ability of the media to facilitate government giving an account, but the media (partially overlapping with some of the above) can play a role in restraining government and holding it to account. Media investigations may lead to government having to concede more information than it would otherwise have done. Primarily, this occurs when government cannot credibly continue to withhold information, without damaging its legitimacy. In the Westland affair, for example (see Oliver and Austin, 1987), the findings of Sir Robert Armstrong's enquiry into the leaked Solicitor General's letter were originally intended to be kept private. But once Tam Dalyell named Trade and Industry Secretary Leon Brittan's Director of Information as the source, intense speculation (emanating partly from and transmitted by the media) led to Mrs Thatcher having little option but to come to the House and confirm that the leak was indeed authorised by Leon Brittan.

Media investigations can also restrain government in its general activities. Certainly, the media can rarely do this alone, and is assisted in crisis-type situations when the agenda is set, according to Kingdon (1984) by the convergence of problems, political events, and the activities of senior participants in the policy sphere. The media, for example,

undoubtedly played a role (Lord Tebbit argued that it was a dishonoura-
ble role) in the downfall of Mrs Thatcher in 1990, and we can identify
each of the factors mentioned by Kingdon. First, there were "problems"
in the form of the Poll Tax and Europe. Second, there were the "political
events" of abysmally low opinion poll ratings for the Conservatives and
Mrs Thatcher in particular. Third, and unlike the situation in 1989 when
Anthony Meyer made a challenge for the leadership, there were now
"senior participants" in the form of both Michael Heseltine and
Margaret Thatcher. All this took place at a time when there was possibly
still a majority preference within the Conservative Party as a whole for
Mrs Thatcher to remain as leader. Through its enquiries and opinions,
therefore, the media played a role in opening up and highlighting
popular discontent. In this regard, it helped restrain a governing party
which might otherwise have settled for the *status quo*.

Overall, this is one perspective from which to view the media, as the
public watchdog (a Fourth Estate of the Realm), ever vigilant and
restraining government when necessary. Once again, however, we must
avoid one-sided views. We must be prepared to shift our vantage point
and consider the ways in which the media is unable to perform these
roles, and therefore unable to hold government to account. Although far
from extensive, there are a number of key factors which we can consider
here.

First, as an illustration of the "mobilization of bias", the media may be
directly censored by government – invoking the nebulous and subjective
justification of the "national interest". One of the earliest manifestations
of this is illustrated by Curran and Seaton (1991) in their description of
the emergence in the late 18th and early 19th centuries of a radical press,
independent of government and the various political groupings within
Parliament.

> Successive governments tried to contain the emergent radical press
> through direct legal repression . . . the seditious and blasphemous libel law
> was framed in a catch-all form that made any kind of fundamental
> criticism of the social order a legal offence.
> (Curran and Seaton, 1991: 12).

In the contemporary political sphere, the media can be directly subject to
censorship in a number of ways. The pivotal feature of press censorship
has been the 1911 Official Secrets Act (supplemented by Acts in 1920 and
1939), and then a successor Act in 1989. The 1911 Act was a wide-

ranging and blunt instrument: Section 2 of the Act made illegal any unauthorised disclosure of government information. The 1989 Act, however, was widely seen simply as a refinement of the earlier legislation. It narrowed the categories of restricted information to areas such as security, intelligence and defence (Oliver, 1991: 172), but did not put in place the freedom of information measures found in countries such as the USA and Australia.

Second, governments can attempt to use the courts in order to obtain interdicts and injunctions to restrain the media (as in the Zircon and Spycatcher affairs), or they may simply use covert and indeed routine pressure for restraint. This is put clearly by Mark Bonham Carter (1988: 29), former Vice Chairman of the BBC.

> It is common practice for ministers – and indeed members of the opposition – to ring up the Director General, or the Chairman of the Board of Governors, to protest about programmes which they fear may be objectionable or contrary to the interests of the country or their party. To assess, to accept or resist such pressures is part and parcel of the duty of the Chairman of the Board of Governors or the Director General.

Third, the accountability of government can be undermined because of media regulation. This takes two main forms. The first is regulation by the state. Here, it is important to distinguish between the electronic media and the print media. Independent television is limited by a legal code of conduct (introduced in 1954 and updated in 1981) which requires that news programmes adhere to such traditions as "accuracy and impartiality" and "proper balance", yet no such restrictions apply to the print media i. e. newspapers (Newton, 1995).

The other form is self-regulation by the media itself. In terms of the press, self-regulation has been reflected in a number of structures down the years, from the Press Council established in 1953, through to the Press Complaints Commission which was set up in 1991. The rationale behind such bodies lies in the law of anticipated reactions. Here, the press regulates itself in the knowledge that if it does not do so statutory controls may follow (or they may follow nevertheless, because of an inability to satisfy government ministers). In terms of the electronic media, the BBC, essentially a creation of the state, has been particularly open to such a charge. Although not legally required to do so, it also adopts the code of conduct which applies to the independent sector. More contentiously, however, there is the matter of the Corporation's self-restraint in scrutiny of government activities. Duncan Campbell (1988: 19), for example, notes how the experience of the Zircon affair in 1985–86 led to the BBC setting up a "political unit" to "pre-check any programme items that might irritate the government."

It can be argued that a further form of self-regulation, and much more subtle than any of the other forms, occurs simply because the vast majority of the electronic and print media accepts the fundamental organising principles of society. The Glasgow University Media Group (1976: 13–14) may not have avoided criticism from some areas of academia and political commentary, but there is more than a grain of truth in their suggestion that

> one must see the news as reflecting not the events in the world "out there", but as the manifestation of the collective cultural codes of those employed to do this selective and judgemental work for society.

To put this in simpler terms, as Sir Charles Greene, ex-Director General of the BBC once remarked – "Yes, we *are* biased. Biased in favour of parliamentary democracy" (quoted in Wagg, 1987: 17).

The fourth factor which serves to restrict the media's capacity to act as a check on government, is the matter of ownership and control in the non-state sector and the press in particular. For those sympathetic to a pluralist diversity of multiple producers catering for a multitude of viewpoints, a recent study by Newton (1995) paints a bleak picture. Whilst he recognises that there are exceptions to general trends, he carefully delineates the dominant tendencies towards a national and centralised newspaper market, a declining number of titles, an increasing concentration of ownership and control, the rise of multi-media concentration (notably the Murdoch empire), and the internationalization of ownership and control. It is aspects of control by so-called "press barons" which are crucial to accountability. From the days of Beaverbrook and Rothermere, through to those of Maxwell and Murdoch, the heavy hand of ownership can be found. Lord Beaverbrook, for example, claimed to run the *Daily Express* "merely for the purpose of making propaganda and with no other motive" (quoted in Curran and Seaton, 1991: 56). Beaverbrook's statement is perhaps overly crude, because the capacity for interference is embroiled with other factors such as personalities, the practicalities of detailed intervention, and the need to maintain profits. Nevertheless, as Tunstall and Palmer's (1991) study *Media Moguls* reveals, individuals such as Berlusconi, Hersant and

Murdoch run their empires in highly prescriptive and political ways. Although the impact of this is highly complex and far from one-dimensional, we should not be surprised that owners whose product relies on deregulation and the avoidance of state interference, tend to be more sympathetic to governments of the right rather than the left. In Britain, the Conservative press accounts for 63% of national Sunday sales, and 67% of national daily sales (Newton, 1995: 167). In terms of popular accountability, the attitude of the Conservative press has been clear – exhibiting a strong tendency to be supportive rather than critical of Conservative Governments since 1979.

Fifth, the media may be unable to promote the popular accountability of government, simply because government may be able to deflect the pressures on it. One reason for this is the sheer numbers of matters raised by the media. Government simply cannot deal with every issue of relevance to it which is raised in every newspaper and television programme, and since the media cannot give the same level of prominence to every item, then a process of selection is already underway. Furthermore, and echoing points made previously in relation to pressure groups and the two-dimensional view of power, government can attempt to delegitimate attempts by the media to hold it to account. John Major's premiership, for example, has seen a number of occasions when he has criticised the press for "talking down" his government's achievements in the interests of mischief-making and selling newspapers.

Sixth and finally, the media may not be a vehicle for popular accountability of government, simply because it does not necessarily reflect popular concerns. It must be said, however, that this is a difficult matter to judge. It would be misleading, for example, to use public accusations of media bias as a surrogate for popular concerns. As Miller (1991: 110) found of his study of the role of the media in the 1987 general election:

> alleged bias was related in a complex way to the critics' own partisanship. People tended to see television as biased against their own party while they thought their paper was biased towards their own party.

An approach which is also of limited use here is to turn to wider allegations that the media is biased. The fact that these come from the both the left (arguing that the media is essentially reactionary and wedded to the existing economic and political system) and the right (arguing the media is full of left-wing journalists out to undermine the political right), says more about political dogma than it does about considered analysis. It seems far more useful, therefore, to concur with the point made by Gouldner (quoted in Eldridge, 1993: 19), when he suggests that

> the media *mediates*, which means they select and edit, dramatising some and repressing other events according to their own standard and rules. They stand *between* the public, on the one side, and, on the other, the official managers of institutions, organisations, movements, or the society's hegemonic elites.

This autonomy means, *inter alia*, that whilst the media can perhaps be considered as a general vehicle for a public which wants to hold government accountable, it cannot be considered to mirror precise views on all issues.

Ultimately, therefore, we are left with an ambivalent view of the media. It is both a facilitator of and obstacle to, the popular accountability of government. Thus, as Eldridge (1993: 20) suggests, "the media occupy space which is constantly being contested." It is this contest which makes it neither wholly a vehicle for governmental rule, nor wholly an unrestricted promoter of enquiry into the activities of government.

Conclusion: Popular Accountability and Parliamentary Principles

The reality of popular accountability appears at first glance to be something of an enigma. Throughout this chapter, no sooner have we observed the various mechanisms of elections, parties, pressure groups and the media as bulwarks of popular rights to hold governments to account, than we find them transmuting into barriers to these self-same rights. We can conclude and go some way towards explaining this tension by utilising pivotal parliamentary principles, and seeing how this tension necessarily flows from these. David Judge's (1993) *The Parliamentary State* is of considerable use to us in this regard. It traces the development of the Parliamentary state from the thirteenth century through to the present day in the UK, and suggests that there is a persistence of three traditions: representation, consent and legitimate government. Judge (1993: 6) argues:

> What the Parliamentary tradition in Britain has been concerned with is the transmission of opinion between "political nation" and governors, the controlling of government to the extent that governmental actions require

the consent of the representatives of that "nation", and the legitimation of changes of governors. These have been the essential characteristics of the British State . . .

These three principles of representation, consent and legitimate government form the building blocks of our analysis here. We can conclude this chapter by looking in turn at each of the two faces of popular accountability, and how they necessarily flow from these principles underpinning the modern British parliamentary state.

First, we can look at elections, parties, pressure groups and the media from the vantage point where we see them as genuine facilitators of popular accountability. Certainly, this view accords closely with what many would see as the positive connotations of the words representation, consent and legitimate government. We have seen in this chapter how there exists a representational dialogue between the people and government. Governments use elections to parade their record of achievement; the adversary party system ensures the promotion of alternative views to those of the government, and the existence of "outer circle" MPs ensures that there is room in this dialogue for the views of those supporting particular interests, independence of mind and so on. Furthermore, the existence of policy communities assists the dialogue with particular interests in a much more extensive way, whilst with respect to the media, the government needs it so that it can engage in dialogue and give an account of its actions.

The matters of consent and legitimation are also bound together. Representatives do not give their consent to government actions if a government is considered illegitimate. At the same time, for a government to be considered legitimate it may at times have to respond to the wishes of these representatives and also other representations of the wider populace (as manifested at election time, and in the activities of both pressure groups and the media). Thus, as we have seen, governments have been subject to popular restraint in their election promises; they have been forced into making concessions in order to maintain their legitimacy, and they have been restrained by the efforts of pressure groups and the media. Overall, therefore, we should not be surprised when we find evidence of popular accountability because it fits neatly with the long-standing parliamentary principles of representation, consent and legitimation.

Second, we can look at elections, parties, pressure groups and the media from the vantage point where we see them as barriers to popular accountability. Here, we may not immediately perceive these as according with the principles of representation, consent and legitimate government, but a more considered approach does indeed lead us to this conclusion. This time, we can link representation with consent, because of the very nature of representation in Britain as an amalgam of the delegate and Burkean traditions and the way that this representation feeds through to the activities of governments. Thus, governments may see their election manifestos and victories as forming the basis of a mandate, and this in turn gives them substantial autonomy to use their independence to respond to changing circumstances, formulate new policies and so on. This is then heightened by the malleability of the British constitution and the substantial freedom that this gives to the government of the day (indeed, to the incumbent prime minister). We have seen in this chapter, therefore, a host of ways in which governments are able to deploy a "mobilization of bias" in order to have an impact upon and sometimes deflect attempts to restrain them and hold them to account. For example, they can choose the timing of elections; they can exploit their dominance within Parliament to reinforce this very dominance (through the whip system, the prime minister's powers of patronage and so on); they can delegitimate pressure groups through the dissemination of key political values; they can censor the media, and they can prompt the media into self-regulation for fear of the sanctions that may follow from impinging on dominant political values. All this is done in complete accordance with the Parliamentary principles of representation (because of the dialogue between the people and government) and consent (because Parliament as a whole accepts the right of government to govern).

There is also the matter of legitimation. Governments can claim constitutional legitimacy through being elected by the people, and they are assisted in getting there by the vagaries of the electoral system, whilst being protected once they get there by the structure of the British Parliamentary state. Once in power they can argue that to legitimately govern, they must have the autonomy to decide what are, or are not, legitimate attempts to restrain them and hold them to account. Still within the parameters of the British constitution, therefore, governments can attempt to withhold information, claiming that this is in the national interest. Governments can also assert the primacy and legitimacy of their right to govern on behalf of the people, and so use their constitutional authority to mobilize against the views of those who did not elect them, and against opposition parties, pressure groups and the media.

In conclusion, therefore, we are able to see that the core Parliamentary principles of representation, consent and legitimation are means by which the people and government are fused together. Modern British government cannot hope to govern without this popular underpinning of representation, consent and legitimation. At the same time, however, it cannot hope to govern without utilising the flexibility that these bring in order to deflect elements of popular concerns. Thus, the fact that, depending on the circumstances, people are able *and* unable to make successful use of popular mechanisms to hold government to account, is not as surprising or enigmatic as it might seem.

References

Arblaster, Anthony (1987), *Democracy*, Milton Keynes: Open University Press.

Bachrach, Peter and Baratz, Morton S. (1970), *Power and Poverty: Theory and Practice*, London: Oxford University Press.

Bealey, Frank (1988), *Democracy in the Contemporary State*, Oxford: Clarendon Press.

Bonham Carter, Mark (1988), "Whose Service?", *Index on Censorship*, Volume 17, Number 8, September.

Brand, Jack (1992), *British Parliamentary Parties: Policy and Power*, Oxford: Clarendon Press.

Butler, David and Kavanagh, Dennis (1992), *The British General Election of 1992*, Houndmills: MacMillan.

Campbell, Duncan (1988), "Paradoxes of Secrecy", *Index on Censorship*, Volume 17, Number 8, September.

Cockerell, Michael *et al*, (1985), *Sources Close to the Prime Minister*, London: Papermac.

Crick, Bernard (1964), *In Defence of Politics*, Harmondsworth: Penguin.

Crick, Bernard (1968), *The Reform of Parliament*, London: Weidenfeld and Nicolson, 2nd Edition.

Curran, James and Seaton, Jean (1991), *Power Without Responsibility: The Press and Broadcasting in Britain*, London: Routledge, 4th Edition.

Dahl, Robert A. (1961), *Who Governs?*, New Haven and London: Yale University Press.

Dahl, Robert A. (1971), *Polyarchy*, New York and London: Yale University Press.

Deutsch, Karl W. (1966), *The Nerves of Government*, New York: Free Press.

Downs, Anthony (1957), *An Economic Theory of Democracy*, New York: Harper and Row.

Easton, David (1965), *A Systems Analysis of Political Life*, New York: John Wiley and Sons.

Eldridge, John (1993), "News, Truth and Power" in Eldridge, John (ed), *Getting the Message*, London: Routledge.

Foley, Michael (1993), *The Rise of the British Presidency*, Manchester: Manchester University Press.

Garrett, John (1992), *Westminster: Does Parliament Work?*, London: Victor Gollancz.

Glasgow University Media Group (1976), *Bad News*, London: Routledge and Kegan Paul.

Grant, Wyn (1989), *Pressure Groups, Politics and Democracy in Britain*, London: Philip Allan.

Hogwood, Brian W. (1987), *From Crisis to Complacency*, Oxford: Oxford University Press.

Hinton, Peter and Wilson, Elizabeth (1993), "Accountability" in Wilson, J. and Hinton, P. (eds), *Public Services in the 1990s*, Eastham, Tudor.

Hood, Christopher C. (1983), *The Tools of Government*, London and Basingstoke: MacMillan.

Jordan, A.G. and Richardson, J.J. (1987), *Government and Pressure Groups in Britain*, Oxford: Clarendon Press.

Jordan, Grant and Richardson, Jeremy (1982), "The British Policy Style or the Logic of Negotiation?" in Richardson, Jeremy (ed), *Policy Styles in Western Europe*, London: George Allen & Unwin.

Judge, David (ed), (1983) *The Politics of Parliamentary Reform*, London: Heinemann.

Judge, David (1990), "Parliament and Interest Representation" in Rush, Michael (ed), *Parliament and Pressure Groups*, Manchester: University Press.

Judge, David (1993), *The Parliamentary State*, London: Sage.

Katz, Richard S. (1980), *A Theory of Parties and Electoral Systems*, Baltimore: The John Hopkins University Press.

Kavanagh, Dennis (1989), "The Timing of Elections: The British Case" in Crewe, Ivor and Harrop, Martin (eds), *Political Communications: The General Election Campaign of 1987*, Cambridge: Cambridge University Press.

Kingdom, John (1991), *Government and Politics in Britain: An Introduction*, Cambridge: Polity Press.

Kingdon, John (1984), *Agendas, Alternatives and Public Policies*, Boston: Little, Brown and Company.

Lawton, Alan and Rose, Aidan G. (1991), *Organisation and Management in the Public Sector*, London: Pitman.

Lenman, Bruce P. (1992), *The Eclipse of Parliament*, London: Edward Arnold.

Lindblom, C. E. (1977), *Politics and Markets*, New York: Basic Books.

Lukes, Steven (1974), *Power: A Radical View*, London: MacMillan.

Macpherson, C. B. (1972), *The Real World of Democracy*, Oxford: Oxford University Press.

McConnell, Allan (1994), "A Concluding Thought: Should Parties be Funded by the State?" in Robins, Lynton *et al.* (eds) (1994), *Britain's Changing Party System*, London and New York: Leicester University Press.

McConnell, Allan and Pyper, Robert (1994), "The Revived Select Committee on Scottish Affairs: A Case Study of Parliamentary Contradictions", *Strathclyde Papers on Government and Politics*, Number 98, Glasgow: University of Strathclyde.

McConnell, Allan (1995), *State Policy Formation and the Origins of the Poll Tax*, Aldershot: Dartmouth.

Marsh, David (1992), *The New Politics of British Trade Unionism*, Basingstoke: MacMillan.

Miliband, Ralph (1973), *The State in Capitalist Society*, London: Quartet.

Miliband, Ralph (1982), *Capitalist Democracy in Britain*, Oxford: Oxford University Press.

Miller, William L. (1991), *Media and Voters*, Oxford: Clarendon Press.

Newton, Kenneth (1995), "The Mass Media: Fourth Estate or Fifth Column", in Pyper, Robert and Robins, Lynton (eds), *Governing the UK in the 1990s*, Houndmills: MacMillan.

Norton, Philip (1993), *Does Parliament Matter?*, London: Harvester Wheatsheaf.

Offe, Claus (1984), *Contradictions of the Welfare State*, London: Hutchinson.

Oliver, D. and Austin, R. (1987), "Political and Constitutional Aspects of the Westland Affair", *Parliamentary Affairs*, Volume 40.

Oliver, Dawn (1991), *Government in the United Kingdom: The Search for Accountability, Effectiveness and Citizenship*, Milton Keynes: Open University Press.

Packenham, Robert A. (1970), "Legislatures and Political Development" in Kornberg, Allan and Musolf, Lloyd D. (eds), *Legislatures in Developmental Perspective*, North Carolina: Duke University Press.

Pross, A. Paul (1992), *Group Politics and Public Policy*, Toronto: Oxford University Press, 2nd Edition.

Pyper, Robert (1991), *The Evolving Civil Service*, Harlow: Longman.

Radice, Lisanne *et al*, (1990), *Member of Parliament: The Job of a Backbencher*, Houndmills: MacMillan, 2nd Edition.

Rhodes, R. A. W. and Marsh, D. (1992), "New Directions in the Study of Policy Networks", *European Journal of Political Research*, Volume 21, Numbers 1–2, February.

Richardson, J. J. and Jordan, A. G. (1979), *Governing Under Pressure*, Oxford: Martin Robertson.

Richardson, Jeremy, J. *et al*, (1992), "The Dynamics of Policy Change: Lobbying and Water Privatisation", *Public Administration*, Volume 70.

Richardson, Jeremy J. (ed) (1993), *Pressure Groups*, Oxford: Oxford University Press.

Riddell, Peter (1993), *Honest Opportunism*, London: Hamish Hamilton.

Robinson, Ann and Sandford, Cedric (1983), *Tax Policy-Making in the United Kingdom*, London: Heinemann.

Rose, Richard (1982), *British MPs: A Bite As Well As a Bark?*, CSPP Paper No. 98, Glasgow (University of Strathclyde): Centre for the Study of Public Policy.

Rose, Richard (1984), *Understanding Big Government: The Programme Approach*, London: Sage.

Rose, Richard (1989), *Politics in England*, Basingstoke: MacMillan, 5th Edition.

Rose, Richard and McAllister, Ian (1990), *The Loyalties of Voters: A Lifetime Learning Model*, London: Sage.

Seymour-Ure, Colin (1991), *The Press and British Broadcasting Since 1945*, Oxford: Blackwell.

SLGIU (1988), *"Opting Out" and the School Boards (Scotland) Bill*, Glasgow: Scottish Local Government Information Unit.

Smith, Martin J. (1993), *Pressure Power and Policy*, London: Harvester Wheatsheaf.

Stewart, John (1993), *The Rebuilding of Public Accountability*, Unpublished Paper.

Stringer, Joan K. and Richardson, J. J. (1980), "Managing the Political Agenda: Problem Definition and Policy Making in Britain", *Parliamentary Affairs*, Volume 33.

Thatcher, Margaret (1993), *The Downing Street Years*, London: Harper Collins.

Tonge, Jon (1994), "The Anti-Poll Tax Movement: A Pressure Movement?", *Politics*, Volume 14, Number 3, December.

Tunstall, Jeremy and Palmer, Michael (1991), *Media Moguls*, London: Routledge.

Wagg, Stephen (1987), "Mass Communications: The Debate About Ownership and Control", *Social Studies Review*, Volume 2, Number 4.

Walkland, S. A. (1983), "Parliamentary Reform, Party Alignment and Electoral Reform", in Judge, David (ed), *The Politics of Parliamentary Reform*, London: Heinemann.

2

PARLIAMENTARY ACCOUNTABILITY

Robert Pyper

Introduction

In 1993, a collection of essays was published in book form under the title *Debating the Constitution. New Perspectives on Constitutional Reform* (Barnett, Ellis and Hirst, 1993). Among the twenty-six chapters in this book, coverage was given to topics such as "Welfare Rights and the Constitution", "Women's Rights in Citizens' Europe", "Making the Police More Accountable", "The Media and the Constitution" and "The Necessity of Regionalism". The place of Parliament in a constitutionally reformed Britain did not merit a chapter in its own right. Indeed, the references to Parliament in the text tended to be fleeting, dismissive in tone, and marginal in context.

By the 1990s, this approach had become increasingly familiar. For many apparently serious academics and political pundits, Parliament was something of an intellectual backwater, and Parliamentary accountability was a concept to be treated as an historical curio, an anachronistic irrelevance. The fundamental premise of this chapter is that such an approach is misguided to the point of distortion. Any discussion of accountability in the context of the British constitution which neglects or minimises the role of Parliament has serious deficiencies.

It might have been expected of Philip Norton that he would answer his own question, *Does Parliament Matter?*, in the affirmative (Norton, 1993). However, he is far from being alone in recognising the central importance of Westminster in any meaningful discussion of accountability. David Judge has argued that the time has come "to take Parliament seriously" once again (Judge, 1993: 2). The accountability of government to Parliament

. . . helps to explain the organisational form as well as the political practice

of the modern British central state. To dismiss it as a "myth" is to eliminate an analytical key capable of unlocking the ambiguities and contradictions inherent within the system of "responsible government" in Britain.
(Judge, 1993: 159).

In a similar vein, Diana Woodhouse, while recognising the importance of extra-Parliamentary foci of accountability (including parties, the electoral process and the mass media) points out that ". . . in a constitution which centres upon the supremacy of Parliament, accountability to the legislature is constitutionally of most significance." (Woodhouse, 1994: 3).

In spite of these reassuring statements about the importance and legitimacy of studying Parliamentary accountability, the enigma of the dismissive approach which we cited earlier remains. In order to understand why this came to be seen as an acceptable mode of analysis (at least to some) we need to examine some strains of constitutional thought on the topic of Parliamentary accountability.

The Traditional Power Model, the Liberal Democratic Model, and Parliamentary Accountability

Various theoretical perspectives and models have emerged in response to the historical development of Parliamentary accountability. In the early part of the 19th century, the concept of accountable government was, as yet, embryonic. However, as the century progressed, the dependence of ministers on a Commons majority for their continuance in office, rather than on the will of the monarch, became clear. The relative weakness and low standing of the monarchy between the final onset of George III's madness and Victoria's marriage, combined with the increasing responsibilities imposed on governments by the rapidly changing social and economic environment to provide the impetus for the final shift away from quasi-monarchical government towards a more rigidly delimited constitutional monarchy. Bagehot, in 1867, could acknowledge as an established fact the consolidated position of the Prime Minister and his Cabinet, as the executive which had clearly become accountable to the legislature, as well as the entrenchment of ministerial responsibility in both its individual and collective forms (Bagehot, 1963 edition: *passim*).

The industrial revolution, with all that it implied for the social balance, combined with the constitutional, economic and social reforms of the 19th century to transform the role of British government. There were new offices and departments to administer, and old ones to expand. As the century progressed, ministers came to be seen increasingly as departmental heads as well as prominent counsellors. They came to be accountable to the people, via Parliament, for something more specific and tangible than merely the conduct of the monarch's business. The doctrine of individual ministerial responsibility, to which we will return later in this chapter, came to represent something which was vital and central to the whole idea of government in Britain. The doctrine would affect almost every aspect of the constitution. However, at its inception in the modern sense, during the period of increasing interaction between government and society in the 19th century, individual ministerial responsibility served the simple purpose of ensuring that the House of Commons could achieve control over the burgeoning bureaucracy by forcing ministers to oversee everything which might lead to trouble, and obliging civil servants to be punctilious about every significant step they took.

The new accord between the executive and the Commons' majority which was reached by means of direct individual ministerial responsibility to Parliament, allowed governments to lead the Commons' legislative activity as they had not done for centuries. Members steadily lost control over their own time in the face of rising legislative output and the increasingly disciplined parties. In return, they were given the power to hold particular ministers to account for action or lack of action in specified spheres of public policy (Chester, 1981: 120–21). The practice of utilising the Privy Council or the Home Office as repositories for every kind of supervisory duty over public services waned, and new departments emerged. As the number and size of departments grew from the early part of the 20th century onwards, so the capacity of Parliamentarians to effectively scrutinise and enforce meaningful accountability came to be stretched to its limit.

In the face of these developments, it is possible to discern the emergence of two broad theories or models of government and Parliamentary accountability. For the sake of convenience, these models can be termed the traditional power model and the liberal-democratic model.

THE TRADITIONAL POWER MODEL

A. H. Birch, writing about the fundamental division between these two perspectives on the constitution (Birch, 1977), noted the differences between the normative theory of what we can term the liberal-democratic model, and the working reality of the constitution which conforms in large measure to the expectations of those who will be viewed as adherents to the traditional power model.

The latter retained its value as a description of what really happens within the constitution, because the transfer of power from Crown to Parliament did not fundamentally change the nature of executive government. The British tradition of monarchical government carried with it certain assumptions about the power of the executive, and these were passed on to the new Parliamentary governors. The ability of a government to do its job depended on it being free from unnecessary restrictions. The duty of government was to govern. Of course, according to this interpretation, Parliament has the right to report on and approve governmental acts, but only with the strict understanding that the government should be allowed to get on with its job until defeated by a vote of the Commons or the electorate.

Birch provideds us with a useful account of the traditional power model:

> It talks of the responsibility of Her Majesty's Government for the administration of the country, of the importance of protecting civil servants from political interference, of Parliament's function as a debating chamber in which public opinion is aired . . . It is . . . usual to employ . . . concepts, such as that the Government has a mandate to put its policies into effect, and is ultimately answerable to the electorate (not Parliament) for their success.
> (Birch, 1977: 165).

The role of Parliament is simply to provide a forum for the ventilation of grievances and the continuation of the party battle.

Birch's view that this interpretation of the constitution is held by those in power or with the prospect of coming to power, is only part of the truth. While most ministers, shadow ministers and ambitious backbenchers would appreciate the benefits which accrue from the traditional power model, some people in these positions are firm supporters of the liberal-democratic viewpoint. Similarly, there are backbenchers with no obvious ambition for, or serious prospects of, attaining office, who take the traditionalist line. Neither were all academic commentators and journalists totally convinced that the traditional power model should be discarded (as Birch assumed they were).

For example, Henry Fairlie argued that the domination of Parliament by the executive is not only real, but actually desirable (Fairlie, 1968). He

perceived the role of the Commons as important, but distinctly limited .
Furthermore, he felt that it would be unrealistic to expect any
government to initiate fundamental change in the balance of power
between executive and legislature. In any case, the ultimate accountability of a government to the electorate provided, according to Fairlie, the
best check on its activities.

When applied directly to the question of accountability, the traditional
power model posits a fairly simple and straightforward relationship
between ministers and Parliament. By answering Questions and partici-
pating in debates, ministers are fulfilling the major part of their
accountability to Parliament. In effect, this amounts to nothing more
than explanatory accountability, or answerability. The accountability of
ministers to their colleagues in government, and in particular to the
Prime Minister, is paramount.

Founded as it is on the concept of the party struggle, the traditional
power model provides a straightforward answer to the question of
sanctions (implicit in the concept of full accountability, as argued in the
Introduction). A minister will normally resign only if the government
stands to lose more from his remaining in office than from his departure.
Again, the important issue is the effect on the government's ability to get
on with the job of governing. As far as civil servants are concerned, the
traditional power model stresses two factors: they must remain essentially
anonymous, and their accountability to ministers (not to Parliament)
should be complete.

THE LIBERAL-DEMOCRATIC MODEL

Birch encapsulated the idealistic nature of this theory, based as it is on a
certain degree of nostalgia for the supposed heyday of Parliamentary
control in the mid-19th century.

> . . . it talks of Parliamentary sovereignty, of the responsibility of ministers
> to Parliament for the work of their departments, of the defence of the
> people's rights through the vigilance of "the Parliamentary watchdog", of
> the democratic advantages of a system in which there is no separation of
> powers between legislature and executive.
> (Birch, 1977: 165).

He made the general point that while the constitutional theory which is
here termed the traditional power model provides the more accurate
description of how the constitution works, it is the language, and in some

senses the mythology, of the liberal-democratic model which pervades the British system of government (Birch, 1977: 237).

The factor which binds the adherents to this model together, and differentiates them from those who favour the traditional power theory, is their belief in the extant or potential power of Parliament to effectively monitor, influence and control the actions of government. This is not to say that the divisions between those we would term liberal-democrats and traditionalists are absolute, or indeed that the divisions among the liberal-democrats themselves, to which we are about to refer, are rigid. We are dealing here with relative terms, in an attempt to tease out some general points of reference in relation to Parliamentary accountability. Bearing this in mind, it can be argued that liberal-democrats can be divided into two broad groupings: "contents" and "malcontents".

The fact that common ground exists between some liberal-democrats and traditionalists can be illustrated with reference to the position of Enoch Powell. He was never in any doubt about the reason why the traditional power model offers the more accurate description of how the constitution works:

> . . . the English have a profound conviction that the Queen's Government must be carried on. In the end, they are on the side of government, in the end they believe that somehow somebody has to do the governing. . . (Powell, 1982: 173).

Notwithstanding this, Powell, Michael Foot and others could reasonably be described as liberal-democrats of the "content" variety because they believe it actually functions in such a fashion as to make these maxims real. Ronald Butt's view of *The Power of Parliament* (1969) epitomised this approach, which attributed to the House of Commons an essentially negative, checking role, which is, nonetheless, far from insignificant.

These people took a similar, generally satisfied view of Parliamentary accountability to that held by the traditionalists, albeit for different reasons. The traditional methods of scrutiny (Questions and debates) were seen to be powerful and effective weapons for the task of enforcing ministerial accountability to Parliament, although the failure of ministers to abide by the interpretation placed by these liberal-democrats on the sanctions element caused some measure of concern.

By the 1950s and 1960s, the complacency of the "content" liberal-democrats was being challenged by others, who were less satisfied with the existing relationship between the legislature and the executive, and aimed to introduce structural reforms in order to redress the balance of power in favour of the House of Commons. The "malcontents" were in the ascendancy; their reformist schemes gained impetus, and were at least partially realised with the advent of new organs of Parliamentary scrutiny in the 1960s. Allowance must be made for the fact that the "malcontents" were not an homogenous group. Their views on the objectives of reform ranged from the extremely vague and highly generalised (achieve a fundamental alteration in the balance of power between the executive and the legislature) to the specific (allow MPs more opportunities and time to question ministers in detail). Nonetheless, at least implicitly, they shared one aim: to enhance the standing and functioning of Parliamentary accountability.

The experience of the 1960s and 1970s resulted in the disillusionment of some liberal-democrat "malcontents". For some, faith in the efficacy of structural reform was weakened by what they perceived to be the disappointing impact of new Commons select committees and the Parliamentary Commissioner for Administration. Consequently, some liberal-democrats no longer placed their hopes in adding to the existing structures and powers of Parliament, but felt that there was still much to be done before the liberal-democratic maxims could be realised.

For Philip Norton, the answer and the key to progress lay in revitalising the dormant powers of the Commons.

> . . . the answer lies with MPs themselves. The means by which the House can achieve a greater degree of scrutiny and influence of (sic) that part of it which forms the government exist already, but those means can be employed only if Members themselves are willing to employ them. The two elements of this approach – the powers available to the House and the willingness of Members to employ them – have been ignored . . . by . . . reformers.
>
> (Norton, 1981: 225).

Norton placed great stress on the need for attitudinal change amongst MPs as a means of reasserting Parliamentary accountability. Others, most notably Nevil Johnson (1970; 1981) and S. A. Walkland (1976; 1981; 1983), agreed with Norton that the liberal-democratic creed could not be fulfilled until attitudes changed. However, this school went further, to argue that only a fundamental constitutional upheaval would serve to loosen the stranglehold of the executive. They saw electoral reform as the most important prerequisite for this. In other words, these liberal-democrat "malcontents" had lost faith in the value of internal structural and even behavioural change on the part of MPs alone. Instead, they now favoured reforms which were external to Parliament in the sense that they stressed the importance of reforming not Parliament *per se*, but, at least in the first instance, the broad political environment.

Thus, it might be argued that through an unholy alliance of two schools of thought (adherents to the traditional power model and an element of the liberal-democratic "malcontents"), the value and importance of Parliamentary accountability came to be played down. The views of Norton, Judge and Woodhouse, cited above, represent a welcome reassertion of the significance of this strain of accountability. For the remainder of this chapter, we shall explore some of the key themes associated with the concept of Parliamentary accountability.

Mechanisms and Agents: A Survey

When establishing the broad parameters of accountability in the introductory chapter of this book, we set out a range of basic ministerial and civil service role responsibilities. It was argued that the ministerial role encompasses responsibility for policy leadership, departmental management, legislative piloting, and the representation of departmental interests in Cabinet, with pressure groups and with departmental clients. For their part, civil servants will have role responsibilities for the provision of policy advice to ministers, administering or implementing policy and departmental or agency management.

The various mechanisms and agents of Parliamentary scrutiny engage with these role responsibilities to secure (at least in theory) the accountability of the executive. A number of important qualifications should be entered at this point, however.

First, certain areas of executive activity (for example, the operation of the security and intelligence services) are not subject to Parliamentary scrutiny in any meaningful sense. No mechanisms exist to examine these areas of work, and Questions about them are rebuffed. Thus, at any given time there will exist a partial lacuna in Parliamentary accountability.

Second, the primacy of the doctrine of individual ministerial responsibility means that, in strict constitutional terms, the accountability of civil servants to Parliament is severely limited. This was given added emphasis, and an additional spin, in the aftermath of the Tisdall, Willmore and Ponting cases in 1984–85 (Pyper, 1985; Ponting 1985) and the case of Colette Bowe during the Westland affair in 1986 (Linklater and Leigh, 1986; Madgwick and Woodhouse, 1989). These cases, together with the publication in 1985 of the "Note of Guidance on the Duties and Responsibilities of Civil Servants in Relation to Ministers" by the then Head of the Civil Service, Sir Robert Armstrong, emphasised the constitutional norms. The Armstrong Memorandum baldly stated that civil servants were accountable to their own civil service superiors, and to ministers. They owed duties of confidentiality and loyalty to the Crown, but since the Crown was equated with the government of the day in modern constitutional terms, the position of civil servants could not be distinguished from that of the government. Accordingly, officials suffering crises of conscience or presented with acute ethical dilemmas could not take refuge in what they might perceive as their overriding accountability to the people or even Parliament, since this accountability did not exist. Despite the significant reservations which have been expressed by former senior civil servants over the years (Wass, 1985; Chipperfield, 1994), the Armstrong Memorandum has become entrenched within the Civil Service Management Code, and stoutly defended by Armstrong's successor (Sir Robin Butler) and the government in the face of close scrutiny by the Treasury and Civil Service Committee of the House of Commons (Treasury and Civil Service Committee, 1993: paragraph 18).

Finally, the mechanisms and agents of Parliamentary scrutiny function with varying degrees of efficacy, to produce a rather mixed result in terms of the overall accountability of the executive. The last point can be illustrated by surveying the range of mechanisms and agents, and offering brief comments about the "coverage" they give to the role responsibilities set out above. A catalogue of parliamentary mechanisms of accountability would be comprised of the following:

- informal contacts utilised by MPs, including personal letters and verbal communications;
- Parliamentary Questions;
- debates;
- standing committees;
- the Public Accounts Committee and the National Audit Office;
- departmentally-based select committees;
- the Parliamentary Commissioner for Administration.

When discussing the functioning of these mechanisms, we shall refer mainly, although not exclusively, to the House of Commons.

INFORMAL CONTACTS

While it is difficult to offer definitive statements about the quantity and quality of scrutiny delivered by informal mechanisms, some general comments can be made. The trend towards increased professionalism amongst MPs, coupled with mounting pressure on members to secure redress of an ever-expanding range of constituents' grievances (stemming in part from the increased impact of the state on people's lives), helped ensure that this aspect of Parliamentary scrutiny developed quite significantly.

Although the research undertaken in this sphere is rather rudimentary, and there are obvious problems associated with attempting to quantify this type of scrutiny, the evidence which is available shows that there has been a steady acceleration in the increase in correspondence between MPs and ministers during the period since 1945 (Marsh, 1985). One illustration of this would be the fact that five ministers in a single department of state were receiving over two thousand letters every month from MPs in the early 1980s (Norton, 1981: 114). There was a substantial increase in the number of letters sent by MPs to ministers during the following decade, to the point where about 250,000 letters per session were being sent (Elms and Terry, 1990; Franklin and Norton, 1993: 118).

Sheer quantity is one matter, but what can we say about the nature of this type of scrutiny? It seems clear that personal letters addressed by MPs to ministers are treated very seriously within departments and agencies. In that sense, one might argue that informal contacts between MPs and ministers produce scrutiny of a relatively high calibre. In simple terms, an MP's letter will elicit a much more specific, detailed response than would be the case if the same matter had been raised on the floor of the House. These letters are immediately afforded preferential treatment within departments and agencies. One former minister encapsulated the aura of importance which surround these missives:

> . . . letters come in from MPs and you look at them and you say, "That dum-dum has written about so-and-so". And to your astonishment, because he's an MP, his letter is given a green folder, it's flagged Urgent – it's got a signal on it saying "For God's sake, answer this tomorrow." (Anonymous MP, quoted in King, 1974: 30–31).

The high-priority investigations of subjects referred to in MP's letters serve to enhance the accountability of both ministers and civil servants for their role responsibilities. Which particular role responsibilities are likely to be the targets of this type of communication? Marsh gives us a clue:

> Members do not write letters now when they previously asked questions: the great increase in the demands for constituency services has been answered by the use of correspondence with ministers. Now such correspondence is the most popular and effective means of seeking redress of grievances . . .
> (Marsh, 1985: 87).

Certain aspects of ministerial role responsibility are likely to be affected by this kind of scrutiny. The minister's role as policy leader could, conceivably, come under examination as a consequence of an MP's letter of inquiry. A detail of departmental policy could require amendment in order to alleviate the type of problem encountered by the MP's constituent. The amendment, initiated by the minister as policy leader, could be said to have resulted from the scrutiny and influence brought to bear by the MP. It should be stressed, however, that major policy issues are much more likely to be raised by means of Parliamentary Questions and debates.

In practice, the main aspects of ministerial role responsibility which would be affected by this type of informal scrutiny are related to the managerial and "ambassadorial" (i.e. dealing with client and pressure groups) functions. Furthermore, when responding to the typical letter, the minister is, in effect, often being held accountable for the actions of officials. Most of the complaints raised by MPs in letters to ministers relate to the way in which departmental policy has been implemented or administered, and, of course, this is a specific role responsibility of the civil servants. As we shall see, one important consequence of the Next Steps initiative has been an attempted disaggregation of policy delivery and implementation from the work of parent departments, and this has produced a new, direct line of communication between MPs and agency chief executives. This raises the problematic issue of civil service accountability to Parliament, to which we shall return in due course.

PARLIAMENTARY QUESTIONS

In terms of sheer volume, there can be no doubt that PQs have assumed increased importance as a means of securing the accountability of ministers over the years since the Second World War. Whereas a total of 17,064 Questions of all types (for oral answer, for written answer, and

Private Notice Questions) were asked in session 1946–47, by 1989–90 the figure had risen to 66,071 (Irwin, Kennon, Natzler and Rogers, 1993: 27). Within this global increase, certain trends were apparent. There was a very significant increase in the number of Questions for written answer, from well below 10,000 during the 1940s and 1950s, to around 40,000 per session by the late 1980s and early 1990s. Over the period as a whole, this type of Question came to be utilised much more frequently than the Question for oral answer: the turning point came in 1972–73, when the "unstarred" Questions (for written answer) formed the majority of PQs for the first time (Borthwick, 1979: 491). Oral Questions also grew numerically, nonetheless, especially in the period since the late 1980s. Whereas the total number of Questions for oral answer in each session between 1946 and 1987 never exceeded 17,500, and was often nearer to half that figure, the number rose to well over 20,000 per session thereafter (Irwin, Kennon, Natzler and Rogers: 27).

The efficaciousness of the Parliamentary Question as a means of enhancing scrutiny of the executive has long been a matter of dispute, as we shall see. Nonetheless, it is easy to comprehend the continuing attraction of this device. All government ministers can be questioned in a number of different ways, about almost any aspect of their departmental responsibilities. In the oral form, PQs can be put to ministers on a rota system which facilitates more frequent appearances by ministers from the departments which attract greatest Parliamentary interest. Those oral Questions not reached in the course of a given Question Time are automatically answered in writing unless those who tabled them request their deferment to a later sitting. MPs are more likely to utilise Questions for written answer, as opposed to oral Questions, when auditing departmental performance, or attempting to discover information which may be hard to get elsewhere (Franklin and Norton, 1993: 109). Private Notice Questions, up to 40 of which are asked in an average-length Parliamentary session (Irwin, Kennon, Natzler and Rogers, 1993: 27), relate to matters of an urgent character. At the discretion of the Speaker, these may be put orally to ministers at the end of Question Time.

Against the superficial attractiveness of PQs, the observer is left with some reservations about the ultimate impact of this type of Parliamentary scrutiny. It must be remembered that ministers can, and occasionally do, plead that the information requested in a PQ is not available, or could only be obtained at disproportionate cost. Furthermore, there is a recognised list of topics on which ministers of successive governments have refused to be questioned (Sedgemore, 1980: 184–87). Beyond these points, the advent of the Next Steps executive agencies brought about a fundamental change to the functioning of PQs as mechanisms of accountability. We shall examine this in the next section of this chapter. In the meantime, it should be borne in mind that our comments about Questions relate to PQs directed at parent departments rather than at executive agencies.

When considering the limitations of PQs, the views of MPs utilising the PQ system should be borne in mind. A survey of MPs who were frequent users of PQs revealed that a relatively low percentage of the group believed Questions performed well in relation to key functions relating to accountability (Franklin and Norton, 1993: 107). For example, only 23% believed PQs performed "well" in relation to the function of holding ministers accountable. A mere 13% believed Questions performed the function of influencing government policy and actions "well".

Part of the problem would seem to be associated with one of the perceived strengths of PQs: the fact that ministers are likely to be called upon to answer Questions about virtually any aspect of their department's work. Because the potential targets for PQs are so numerous, they can be a rather inefficient and ineffective means of holding ministers to account. William Waldegrave once commented: "Parliamentary Questions are really a scatter-gun approach to scrutiny: most Questions are fairly harmless and easily dealt with." (Quoted in Pyper, 1983: 87).

Notwithstanding these weaknesses, the PQ's "scatter-gun approach" does at least have the merit of ensuring that all aspects of ministerial role responsibility can be touched upon. What is more, this approach, for all its deficiencies, does sometimes result in a direct hit, as Waldegrave was prepared to admit.

> . . . occasionally a questioner has done some good background work, and can through asking a series of Questions, reveal something important. Perhaps only one in ten is a "good" Question, but these tend to be very good. Tam Dalyell is excellent at researching such Questions – I have learned from him on various technical matters.
> (Quoted in Pyper, 1987: 87–88).

William Rodgers, a Minister in the Labour Governments of the 1960s and 1970s, has supported this general point.

> As a backbencher, I often felt deflated when my well thought-out Questions elicited only a bland reply from the minister. As a minister, I

learned that the bland reply is often given when the backbench questioner has come very near the mark! I recall on some occasions giving just such a reply, then going back to the department and saying to my officials, "Well, we got away with it this time, but only just."
(Quoted in Pyper, 1987: 88).

Whether Questions are viewed as "good" or "weak", it cannot be denied that they have a continuous impact on the work of every government department.

The task of overseeing the process of preparing answers to PQs falls to the Parliamentary Unit, normally located within the Secretary of State's Private Office, and headed by the department's Parliamentary clerk, a middle-ranking civil servant (Giddings, 1993: 125). In all cases, the PQ work assumes priority over other business. Draft answers, together with supporting documents, are passed up the departmental hierarchies. Normally, the minister concerned, along with his or her private secretary and the permanent secretary of the department, will consider the draft answer and the accompanying notes, which, in the case of a Question for oral answer, will provide information on points which might arise in supplementary Questions. Oral Questions are ultimately answered by the minister on the floor of the House. In the course of Question Time, the minister will be watched by his or her private secretary, sitting in the official box at the side of the chamber and making notes of any last-minute adjustments made by the minister, as well as the supplementaries.

> . . . however much preparatory work there may have been done in the Department, the answer in the House, whether to the main Question or to any supplementary, is that of the Minister, personally and in full hearing of a well-attended Chamber. It is his responsibility, therefore, to decide the final form of the answer . . .
> (Chester and Bowring, 1962: 235–36).

The PQ, whether for oral or written answer, is therefore designed to bring about the accountability of ministers for their role responsibilities as policy leaders, departmental managers, departmental ambassadors and legislative pilots. However, officials also find themselves under scrutiny, albeit not from Parliament directly. Each PQ attracts ministerial attention to the work being done by departmental civil servants. Thus, the minister, in his or her capacity as departmental manager, brings an internal form of accountability to bear on the officials. The latter are effectively answering to their minister for the conduct of their own role responsibilities as policy advisers, departmental managers and departmental administrators: the minister, in turn, answers to Parliament.

We are left with the impression that, in the hands of shrewd MPs, Parliamentary Questions can be useful weapons of Parliamentary scrutiny. This is perhaps particularly true when PQs are used as one weapon in the formidable armoury of a Tam Dalyell, or as part of a concerted campaign by a number of MPs (Giddings, 1993: 142–48). However, with the full range of a department's work at which to aim, with no time to expose a minister to lengthy and frequent interrogation, with no opportunities to question civil servants in person about their own role responsibilities, the limitations of the PQ as a regular instrument of detailed scrutiny are obvious.

Again, as with the informal contacts, the advent of the Next Steps executive agencies brought a basic change in the operation of this mechanism of Parliamentary scrutiny, and this will be examined in due course.

DEBATES

Parliamentary debates come in a wide range of different forms. A simple categorization would divide debates into two broad types. General debates take place on opposition days, estimates days, private members' motions, adjournment motions (general adjournment, daily half-hour adjournment, emergency debate, recess adjournment), and government motions. Legislative debates take place on the second and third readings of bills, as well as at the report stages, and when considering amendments introduced by the other chamber. Excluding legislative debates and the daily half-hour adjournment debates, it has been estimated that approximately a quarter of the time available in the House of Commons is taken up by debates (Norton, 1993: 94).

Viewed in terms of accountability, we can say that debates serve the purpose of bringing ministers to the despatch box, to answer for their role responsibilities. During general debates, any aspect of the ministerial role might be the focus of attention. For example, during opposition days between December 1990 and March 1991, a series of debates was staged on the abolition of the Community Charge, and these clearly focused attention on the policy leadership role of the ministers who had conceived the abortive policy. In other cases, the minister's role as departmental manager or departmental ambassador might be the principal subject of attention. Legislative debates obviously relate specifically to the minister's role as legislative pilot.

As with PQs, the process of preparing for and conducting "post mortems" on, debates can serve to enhance the internal accountability of departmental civil servants to their official and ministerial superiors.

Debates do not take place in a political vacuum. The nature of the issue under consideration, the extent of extra-Parliamentary concern about the issue, the party balance in the House of Commons at any given time, the effectiveness of party discipline and the role of the whips, can all play a part in influencing the nature and outcome of debates. It would be foolish to argue that ministers (and their officials) cannot be held to account through the medium of debate. However, the atmosphere which prevails during many debates is not conducive to sustained and detailed interrogation. Backbenchers and ministers alike tend to deliver prepared speeches rather then participate in genuine debate. Party political point-scoring is the name of the game during debates on major issues of policy, and the power of the whips ensures that, exceptional circumstances apart, governments can depend on securing a majority in the division.

STANDING COMMITTEES

The great majority of government bills are sent to standing committees for detailed consideration, once the House has approved the principles which lie behind the bills. These committees are comprised of between sixteen and fifty members, reflecting the party composition of the Commons. Membership is for the duration of the particular bill under consideration, so the very name "standing" committee is something of a misnomer. Only in the case of the Scottish standing committees can membership be described as permanent or specialised (that is, lasting for a complete Parliamentary session).

Members of standing committees are technically nominated by the Committee of Selection, although the party whips play a major part in the process of selection. A chairman is appointed by the Speaker. The opposition front bench will be represented, and MPs from each side of the House with particular knowledge of, or expertise in, a bill's subject matter will normally find themselves on the standing committee dealing with that bill.

From the government side, the minister in charge of the bill, together with one or more of his junior ministers, his Parliamentary private secretary and a whip, will be members of a standing committee. In some cases, ministers from other departments, whose interests might be affected by a bill, could be members of a committee.

Standing committees carry out their task of scrutinising bills by discussing each clause, and suggesting possible amendments. Witnesses are not called, and there is no cross-examination of either ministers or civil servants. Instead, the work of a standing committee resembles that of the Commons as a whole. Debate within committee tends to be slightly less formal than that which takes place on the floor of the House, but the atmosphere in each arena is broadly similar.

In his or her roles as legislative pilot and policy leader, the minister is undoubtedly exposed to scrutiny through the medium of the standing committee. Indirectly, the role of senior civil servants as policy advisers is also being scrutinised, although the key word here is indirectly.

> . . . the Member in committee who wishes to elucidate a question of fact from the administrator (in charge of steering a bill through) . . . has to ask, and receive an answer to his question through the Minister.
> (Wiseman, 1970: 181).

The task of the minister is to bring the bill through its committee stage with all its fundamental principles intact, and as many of its detailed provisions as possible free from amendment. In this task, the minister is aided by the whip, who will endeavour to secure the cooperation and the votes of government members. Of course, there will be occasions when the minister will be prepared, or obliged, to accept amendments.

> But more important than the making of amendments is the scrutiny to which Ministers and their policies are subjected . . . For hour after hour and for week after week a Minister may be required to defend his bill against attack from others who may be only slightly less knowledgable than himself. His departmental brief may be full and his grasp of the subject considerable but even so he needs to be constantly on the alert and any defects he or his policy reveals will be very quickly exploited by his political opponents.
> (Griffith, 1981: 130–31).

This point notwithstanding, the limitations of standing committees as agents of accountability are obvious. Standing committees have been described as "the Achilles heel" of the legislative process (Drewry, 1988: 128). The work is time-consuming, the quality of scrutiny highly variable (but all too often rather superficial), and for most of the time these committees simply provide another forum for the continuation of the party battle (Griffith, 1984; Norton, 1993: 82).

Due to the fact that ministers have access to a wealth of detailed information, as well as the expertise of their officials, even the best informed member of a standing committee is unlikely to be able to match the resources which the minister can muster when the going gets rough. This means that "the scrutiny of ministers has about it a measure of superficiality based on an inadequacy of information" (Griffiths, 1981: 131).

Thoroughgoing reform of standing committee procedure has been a perennial theme for Parliamentarians. In practice, however, there have been only limited experiments which have seen small numbers of standing committees taking evidence in select committee fashion before reverting to the traditional format to examine the bill.

It is worth noting that, in some respects, legislative scrutiny can be even more intensive in the House of Lords than in the Commons (Shell, 1992: chapters 5 and 6). A number of factors contribute to this, including the existence of a relatively large number of crossbenchers, the general tendency amongst peers to be independent-minded and the fact that there is no automatic government majority. In addition, because bills cannot be guillotined in the Lords, there is an increased tendency for governments to offer concessions in standing committee, if the timetable for passage is likely to be tight.

PUBLIC ACCOUNTS COMMITTEE AND NATIONAL AUDIT OFFICE

It is only in the realm of external financial audit that we can discern a systematic attempt by Parliament to bring civil servants to account, directly and constitutionally, for an aspect of their role responsibility. The accounts of government departments and executive agencies (once again, changes in the mode of operation of this strain of scrutiny, which were consequent upon the advent of Next Steps, will be examined in due course) are subjected to regular financial auditing and value for money auditing by the Comptroller and Auditor General and his staff in the National Audit Office. Under the terms of the 1983 National Audit Act, the C&AG and the NAO (successor to the former Exchequer and Audit Department) were given a new constitutional basis as servants of the House of Commons, rather than adjuncts of the executive.

Following audit, reports are filed with the Public Accounts Committee of the House of Commons, which conducts detailed examinations of the accounting officers, paying special attention to any problematic items which have been identified by the NAO. These accounting officers are invariably senior civil servants. Unless they have specifically dissociated themselves from any item of account (on the grounds that this has been carried out under ministerial instructions), these officials are formally and directly accountable to the House of Commons, through the PAC. Ministers may also be required to furnish the PAC with oral or written evidence relating to the departmental finances.

In our terms, therefore, ministers and civil servants are being held accountable to Parliament for the proper discharge of their roles in relation to departmental management in general, and financial management in particular.

Opinions vary regarding the effectiveness of this form of Parliamentary scrutiny (Flegman, 1980; 1985; Latham, 1986; Robinson, 1988). Senior civil servants conventionally pay tribute to the rigour of the PAC and the discipline this imposes upon the internal lines of accountability within government departments. Sir Antony Part, former Permanent Secretary at the Department of Trade and Industry, encapsulated this view:

> The Permanent Secretary . . . will spend about three weeks concentrating solely on PAC work . . . Such a concentrated dose of information relating to particular aspects of his Department's work can do no harm to any Permanent Secretary. Indeed, most of them believe that as a result they are better informed . . . Occasionally such preparatory work takes the Permanent Secretary to sites of projects he would not otherwise visit, to meet members of his Department he would not otherwise have met. (Quoted in Pyper, 1987: 104).

While the impact of the reports produced by the PAC and the NAO are often praised for, *inter alia*, their "pervasive influence on . . . accountability" (Bates, 1988: 193), some observers point to the huge task confronting the PAC and the NAO, the highly variable nature of the scrutiny brought to bear by the PAC, and the lack of skill or inclination on the part of some of its members (Robinson, 1988: 154).

It remains for us to offer some comments on select committees and the Parliamentary Commissioner for Administration. While select committees beyond the PAC figured from time to time as elements of the system of Parliamentary scrutiny (for example, there was an Estimates Committee between 1912–39 and 1945–70, and a Select Committee on Nationalised Industries between 1955–79), it is fair to say that there was no attempt to introduce a system of select committees until 1966 at the earliest. Around the same time, the office of Parliamentary Commissioner for Administration came into being. It would be appropriate to consider these mechanisms in the context of the new regime of Parliamentary accountability which began to take shape in the mid-1960s.

The Changing Landscape of Parliamentary Accountability

When attempting to analyse the changes which have taken place in the theory and practice of Parliamentary accountability over recent times, the observer is confronted with the need to explain two broad developments. The first is the emergence of what might be described as a new regime of accountability, predicated upon the advent of new organs of scrutiny. The second is the collection of structural and managerial reforms within the machinery of government, which have had implications for accountability. In each case, the developments proceeded without overt, formal constitutional change, although their impact on the constitution was to be highly significant. Let us examine these developments in turn.

A NEW REGIME OF ACCOUNTABILITY

The progenitors of the new regime of Parliamentary accountability, which began to take shape in 1966, and was given a major boost in 1979, were many and varied. Those we have described as liberal-democrat "malcontents", together with such curious bed-fellows as Richard Crossman and Norman St John Stevas, can be credited with a share in the parentage. What was this regime, what was "new" about it, and what impact did it have upon Parliamentary accountability?

The components of the new regime are easy to describe. In addition to the traditional methods of Parliamentary scrutiny (informal contacts, Parliamentary Questions, debates, standing committees, the PAC and NAO, and the hotch-potch of extant select committees) Parliament had at its disposal from 1966 onwards new devices designed to enhance the accountability of ministers and civil servants for the work being done in the departments of state. Specifically, a range of new experimental Commons select committees evolved from 1966 into a fully-fledged system by 1979 (with key roles being performed by Richard Crossman and Norman St John Stevas as Leaders of the House of Commons at crucial junctures), while the Parliamentary Commissioner for Administration was established in 1967 (again, Crossman played a significant role, despite his private scepticism regarding the limited powers of the UK "ombudsman").

It is difficult to be precise about the motivations which lay behind the creation of the new regime, partly because there was never a conscious and concerted attempt to give it life: instead, the new organs of scrutiny can be seen to have developed and evolved in an incremental fashion typical of the British constitution. However, we can identify at least some contributing factors.

- The Crichel Down affair of 1954, and its extended aftermath (which included the British lecture tour of the Danish Ombudsman in 1958 and the publication of the Whyatt Report in 1961), served as a catalyst for change, by highlighting the inherent weaknesses of the traditional system of Parliamentary accountability, and the need for new mechanisms designed to secure redress of citizens' grievances against the government machine (Griffith, 1987; Justice, 1961; Nicolson, 1986).
- The initial reforming impulse of the Wilson Government, particularly in relation to Parliamentary systems and structures, coupled with Crossman's personal commitment to change.
- The intellectual inspiration of the liberal-democrat "malcontents", which hovered over the early developments.
- The Thatcher Government's antipathy towards the state bureaucracy, which bore at least one curious fruit in the form of the 1979 select committee system, geared as it was for the purpose of scrutinising departments of state.
- The personal commitment of St John Stevas in favour of redressing the imbalance of power between Parliament and the executive (this contributed to an admixture of motivations within the first Thatcher Cabinet in support of the 1979 reform).

Whatever the contributing factors, the new regime of Parliamentary scrutiny took its fundamental form in the period between 1966 and 1979. By the latter date, the Parliamentary Commissioner for Administration was well established, and there were fourteen new Commons select committees scrutinising the work of the main government departments. The structure and content of the select committee system continued to evolve thereafter, and by 1995 seventeen committees were in operation. The novel aspects of the new regime can be simply delineated.

First, there was now a wider breadth of Parliamentary scrutiny of the executive than ever before. With only a few exceptions, government departments, across the board, were open to investigation by the PCA in cases of alleged maladministration, and the select committees for the purpose of on-going scrutiny.

Second, the new mechanisms facilitated a greater depth of scrutiny.

The sustained questioning of ministers and civil servants during select committee hearings, the close examination of departmental papers by committee members, coupled with the detailed investigation of personnel and documents in an average of 220 cases handled by the PCA each year, produced a level of scrutiny which could not be matched by the traditional mechanisms. While the PCA would focus primarily on the role responsibilities relating to departmental management and the administration or implementation of policy, the select committees would range across the full panoply of ministerial (and civil service) role responsibilities.

Over the years, debate has raged regarding the impact of the select committees and the Parliamentary Commissioner for Administration. The powers, remit and jurisdiction of these mechanisms, together with their performance in key cases, have been pored over by academics and Parliamentarians (a flavour of the debates and issues may be derived from Drewry, 1988a; Gregory and Hutchesson, 1975; Gregory and Pearson, 1992; Judge, 1992; Judge, 1993; McConnell and Pyper, 1994). Given the limited focus of this chapter, it would be inappropriate to engage in a substantive account of the major issues and themes surrounding these organs of scrutiny. Notwithstanding this point, it should be noted that some of the broader issues and themes, as they relate specifically to accountability, will be discussed in the next section.

At this stage, however, it is possible for us to identify what is arguably the single most significant contribution made by the select committees and the PCA to accountability. Under the new regime, civil service accountability to Parliament was substantially enhanced, to the point where it became possible to argue that officials were now, *de facto*, directly accountable for their role responsibilities. We should immediately add that there was no change in the formal constitutional position of civil servants: the governments of the 1980s and 1990s were keen to stress that officials were accountable only to their ministerial and civil service superiors, and not to Parliament (except for the special case of accounting officers and the PAC). In other words, the *de facto* accountability was not accompanied by *de jure* accountability. Nonetheless, it was difficult to avoid the conclusion that the combined operation of the PCA and the Commons' select committees had produced a change in the relationship of accountability between the civil service and Parliament.

Investigations into cases of alleged maladministration by the Parliamentary Commissioner triggered internal scrutiny by senior civil servants and ministers of the work being carried out by middle to low ranking officials. Beyond this strengthening of internal lines of account-ability, however, the PCA facilitated a limited, but definite movement in the direction of external accountability of civil servants to Parliament. The limitation was due to the fact that the Parliamentary Commissioner and his staff were not Parliamentarians as such, but servants of Parliament. Nonetheless, when answering questions before the PCA, officials were effectively answering to Parliament. These officials were not simply senior civil servants: they came from every grade, and they answered questions relating to their role responsibilities for departmental management and the administration and implementation of policy. Moreover, in certain circumstances, there was the possibility that officials might be called to account for their actions before real Parliamentarians sitting on the body which functioned as the PCA's political arm, the Select Committee on the Parliamentary Commissioner for Administration.

The work of the select committees similarly enhanced the functioning of internal lines of accountability, as ministers and senior civil servants oversaw the gathering of documentary evidence and the performance of their own staffs before the committees. However, a clear statement of the non-accountability of civil servants to Parliament came with the advent of the 1979 select committee system. A Memorandum of Guidance for Officials Appearing Before Select Committees, usually referred to as the Osmotherly Memorandum, attempted to set the agenda for the conduct of relations between the select committees and the civil service. Fundamentally, the Osmotherly Memorandum represented a statement of constitutional orthodoxy: civil servants are not, and cannot be, accountable to Parliament. When appearing before select committees, they are effectively only helping their ministers to be accountable. Osmotherly has been described as "twenty five pages of how to say 'I'm sorry, Chairman. I can't answer that question. May I refer you to my Minister?' " (Hennessy and Smith, 1992: 16).

The general effect of the Osmotherly Memorandum was to cloud the accountability of civil servants with an element of uncertainty. It seemed clear that they were accountable (*de facto*) on a fairly regular basis, directly to Parliament, as well as indirectly through their ministers. The issue of precisely what they were being held accountable for was fudged by the fact of the perennially hazy divide between matters of policy and administration, coupled with Osmotherly's intimation that the civil servant's role responsibility as a policy adviser should be out of bounds for the select committees.

Although the traditionalist ethos conjured up by Osmotherly was antipathetic towards the whole concept of accountability, and in the early years of the post-1979 system there were a few *causes célèbres* involving officials who chose to hide behind the skirts of Osmotherly, as the years went by the Memorandum was rarely invoked by officials giving evidence. Indeed, there was some expectation that the Procedure Committee would recommend the ditching of the anachronistic Osmotherly when it embarked on a major review of the functioning of the select committee system in 1990. Much to the disappointment of the system's father-figure, Norman St John Stevas (Hennessy and Smith, 1992: 16), the Procedure Committee took the view that it would be better to let sleeping dogs lie, on the grounds that Osmotherly had not adversely affected the select committees heretofore, and any revamped Memorandum might be more rigorously enforced (Judge, 1992).

In brief, it can be argued that, Osmotherly notwithstanding, civil servants appeared in increasing numbers before House of Commons select committees in the years after 1966 (and especially after 1979) to be held accountable by MPs for their various role responsibilities. When this observation is added to our view of the PCA's impact on civil service accountability, the contribution of the new regime of Parliamentary accountability seems clear.

MANAGERIAL AND STRUCTURAL REFORM IN GOVERNMENT

> . . . Next Steps indirectly and directly affects both the ways in which parliamentary accountability is upheld and the fundamental principles of parliamentary accountability.
> (Greer, 1994: 94).

The landscape of Parliamentary accountability was to shift significantly as a consequence of the new public management. In particular, the Next Steps initiative raised serious issues regarding the philosophy and functioning of accountability.

From the time of its launch in 1988, the Next Steps programme has fundamentally changed the processes, shape and structure of British central government. This programme should not be viewed in isolation. In some senses, it had its origins in the Fulton Report's prescriptions for "hiving-off", and it certainly built upon the initial Thatcherite attempts to reform the civil service, especially "Raynerism" and the Financial Management Initiative. The precise motivations behind, and managerial implications of, the drive towards the creation of executive agencies need not concern us here. The implications for Parliamentary accountability must. Our immediate task is to explain the practical impact of Next Steps on the mechanisms of Parliamentary scrutiny.

At its heart, the Next Steps initiative was an attempt to improve the management and delivery of services (within the government machine, and to the public) through a combination of structural change and the application of new managerial methods. Traditional government departments were restructured, with policy-making functions remaining within the province of the core, parent departments, and policy execution or service delivery functions carried out by new executive agencies. The agencies were headed by chief executives, who were given substantial managerial autonomy, within the terms of their agencies' Framework Documents.

In our terms, the proliferation of executive agencies which accompanied the implementation of the Next Steps programme had an impact upon the role responsibilities of civil servants, both in the parent departments, and in the agencies themselves. The policy advice role remained as significant as ever for the senior civil servants in the parent departments, while agency chief executives were allocated either a "sleeping" or pro-active role in this sphere, according to the nature of the agency and the terms of the Definitive Document (Pyper, 1995: 24). Departmental and agency management roles were central to the working activities of officials in parent departments and agencies alike, while effective despatch of the policy implementation/service delivery role was the *raison d'être* for officials in the agencies. Ministerial role responsibilities remained as before, although it might be argued that the departmental management function had effectively been narrowed through the creation of the semi-autonomous agencies (the management of which was a ministerial concern in only the strategic sense).

In theory, Next Steps facilitated an explicit division of the policy-making and policy-execution functions of government. In practice, these functions are simply not amenable to such definitive distinction. In any case, it became clear that the government was not prepared to follow this supposed division through to its logical conclusion, by making civil servants based in executive agencies constitutionally accountable to Parliament for the management and operation of their agencies. This resulted in a series of skirmishes between Parliament and the executive in relation to the functioning of key mechanisms of Parliamentary scrutiny.

While the Parliamentary Commissioner for Administration and the

Commons' select committee system continued to function as organs of accountability in relation to the agencies in much the same way as they had previously in relation to old-style departments (Giddings, 1995; Natzler and Silk, 1995), complications emerged in relation to the three other avenues of Parliamentary scrutiny which would touch the executive agencies: informal contacts, Parliamentary Questions and the Public Accounts Committee.

In the spirit of the policy and administration dichotomy which appeared to lie behind the Next Steps initiative, new rules were established to govern the scrutiny of executive agencies through the media of MPs' letters and PQs. Letters and PQs on executive agencies would be examined by officials in the relevant minister's Private Office in order to ascertain whether the matter of inquiry related to the legitimate sphere of the parent department (strategic policy or finance, for example) or of the agency (the service delivered to an MP's constituent by a local branch of the agency, for example). If the latter, the PQ or MP's letter would simply be passed on to the relevant agency chief executive, who would reply directly to the MP.

A minority of MPs, epitomised by Gerald Kaufman, objected to all aspects of this system, on the grounds that, in Kaufman's words, it was "diminishing democracy" (Kaufman, 1992). However, most MPs did not appear to have fundamental objections to receiving replies to their letters from chief executives: it was the new arrangement for answering PQs which provoked their ire. In place of the former system whereby PQs on virtually all matters would be published in Hansard (and therefore open to full public scrutiny), chief executives' replies to PQs were at first only placed in the library of the House of Commons when this was specifically requested by the MP concerned. In the wake of sustained protests from MPs, the government relented in 1990, to the extent that all chief executives' replies were to be deposited in the library as a matter of course. However, this was still far removed from the old system, and it took a further series of protests from MPs and the regular unofficial publication of chief executives replies by a Labour MP and an academic, before the government finally relented and sanctioned the formal publication of these replies in a supplement to Hansard starting in 1992 (Evans, 1995).

The tensions between the government's view that Next Steps represented a clarification of role responsibilities, and its determination to avoid countenancing changes in the operation of Parliamentary accountability, were exposed in the realm of financial accountability. For the government, Next Steps necessitated no change in the arrangement whereby the permanent secretary of a department answered to the Public Accounts Committee for all aspects of financial management. For observers, and many MPs, this view seemed to contradict the ethos of Next Steps, within which financial management responsibilities were allocated to agency chief executives. Following pressure from the Treasury and Civil Service Select Committee, the government agreed that chief executives could become accounting officers for their agencies, within two categories. Chief executives of agencies which enjoyed significant financial autonomy (that is, those designated as Trading Funds or funded through a separate Parliamentary vote) would become accounting officers in their own right. Chief executives of agencies which were funded through one or more of the parent department's Parliamentary votes would be designated agency accounting officers, and would accompany the permanent secretary of the parent department when appearing before the PAC.

It can be argued that the overall impact of the Next Steps initiative on Parliamentary accountability has been to confirm and build upon the key developments facilitated by the new regime of Parliamentary accountability. The Thatcher Government was keen to stress that Next Steps necessitated no change to either the theory or practice of Parliamentary accountability (arguably in contradiction to the recommendations of the original, unpublished version of the Ibbs Report which, in its final form, was the blueprint for Next Steps). The new arrangements for handling informal inquiries from MPs, Parliamentary Questions, and the financial auditing of agencies, demonstrated that the practical operation of Parliamentary accountability *did* adjust in some respects to accommodate the new executive agencies. More than this, the theoretical underpinning of Parliamentary accountability has been affected by Next Steps.

It would be easy to underestimate the significance of this development. After all, the government which originated Next Steps was at pains to deny that the initiative would involve any changes to the constitutional status quo, while academic critics with their eyes on broader constitutional reform asserted that the initiative was doomed to fail because it was not accompanied by a new conception of Parliamentary accountability (Davies and Willman, 1991; McDonald 1992). Nonetheless, in the real world, something of significance was happening:

... there is emerging a form of direct accountability of agencies to

Parliament which by-passes traditional notions of accountability through ministers . . . the new arrangements do in fact bring the responsible officials (chief executives) much closer to Parliament.
(Giddings, 1995a: 230).

In other words, the emerging *de facto*, direct accountability of agency chief executives to Parliament would seem to be in line with the theme we identified when examining the new regime of Parliamentary account-ability. A subtle, crab-like growth in civil service accountability to Parliament can be discerned, even in the face of repeated assertions of constitutional, *de jure*, non-accountability and academic carping.

Conclusion: Issues and Debates
Having examined the theoretical models which underpinned some of the important developments in the sphere of Parliamentary accountability, set out the mechanisms of scrutiny, and described the changing landscape of Parliamentary accountability with reference to the new regime and managerial reform, we will end by addressing a series of key questions touching some of the major issues and themes of Parliamentary accountability.

ACCOUNTABILITY OR MERE ANSWERABILITY?
A case might be assembled for the proposition that Parliamentary accountability is a misnomer. The basis of this case would be that Parliamentary accountability is accountability *sans* sanctions, *sans* redress, *sans* teeth: in other words this is not true accountability at all, but merely answerability or explanatory accountability. The case could be developed with reference to the dominance of the traditional power model, the importance of internal party discipline, the deployment of collective responsibility as a cloak for ministerial malfeasance, the rarity of the sanctions imposed on erring ministers being influenced by Parliament, and the constitutional non-accountability of the civil service.

This would be a strong case, but it would be fundamentally flawed. Despite all the limitations stemming from the nature of the constitution and the imperatives of *Realpolitik*, Parliamentary accountability still has a meaning. Ultimately, governments which fail to carry a Commons majority behind their key policies can be obliged to change tack or relinquish power. Ministers and civil servants whose policies and actions fail to survive the scrutiny imposed by Parliamentary mechanisms may have sanctions imposed upon them by their political or official superiors. The fact that the nature of these sanctions can be concealed by political manoeuvring (reshuffles are a convenient means of dispensing with the services of ministers whose failings have been exposed by PQs, debates, select or standing committees) or the natural secrecy of civil service personnel management, does not mean that they have not been imposed.

Furthermore, the proposition that Parliament cannot secure redress of grievances, even against the wishes of the government of the day, is palpable nonsense. One need only examine the record of the organ of Parliamentary accountability which is most obviously concerned with the issue of redress, the Parliamentary Commissioner for Administration, to find evidence which disproves the "prosecution" case. Leaving aside the minutiae of the PCA's caseload, from which numerous examples of redress can be found, year in and year out, the major highly politicized cases handled by the PCA include Sachsenhausen (1968) and Barlow Clowes (1989). In each of these, governments reluctantly agreed to dispense substantial sums of compensation to complainants following critical reports from the PCA (Parliamentary Commissioner for Administration, 1968; Parliamentary Commissioner for Administration, 1989).

In brief, parliamentary accountability is real, and has a meaning beyond mere answerability.

FAULTY AND INADEQUATE MECHANISMS AND AGENTS OF ACCOUNTABILITY?

Acceptance of the argument above need not blind us to the flaws which mark many of the mechanisms and agents of Parliamentary accountability. The most coherent and constructive analysis of these flaws to have been published in recent years is that of John Garrett. If we were to locate Garrett within one of theoretical schools to which we referred in the early part of this chapter, he would undoubtedly be a liberal-democrat "malcontent". He would, however, be a member of that group who retained faith in the potential of further structural and behavioural change, rather than one of the "new constitutionalists" (Garrett, 1992: 25).

Garrett's observation is that Parliament's weakness in relation to the executive stems in part from the traditional ethos and atmosphere of the House of Commons, and partly from the inherent flaws and weaknesses of at least some of the mechanisms of scrutiny. He argues that the Commons is characterised by the "dominance of the debating chamber and the more lowly status of investigatory and legislative committees". In addition, the prevalent style of the Commons is antipathetic towards detailed scrutiny because it is based on "theatre", and "concentrates much more on events and exploits than on systems" (Garrett, 1992: 16).

In this environment, the mechanisms of scrutiny generally operate inefficiently and ineffectively. Legislative scrutiny is hampered by, *inter alia*, tight timetabling and the paucity of specialist advice. Questions and debates "are not particularly daunting for a competent and well-briefed minister, especially if he or she can produce a flippant reply." (Garrett, 1992: 18) The select committee system is inadequately supported and lacks coordination: "They have not grasped the idea of moving like a flotilla instead of as individual raiders" (Garrett, 1992: 18). Parliament is well served by some elements of the system of accountability, nonetheless. Garrett cites the procedures for securing redress of citizens' grievances, and the functioning of the state audit system (the PAC and the NAO).

John Garrett offers an extended prescription for reform. The detailed changes he favours need not concern us here. The important point is that his proposals effectively combine behavioural change on the part of MPs (cf. Norton) with organizational and structural change in Parliament as a whole, and the further development of the extant organs of scrutiny. In this sense, they fall squarely within the school of thought which stresses the importance of Parliament *per se*, and the evolutionary nature of the mechanisms and agents of Parliamentary accountability.

FAULTY AND INADEQUATE DOCTRINE, AND CONSTITUTION?
We have already indicated that there are academic observers and practical political actors who denigrate the development, reality, and potential of Parliamentary accountability. For these liberal democrat "malcontents", who have lost (or who never had) faith in the efficacy of behavioural and structural change, there is a simple answer to the perceived failings of Parliamentary accountability. This is to be found by ditching the doctrine of individual ministerial responsibility and embarking on a programme of thorough-going constitutional reform.

These critics view individual ministerial responsibility in a single dimension. They do not subscribe to the conception of the doctrine as a complex interaction of ministerial and civil service role responsibilities and accountabilities, they cannot discern Woodhouse's "multi-layered convention" (Woodhouse, 1994: 38). Instead, they see individual ministerial responsibility primarily as a weapon wielded by the executive in order to obfuscate Parliament. It must be admitted that there was an element of this in the Thatcher Government's presentation of Next Steps as a development which fitted securely within what had already become an outmoded interpretation of ministerial responsibility, but, as we have seen, the government did not have the last word on this matter.

While a wide, encompassing interpretation of individual ministerial responsibility pays dividends by opening our eyes to the working reality of Parliamentary accountability, the critics retain only an impoverished notion of the doctrine. Their tunnel vision tends to focus upon isolated aspects of the doctrine, such as the sanctions element of accountability. Eschewing close analysis of the patterns of ministerial resignation and the imposition of sanctions, and turning their blind eyes to changes wrought by the new regime of Parliamentary accountability they take comfort from sweeping generalisations. Thus, McDonald says: "Public accountability should be substituted for the empty notion of ministerial accountability." (McDonald: 1992: 9). Thus, Davies and Willman:

> Accountability of the Executive, including departments, Agencies . . . will be unattainable as long as we persist with the myth of Ministerial responsibility which requires civil servants to be anonymous and unaccountable . . .
> (Davies and Willman, 1991: 41).

Those who reach for words like "myth" and "empty notion" when considering Parliamentary accountability and ministerial responsibility tend to find wondrous blueprints for constitutional upheaval just within their grasp. It can be argued that those who have been described by Garrett as the "new constitutionalists" have contributed to the neglect which has come to characterise academic attitudes towards Parliament. Seemingly blind to the fact that problems of accountability remain even in states with written constitutions, these idealists turn their faces away from the flawed but functioning reality of Parliament, in the search for the El Dorado of a constitutionally reformed UK (their writings are voluminous, but, in addition to those already cited, a flavour can be derived from Bogdanor, 1989; Crick, 1989). At the outset of this chapter, we sought to illustrate this point. We have now come full circle.

References

Bagehot, (1963), *The English Constitution*, Glasgow: Fontana Edition.

Barnett, Anthony, Ellis, Caroline, and Hirst, Paul (eds) (1993), *Debating the Constitution. New Perspectives on Constitutional Reform*, London: Polity Press.

Bates, St John (1988), "The Scrutiny of Administration", in Ryle, Michael and Richards, Peter G. (eds), *The Commons Under Scrutiny*, London: Routledge.

Birch, A.H. (1977), *Representative and Responsible Government*, London: Allen and Unwin.

Bogdanor, Vernon (1989), "The Constitution", in Kavanagh, Denis and Seldon, Anthony, *The Thatcher Effect*, Oxford: Clarendon.

Borthwick, Robert (1979), "Questions and Debates", in Walkland, S. A. (ed), *The House of Commons in the Twentieth Century*, Oxford: Clarendon.

Butt, Ronald (1969), *The Power of Parliament*, London: Constable, 2nd Edition.

Chester, Sir Norman (1981), *The English Administrative System 1780–1870*, Oxford: Clarendon.

Chester, D. N. and Bowring, Nona (1962), *Questions in Parliament*, Oxford: Clarendon.

Chipperfield, Sir Geoffrey (1994), "The Civil Servant's Duty", *Essex Papers in Politics and Government, Number 95*, Colchester: University of Essex.

Crick, Bernard (1989), "Beyond Parliamentary Reform", *The Political Quarterly*, Volume 60, Number 4.

Davies, Anne and Willman, John (1991), *What Next? Agencies, Departments and the Civil Service*, London: Institute for Public Policy Research.

Drewry, Gavin (1988), "Legislation", in Ryle, Michael and Richards, Peter G. , (eds) *The Commons Under Scrutiny*, London: Routledge.

Drewry, Gavin (1988a), (ed), *The New Select Committee. A Study of the 1979 Reforms*, Oxford: Clarendon 2nd Edition.

Elms, T. and Terry, T. (1990), *Scrutiny of Ministerial Correspondence*, London: Cabinet Office Efficiency Unit.

Evans, Paul (1995), "Members of Parliament and Agencies: Parliamentary Questions", in Giddings, Philip (ed), *Parliamentary Accountability. A Study of Parliament and Executive Agencies*, Houndsmill: Macmillan.

Fairlie, Henry (1968), *The Life of Politics*, London: Methuen.

Flegman, Vilna (1980), "The Public Accounts Committee: A Successful Select Committee", *Parliamentary Affairs*, Volume 33.

Flegman, Vilna (1985), *Public Expenditure and Select Committees of the House of Commons*, Aldershot: Gower.

Franklin, Mark and Norton, Philip (1993), "Questions and Members", in Franklin, Mark and Norton, Philip (eds), *Parliamentary Questions*, Oxford: Clarendon.

Garrett, John (1992), *Westminster. Does Parliament Work?*, London: Victor Gollancz.

Giddings, Philip (1993), "Questions and Departments", in Franklin, Mark and Norton, Philip (eds), *Parliamentary Questions*, Oxford: Clarendon.

Giddings, Philip (1995), "Agencies and the Ombudsman", in Giddings, Philip (ed), *Parliamentary Accountability. A Study of Parliament and Executive Agencies*, Houndmills: Macmillan.

Giddings, Philip (1995a), "Next Steps to Where?", in Giddings, Philip (ed), *Parliamentary Accountability. A Study of Parliament and Executive Agencies*, Houndmills: Macmillan.

Greer, Patricia (1994), *Transforming Central Government. The Next Steps Initiative*, Buckingham: Open University Press.

Gregory, Roy and Hutchesson, Peter (1975), *The Parliamentary Ombudsman*, London: Allen and Unwin.

Gregory, Roy and Pearson, Jane (1992), "The Parliamentary Ombudsman After Twenty Five Years", *Public Administration*, Volume 70, Number 4.

Griffith, J. A. G, (1981), "Standing Committees in the House of Commons", in S. A. Walkland and Michael Ryle (eds), *The Commons Today*, Glasgow: Fontana.

Griffith, J. A. G. (1984), *Parliamentary Scrutiny of Government Bills*, London: Allen and Unwin.

Griffith, J. A. G. (1987), "Crichel Down: The Most Famous Farm in British Constitutional History", *Contemporary Record*, Volume 1, Number 1.

Hennessy, Peter and Smith, Frank (1992), "Teething The Watchdogs: Parliament, Government and Accountability", *Strathclyde Analysis Paper Number 7*, Glasgow: University of Strathclyde.

Irwin, Helen, Kennon, Andrew, Natzler, David and Rogers, Robert (1993), "Evolving Rules", in Franklin, Mark and Norton, Philip (eds), *Parliamentary Questions*, Oxford: Clarendon.

Johnson, Nevil (1970), "Select Committees as Tools of Parliamentary Reform", in Hanson, A. H. and Crick, B. (eds), *The Commons in Transition*, Glasgow: Fontana.

Johnson, Nevil (1981), "Select Committees as Tools of Parliamentary Reform: Some Further Reflections", in Walkland, S. A. and Ryle, Michael (eds): *The Commons Today*, Glasgow: Fontana.

Judge, David (1992), "The 'Effectiveness' of the Post-1979 Select Committee System: The Verdict of the 1990 Procedure Committee", *The Political Quarterly*, Volume 63, Number 1.

Judge, David (1993), *The Parliamentary State*, London: Sage.

Justice (1961), *The Citizen and the Administration. The Redress of Grievances*, London: Stevens.

Kaufman, Gerald (1992), "Privatising the Ministers", *The Guardian*, 7 December.

King, Anthony (1974), *British Members of Parliament: A Self-Portrait*, London: Macmillan.

Latham, Michael (1986), "A Watchdog With Teeth: The Committee of Public Accounts", *Social Studies Review*, Volume 1, Number 4.

Linklater, Marcus and Leigh, David (1986), *Not With Honour: The Inside Story of the Westland Scandal*, London: Sphere.

Madgwick, Peter and Woodhouse, Diana (1989), "The Westland Affair: Helicopter Crashes into British Constitution", *Social Studies Review*, Volume 4, Number 4.

Marsh, James, W. (1985), "Representational Changes. The Constituency MP", in Norton, Philip (ed), *Parliament in the 1980s*, Oxford, Blackwell.

McConnell, Allan and Pyper, Robert (1994), "The Revived Select Committee on Scottish Affairs: A Case Study of Parliamentary Contradictions", *Strathclyde Papers on Government and Politics Number 98*, Glasgow: University of Stratchclyde.

McDonald, Oonagh (1992), *Swedish Models: The Swedish Model of Central Government*, London: Institute for Public Policy Research.

Natzler, David and Silk, Paul (1995), "Departmental Select Committees and the Next Steps Programme", in Giddings, Philip (ed), *Parliamentary Accountability. A Study of Parliament and Executive Agencies*, Houndmills: Macmillan.

Nicolson, I. F. (1986), *The Mystery of Crichel Down*, Oxford: Clarendon.

Norton, Philip (1981), *The Commons in Perspective*, Oxford: Martin Robertson.

Norton, Philip (1993), *Does Parliament Matter?*, London: Harvester Wheatsheaf.

Parliamentary Commissioner for Administration (1968), *Sachsenhausen*, 3rd Report, 1967–8, HC 54.

Parliamentary Commissioner for Administration (1989), *The Barlow Clowes Affair*, 1st Report 1989–90, HC 76.

Ponting, Clive (1985), *The Right to Know. The Inside Story of the Belgrano Affair*, London: Sphere.

Powell, Enoch (1982), "Parliament and the Question of Reform", *Teaching Politics*, Volume 11, Number 2.

Pyper, Robert (1985), "Sarah Tisdall, Ian Willmore and the Civil Servant's 'Right to Leak' ", *The Political Quarterly*, Volume 56, Number 1.

Pyper, Robert (1987), *The Doctrine of Individual Ministerial Responsibility in British Government: Theory and Practice in a New Regime of Parliamentary Accountability*, Unpublished Ph D Thesis, University of Leicester.

Pyper, Robert (1995), "Ministerial Responsibility and Next Steps Agencies", in Giddings, Philip (ed), *Parliamentary Accountability. A Study of Parliament and Executive Agencies*, Houndmills: Macmillan.

Robinson, Ann (1988), "The House of Commons and Public Money", in Ryle, Michael and Richards, Peter G. (eds), *The Commons Under Scrutiny*, London: Routledge.

Sedgemore, Brian (1980), *The Secret Constitution*, London: Hodder.

Shell, Donald (1992), *The House of Lords*, Hemel Hempstead: Harvester Wheatsheaf 2nd Edition.

Treasury and Civil Service Committee (1993), *The Role of the Civil Service. Interim Report*, 6th Report, 1992–93, HC 390.

Walkland, S. A. (1976), "The Politics of Parliamentary Reform", *Parliamentary Affairs*, Volume 29.

Walkland, S. A. (1981), "Whither the Commons?", in Walkland, S. A. , and Ryle, Michael (eds), *The Commons Today*, Glasgow: Fontana.

Walkland, S. A. (1983), "Parliamentary Reform, Party Realignment and Electoral Reform", in Judge, David (ed), *The Politics of Parliamentary Reform*, London, Heinemann.

Wass, Sir Douglas (1985), "The Civil Service at the Crossroads", *The Political Quarterly*, Volume 56, Number 3.

Wiseman, H. Victor (1970), "Standing Committees", in Hanson, A. H. , and Crick, Bernard (eds), *The Commons in Transition*, London: Collins.

Woodhouse, Diana (1994), *Ministers and Parliament. Accountability in Theory and Practice*, Oxford, Clarendon.

3

LEGAL AND QUASI-LEGAL ACCOUNTABILITY

Aidan ODonnell

Introduction
The purpose of this chapter is to examine the role of the courts in the process of accountability of both government and public sector organizations in relation to those they are intended to serve. "Courts" will be construed widely to include tribunals and inquiries. We shall also examine the role of the Parliamentary Commissioner for Administration in the process of accountability. The significance of British membership of the European Union will be considered through the impact of decisions of the European Court of Justice. The daily increasing importance of the judicial review procedure will be examined. Hopefully the advantages, disadvantages, appropriateness (or not), and effectiveness (or not) of the procedures will be clearer at the end. There is no escaping the legal nature of the content of this chapter and it is recognised that many readers will not have studied law either at length or in depth. It is intended, therefore, that explanations should be as clear and straightforward as is consistent with factual correctness. Law is of course an area of professional and technical expertise with all the loss of plain English so commonly associated with such areas. Hopefully the move in recent years towards "Law in Plain English" will make the subject more accessible!

The Constitutional Context
Recognition will be given to the separate legal systems that co-exist within the United Kingdom. Most of the discussions will centre on English law because that is where the procedure is most frequently used but Scottish cases will be discussed where appropriate. The discussion of the processes and procedures involved will similarly concentrate on England. Where these differ significantly elsewhere this will be high-

lighted. Before beginning on examination of the role of legal and quasi-legal mechanisms, etc. in the process of accountability it is necessary to understand the unique nature of the rules that regulate government in the United Kingdom. Whereas in other states the body of rules that relate to the structure, function and powers of the organ of the state, their relationship to one another, and to the private citizen are contained in a written constitution, this is not the case in the United Kingdom (and is unlikely to be the case in the near future despite pressure from groups such as Charter 88). In the United Kingdom unlike, for example, the United States or the Irish Republic there is no single document or series of documents from which is derived the authority of the main organs of the state such as (in the UK) the Crown, Parliament, Cabinet, and Judiciary. There is no single document that defines the relationships between these organs or between them and the citizen. The lack of a document akin to the American Constitution has led some observers of the British State to claim that Britain has no constitution (Ridley, 1988: 340). The UK does of course have a constitution (in the sense of a body of rules that regulates the state-citizen relationship and it is within the framework of these rules that the issue of accountability in a legal sense will be addressed. Written constitutions are often mistakenly seen as a one stop panacea. This is far from the truth as most written constitutions are both subject to amendment and are accompanied by a body of changing rules and customs that allow the constitution to operate on a day to day basis, without the need for upheaval occasioned by the requirements for amendment.

Another feature of UK administrative law that sets it apart from its other European neighbours is the absence of a formal separation between private law and public law. Government and public authorities are subject to the same law as private citizens and their actions will be reviewed in the ordinary courts as are the actions of the private citizens. Given the lack of a written constitution in the UK it is important to understand the basic characteristics of our constitution as it is these characteristics that will dictate the system of legal (and indeed other) forms of accountability.

There are several fundamental characteristics and theories of our constitution which have evolved over the centuries. These are the Rule of Law, the Separation of Powers (we shall place particular emphasis on the doctrine of judicial independence) and perhaps the most fundamental of them, the doctrine of Parliamentary Sovereignty (or Legislative Supremacy). The first two of these have a role to play in the process of legal accountability but ultimately as we shall see they may find themselves up against the hard won and unlikely to be easily surrendered power of Parliament.

The Rule of Law will be forever associated with the Victorian academic A.V. Dicey (Dicey, 1959), although it has a pedigree stretching as far back as Aristotle who expressed his belief in the superiority of a higher form of law than that made by man. While belief in some form of pre-ordained natural law would not be commonly held today (although there has been a resurgence of such belief, particularly in the USA), Dicey's view was that the state (and public organizations) should be subject to the same laws as the ordinary citizen, administered in the ordinary courts. Dicey believed that in most continental European systems the Rule of Law (as defined by himself) did not apply as the state was given a special position in law and could only be challenged in special courts. He saw this as especially true in France, where there is a separate system of administrative courts. Most would accept that while Dicey's analysis of the Rule of Law no longer holds, it is a central characteristic of the UK constitution that state power is not exercised in an arbitrary way. A more recent definition of the Rule of Law can be seen in *The Road to Serfdom* (1944) where Hayek says

> government in all its actions is bound by rules fixed and announced beforehand. Rules which make it possible to foresee with fair certainty how the authority will use its coercive powers in given circumstances, and to plan one's individual affairs on the basis of this knowledge.

The case of *Congreve v Home Office* (1976) (Hayek, 1944) would be a simple but classic example of the need for government "to play by the rules". In *Congreve* the Government had increased the television licence fee from £12 to £18. The increase took effect on April 1 1975. As it was known before this date that there would be an increase, seventeen thousand licence holders, whose licences were due to expire after April 1, took out new licences at the old rate, thus saving themselves money. The Home Office upset by this entrepreneurship sought to stem this loss of revenue. They told those concerned that they would have to pay the extra £6 or the Home Secretary would use his power under the Wireless Telegraphy Act 1949 to revoke the licences. They then modified this saying that if the extra £6 was not paid then the licence would be revoked after eight months. Congreve, a solicitor, refused to pay the extra £6 and brought a case against the Home Office. The Court of Appeal said that the decision to revoke the licences after eight months was unlawful, as the Home Secretary had to have a valid reason for revoking licences. The quick thinking of Congreve and the others was not such a reason. The actions of the Government in this case were also subject to the attention of the Parliamentary Commissioner on the grounds that there had been maladministration (see *The Parliamentary Commissioner* below.) The reality, however, is that frequently the state will be granted powers which allow them a very wide range of discretion. The existence of such discretion, no matter how widely expressed (for example, as the minister sees fit) will not, however, allow the power to be exercised solely according to whim, prejudice or irrational opinion. In *Padfield v Minister of Agriculture* (1968) (see below) the House of Lords used its power to adjudicate upon the legality of the minister's actions and said they would not be inhibited from invalidating a minister's decision even where he had a seemingly wide discretion granted him by statute. There are, however, areas where the courts feel less able to intervene with the exercise of ministerial discretion. The most contentious contemporary example is almost certainly the exercise of powers under the Prevention of Terrorism Act 1984.

In summary, the essence of the Rule of Law is the objective of curtailment of the arbitrary exercise of power by making everyone subject to impartially enforced legal rules. The importance of the Rule of Law in the process of accountability is surely obvious. The Rule of Law sets the parameters within which officials must operate.

It has long been recognised that the state has three main branches or functions: the legislative or law making function, the executive function and the judicial function. The idea that these functions should not be exercised by the same group within the state echoes back at us through history. John Locke argued that if these functions were to be concentrated in one set of hands, then tyranny would inevitably result (Locke: Chapter XII). Today the doctrine is seen as having the three-fold meaning articulated by Montesquieu in *De L'Esprit Des Lois* (Montesquieu: Book X1.6).

- The same people should not be members of more than one organ
- Each organ should be independent, i.e. it should not be controlled by another organ
- Each organ should only exercise its own function, not that of the other two.

The basis for the doctrine is the prevention of despotism but the doctrine would seem to be totally inoperative today as the brief examples below will illustrate.

- The Lord Chancellor is head of the judiciary, a Cabinet minister, a member of the House of Lords. He is therefore a member of all three organs of the state.
- It can be argued that the executive is controlled by the legislature because MP's can vote to bring down the government. This will, however, rarely happen, particularly if the government has a strong majority. It can be argued that in fact the executive controls the legislature through patronage, party discipline, control of the legislative timetable and so on. The judiciary are controlled by the executive in that the power of appointment rests with the executive, but once appointed (with the exception of the lower judges) the judiciary are virtually irremovable (a topic we shall return to below). The process of judicial review or indeed judicial decisions in general may be said to be evidence of judicial control over the executive but judicial decisions can be invalidated by subsequent legislation. (See *Burmah Oil* below). As far as primary legislation is concerned the judiciary exercise no control over the legislature although the position is different where delegated legislation is concerned.
- It is in the third of Montesquieu's meaning that the doctrine breaks down almost entirely. Ministers (the executive) legislate through delegated legislation. Many "judicial" decisions will be made by ministers (e.g. planning permission). Judges should in theory only "declare" law, that is merely say what the law is, but there are examples of judges creating offences either not known in the law at all, for example *Shaw v DPP* (1962), where the House of Lords created the previously unknown offence of conspiring to corrupt public morals, or expanding the parameters of the law to encompass new variants of an offence, such as the decision by a Scottish court, that it was an offence to sell "glue sniffing" kits to children (*Khaliq* 1984).

It is almost certainly the case that a strict system of separation of powers is impractical in the modern state although it may ostensibly be more strictly adhered to in the constitutions of France and the USA. (Even in the United States where the 1787 Constitution clearly expresses separate powers, each of the organs of state does not operate in isolation). What we have in the UK is a system of checks and balances whereby each organ does have the right to exercise control over others, albeit a limited right.

Hopefully the result of such a system of checks will be to prevent abuse of power by one organ and thereby achieve Locke's aim of preventing tyranny. These checks and balances also play a part in making each organ accountable to the others and to individual citizens.

Perhaps the most obvious defining characteristic of the UK constitution, the one that differentiates it from other countries apart from Israel and New Zealand, is the doctrine of legislative (or Parliamentary) supremacy. Unlike those States with written constitutions where the constitution is the supreme or ultimate source of law, in the UK, Parliament is the supreme or ultimate source of law. Basically this means that Parliament is legally competent to legislate on any issue at all. We mean by this that there are no legal restraints on its law-making ability. For example, to use an oft-quoted example, there is no legal impediment to Parliament passing a law making it unlawful to smoke on the streets of Paris. The law could not, of course, be enforced except in the UK courts and would for all practical purposes be completely ineffective. (Such a law seems equally ineffective even when passed by the French Legislature). It is still within their legal power to pass such a law. However legality and practicality are not the same. Another aspect of this supremacy is that Parliament cannot bind or be bound by successor or predecessor Parliaments. Parliamentary supremacy also means that Parliament can overrule any judicial decision and that the judges do not have the authority to rule on an Act of Parliament (but see below). A classic example of the former would be the case of *Burmah Oil v L. Advocate* (1965) where the House of Lords decided that Burmah Oil were entitled to compensation from the Government for damage caused to its property. Parliament, however, reversed this somewhat inconvenient decision by retrospectively passing the War Damage Act 1965. In practice this will rarely happen, but the fact that it can obviously has a potentially major impact on the much vaunted doctrine of judicial independence outlined below. Judicial independence has also been affected by the ever closer relationship between legislature and executive, which has seen Parliament's hard-won role as a check on the executive being severely eroded. In theory the executive should be accountable to Parliament but, as was reported by the House of Commons Select Committee on Procedure some seventeen years ago:

> the balance of advantage between Parliament and the government in the day to day working of the constitution is now weighted in favour of the government to a degree which arouses wide spread anxiety and is inimical

to the proper working of our parliamentary democracy. (HC 588 of 1977–78).

Judicial Independence and Accountability

The impact this has on accountability is addressed in chapters 1 and 2 of this book. What we are concerned with in this chapter is how the legal system in the UK plays a direct role in the process of accountability which is one of the central precepts of public administration. It might be asked if there can ever be truly effective legal accountability given the lack of an American-style Supreme Court which has the power to declare legislation as unconstitutional and devoid of legal effect. A Supreme Court system can however involve handing over the process and procedures of accountability to unelected officials who may in turn be unaccountable in any meaningful sense.

We argued earlier that separation of powers was one of the major fundamental features of our constitution. Hopefully, we also managed to demonstrate the theory in its strictest sense is not adhered to in the UK. The UK's application of the theory does not relate to an artificial separation of organs and personnel but relies more on a system of checks and balances whereby the exercise of any governmental power is subjected to the scrutiny and practical control of other bodies. Most writers would agree with this. They would also agree that (in spite of what we said above) that the main manifestation of separation of powers lies in the independence of the judiciary in the UK. If the judiciary is indeed independent this will play a significant part in its ability effectively to manage the process of legal accountability. On the other hand, if it is not independent but is controlled by the legislature or executive (or both) then its ability to hold them accountable will be seriously weakened. Professor Wade has written: The separation of powers means little more than an independent judiciary. (Wade 1988). Is our judiciary truly independent? Most would agree that there are three main aspects of judicial independence.

- The judges have security of tenure;
- The judges are immune to criticism;
- The judges are immune from civil and criminal liability.

TENURE

The rules relating to judicial tenure vary according to on the judicial office held. We shall not concern ourselves with the judges in the lower or inferior courts as their role in the procedure of accountability is minor or in many cases non-existent. Judges of the superior courts, namely the High Court and the House of Lords hold office during what amounts to good behaviour (which is not defined). In England judges may be removed by the Queen or an address to the Queen by both the Houses of Parliament. In Scotland superior judges hold office "aut vitam aut culpam" (for life or blame) which is much the same as good behaviour. Until recently, judges in both jurisdictions had a retirement age of 75. This has been changed in England to 70, since the passing of the Judicial Pensions and Retirement Act 1993, with the possibility of extending this to 75. The power of removal for England does not apply in Scotland and the best that can be said is that the procedure for removal is unclear. The reality is that only one superior judge has been removed and that was in 1830 when an Irish judge was removed for misappropriation of litigants' money. It is certainly the case that if it was felt removal was appropriate strenuous attempts would be made to handle the situation in a low-key manner, by, for example, obliging the malefactor to resign.

Criticism

It is not uncommon for judges to feature in the popular press. This usually arises from what is felt to be inappropriate sentencing or comment. It is, however, a convention of the constitution that the conduct of judges may not be debated in Parliament (except in the context of a removal address). Breach of this convention may amount to a contempt of Parliament and may also amount to contempt of court.

Immunity

Judges are immune from being sued for what they say in court. They cannot be sued even if what they have said would have constituted slander if said outside the court. Judges of the superior courts are not liable for their wrongful or negligent acts provided they have acted in good faith. An example would be wrongfully ordering arrest and detention. If the judiciary are not independent then their ability to play a role in the process of accountability must seriously be questioned. While there are many critics of the judiciary and indeed the whole judicial system it would generally be agreed that the judges are not in thrall to the government, although one might agree with he Russian jurist Krylenko who said "that the judge is above all a politician". (Krylenko, 1927–30). Krylenko also saw the judge as a servant to the government, there to do its bidding. That would not be the view of the judges in the UK. Much of the criticism of the judiciary centres in any case on the narrow social and educational caste from which they are recruited. There are numerous decisions, as we see below, that indicate that judges do not see themselves as servants of the government.

Judicial Review

The courts in the UK have a long history of attempting to ensure that the exercise of power is subject to and constrained by the ordinary principles and rules of law, emanating from the statute or common law. Thus it is possible to see many examples of situations where public authorities have been prevented from acting in breach of the private rights of individual persons (human or legal) through the intervention of the ordinary courts. The common law of contract and tort/delict has often been evoked in the ordinary courts to ensure that authorities comply with their duties in the same way as ordinary citizens. Thus they are required to adhere to their contractual obligations and to compensate those who sustain loss, injury or damage as a result of a breach of duty of reasonable care. These are issues of what is called private law, which is the regulation of legal relationships between individuals, and they can be contrasted with issues which arise between government and the governed, which is the domain of what is known as public law.

Crown Liability

Before examining the liability of Crown and public authorities, we should be aware of a potential problem. There are major difficulties facing the individual who feels he has a lawful grievance arising from the decision of a government or local authority. Perhaps the main one lies in the very nature of the judicial process in the UK. Most European countries have an inquisitorial system. The judge takes an active part in seeking out the truth by, for example, questioning both the parties involved and any witnesses. In the UK, however, the judge does not assume such a role. He is more aloof and could be seen as a referee. He makes no active attempt to discover the true facts. It is up to the parties involved to argue their case on the basis of what they believe the law to be. The burden of proof is on the party who has raised the case (the pursuer or plaintiff), who will have to prove his case on the balance of probabilities. This is not as high a standard as that required in the criminal courts where a case must be proven beyond reasonable doubt but it may still be a difficult hurdle to overcome. This is all the more so because the plaintiff will often be a private individual who will have limited financial and usually, consequently, legal resources available. The public authorities will of course have the resources of the tax payer behind them.

CROWN LIABILITY IN CONTRACT

Judicial examination of Crown liability can be seen in the case of *Rederiaktiebolaget Amphitrite v Rex* (1921) where the British government had, through its embassy in Stockholm, given a Swedish shipping company an undertaking that their vessels would not be requisitioned while delivering goods to Britain during World War I. The Swedes made the mistake of believing this to be a binding obligation. A vessel belonging to the shipping company was, however, requisitioned for war use when it docked in Britain and the Swedes sued for breach of contract. The judge in the course of his judgement said that he was in no doubt that "the government can bind itself through its officers by a commercial contract and if it does so it must perform it like anyone else or pay damages for the breach." In the event the judge held that there had been no obligation to breach but merely an expression of intention to act in a particular way and, therefore, no liability. His reason for reaching this conclusion was that the government cannot fetter its future freedom of action in matters which affect the welfare of the state. This does seem to contradict what he said earlier but it is likely the exception would only apply where the welfare of the state was involved and that this would be narrowly interpreted. This decision does seem to indicate that while it may be dangerous to contract with the government, it is theoretically bound by the same rules as the rest of us. Another example can be seen in *Commissioner of Crown Lands v Page* (1960). Page had been granted a 25-year lease of land by the government. However, the Ministry of Defence requisitioned the land for ten years starting during World War II. Page, as one could imagine, did not feel obliged to pay any rent during this period. The Commissioners responded by suing for the arrears. Page argued that the contract had been breached by the requisitioning which had ended the obligation to pay the rent. It was held that this was not the case and that in spite of their contractual obligations under the lease the Crown could not fetter its future action provided that the reason for the breach is one of public interest. It would, however, seem to be accepted that this exception will not apply to commercial contracts and that it will be limited to the context of the need to allow the Crown freedom of action in time of war. These rulings have been described as unjust and unnecessary because they deprive the innocent party of damages for the Crown breach of contract (Hogg, 1971: 129–140). The cases quoted above, in spite of their conclusions, did establish that the Crown was, generally speaking, liable in contract.

Another legal minefield for individuals contracting with the government is that the Crown will not be liable for breach of contract where the reason for the breach is that Parliament has refused to vote money for that specific contract. This will, however, be unusual. In *Churchward v R* (1865), Churchward had contracted with the Commissioners of the Admiralty to provide a mail service between England and the Continent. The contract was to last eleven years. After four years the Admiralty terminated the contract. The Appropriation Act for that year provided that none of the money appropriated for the post office packet service was to be paid to Churchward after a specified date. Churchward sued for the monies due for the remaining seven years. The court held that the provision of money by Parliament was a condition precedent to the enforceability of such a contract against the Crown. The decision in Churchward may seem "Crown-friendly" but the rule laid down by the court in Churchward will only apply where the terms of the contract expressly provide that the supply of money by Parliament shall be a condition precedent to the validity of the contract, or where the Appropriation Act expressly provides that no money is to be provided. More "citizen-friendly" however is the general rule that "the prior provision of funds by Parliament is not a condition preliminary to the obligation of the contract" (*New South Wales v Bardolph* (1934) where the reasoning in Churchward decision was followed. However, in *Bardolph* the court found that the money had been provided by Parliament and, therefore, the action for breach of contract succeeded. These judgements obviously provide little succour to those who enter into contracts with the government, particularly those whose contracts will run over many years, for example defence contracts. There may even be a different government which does not approve of some contracts entered into by its predecessor. If Parliament refuses to vote the money there is nothing that can be done. Given the doctrine of Parliamentary sovereignty, it is hard to see how it could be otherwise as, in theory, Parliament cannot be forced to vote money against its will. In any event, there is usually such a close identity of interests between the government and Parliament that it is likely that money will not be voted if the government so wishes and will be voted for if it so wishes.

The Crown is still, despite cuts in the armed forces and the civil service, a major employer. Employees are employed under the prerogative and may be dismissed without notice. Unlike most other employees, Crown employees have no remedy if they are wrongfully dismissed (i.e. if the Crown breaches its contract with them). Indeed, for a long time it was the view that Crown employees did not have a contractual relationship to breach in any case, but there have been decisions which suggest that this is not the case (*Reilly v R*) (1934). It seems that members of the armed forces cannot sue for arrears of salary (*Mitchell v R*) (1896) but that civil servants can (*Kodeeswaran v Attorney-General of Ceylon*) (1970). The major problem in this area is that the Crown itself seems unsure. Civil Service Pay and Conditions Code paragraph 14 provides that "a civil servant does not have a contract of employment enforceable in the courts". This provision, it was successfully argued in *R v Civil Service Appeal Board, ex parte Bruce* (1984), was evidence that the Crown did not intend to enter into legal relations with its employees and, therefore, there was no contract (to break). However, in *R v Lord Chancellors Department, ex parte Nangle* (1991) the decision in Bruce was not followed, the Court being of the view that Nangle did have a contract of employment with the Crown that gave him the right to a private law remedy for breach of contract. Within the field of statutory employment law, Section 138 of the Employment Protection (Consolidation) Act 1978 defines Crown employment as "employment under or for the purposes of a Government department or any officer or body exercising on behalf of the Crown functions conferred by an enactment". There is, however, no mention of the existence or otherwise of a contract of employment. The position is clearly unsatisfactory as it seems to be left to the uncertainties of judicial law-making. It should be noted that Crown employees can bring cases before Industrial Tribunals if they feel they have been unfairly dismissed.

Crown Liability in Delict and Tort
Put very simply, the law of Delict (in Scotland) and Tort (in England) is the law that is concerned with liability for negligent actions. Since the passing of the Crown Proceedings Act in 1947, the general position is that the liability of the Crown and Public Authorities under the law of Delict and Tort is the same as it is for any other individual. There are some differences but we have not had in the UK the development of a completely different set of principles for government and public authorities as has been the case, for example, in France. There is an argument that they should be treated differently. Some would argue that, given their enormous responsibility, they should have imposed on them a narrower liability than normal while others argue that the enormity of their power demands broader rather than narrower liability. Under

Section 2 Crown Proceedings Act 1947 the liability of the Crown in delict and tort is:

- it is vicariously liable for delicts and torts committed by its employees or agents
- it has employer's liability at common law
- it has liability at common law for dangerous things or premises.

It has long been accepted as a matter of public policy that an employer should be liable for the wrongful or negligent acts of his employers while carrying out their work. The doctrine of vicarious liability is more complex than this simple statement suggests but it will suffice for the moment. It has also long been established that public authorities are vicariously liable for negligent acts committed by their employees. In *Mersey Docks and Harbour Board Trustees v Gibbs* (1866), a ship was damaged when it ran aground on a mudbank that should have been cleared by the Board. The trustees argued that, as they were agents of the Crown, they could not be liable. The House of Lords said that statutory bodies such as the Trustees had the same liability as commercial companies, and that if they acted negligently they would be so liable. Hospitals have been held to be vicariously liable for the negligent acts of surgeons and nurses and chief constables are liable for negligent acts committed by their officers in the course of their functions (Police Act 1964 s48, Police (Scotland) Act 1967 s39). It should be noted that if the individual concerned is what the courts quaintly refer to as "on a frolic of his own," (for example a nurse carrying out the surgeon's job) then there will be no vicarious liability.

The courts will, however, be reluctant to impose liability if loss or damage is caused by what is seen as a policy decision. The basis for this exception is the case of *Home Office v Dorset Yacht Co* (1980). Seven inmates of a borstal had escaped from a summer camp and damaged a boat belonging to the yacht company. The summer camp was part of a policy decision by the Home Office to teach the boys self-discipline. The Lords said there was a distinction between negligent policy-making and negligence in the execution of that policy, i.e. while actually supervising the boys. Had there merely been negligent policy-making the Yacht Co. could not have sued, as the Home Office, as policy-makers, owed no duty or care to them. In this case, however, in addition to negligent policy-making there had been negligence at the supervisory level. The Home Office were vicariously liable for the borstal officers' negligence, as the officers owed a duty of care to the yacht owners, as it was reasonably foreseeable that damage would result from their negligent supervision of the inmates.

One of the difficulties that may be encountered in taking action against the Crown or public authorities is that it may prove difficult to have documents produced if the Crown claims privilege on the grounds that production of the documents is injurious to the public interest. English courts had always been readier to refuse production of documents on a minister's bare statement that their production would be so injurious. While there certainly have been situations where this was the case, blanket application of the rule allowed ministers to refuse to allow production of any document at all. This was not, however, the case in Scotland (*Glasgow Corporation v Central Land Board* (1956), *Whitehall v Whitehall* (1957)) and indeed has not been the case in England since *Conway v Rimmer* in 1968 when the House of Lords decided that while the court would give full weight to a minister's view they still had jurisdiction to order the production of documents.

The European Dimension
British membership of the European Union has extended the possible remedies available to individuals aggrieved by the actions of governments or local authorities. It is clear from the interpretation of the founding treaties of the Community of the European Court of Justice that community law should prevail over inconsistent domestic law. The treaties themselves do not specifically say that this should be the case. The doctrine of supremacy of Community law can be seen in cases stretching back as far as 1963 where the ECJ said:

> The conclusion to be drawn . . . is that the Community constitutes a new order of international law for the benefit of which the States have limited their sovereign rights, albeit within limited fields.
> (Van Gend en Loos, 1963).

The following year in *Costa v Enel* (1964) the ECJ further developed the doctrine of the supremacy of Community law over conflicting domestic law. That these are obvious implications for the doctrine of supremacy of Parliament is beyond doubt and this has been accepted by our judiciary. In *Stoke-on-Trent County Council v B&Q plc* (1991) the judge stated: "The EEC Treaty is the supreme law of this country, taking precedence over Acts of Parliament".

We are not concerned with the issue of sovereignty but with the extension of remedies available to those with a grievance. An examination of what has become known as the Factortame litigation (1989, 1990,

1991) may illustrate the usefulness of a remedy under Community law. Factortame was a British registered company which owned 95 fishing boats. These boats were operated from the UK although most of Factortame's directors and shareholders were Spanish. Many Spanish fishing companies operated in this fashion to gain access to the UK fishing quota. In an attempt to stop what was seen as "quota hopping" Parliament passed the Merchant Shipping Act 1988. Under the Merchant Shipping (Registration of Fishing Vessels) Regulations made under the Act, Factortame's vessels could no longer be registered as British. The regulations required that the whole legal title and 75% of the beneficial ownership of the vessels had to be vested in UK citizens or companies whose principal place of business was the UK. Factortame challenged the validity of the regulations and sought judicial review. The European Commission brought an action against the UK for a declaration that the nationality provisions contained within the regulations were in breach of provisions of the Treaty of Rome. The UK were obliged to change the regulations. The several Factortame cases covered issues which we need not discuss here but it is important to note that the decision of the ECJ had the effect of disapplying secondary or delegated legislation. It would seem from some of the judges' statements in the European Court of Justice that where there is a European element involved, even an Act of Parliament may be set aside by a UK court if it considers that it is in violation of Community law.

Tribunals and Inquiries
The main purpose of any civil judicial system is to resolve disputes between individuals. Whether it is able to do this well will depend on a variety of factors. One of these is the sheer volume of disputes that come before the courts. The traditional court system we have in the UK evolved in a time when the resolution of a dispute involving the "average citizen" by the ordinary courts would be unusual. A system evolved which was not "user-friendly" – it was aloof, remote, spoke a language of its own and was slow and, therefore, expensive. For the "average" citizen this mattered little as he would have little contact with the state and little likelihood of a grievance requiring legal resolution. With the creation and growth of the Welfare State, points of contact between citizen and State increased, and with them came an increase in potential and actual grievances (for example, disputes about benefits). Experience with early manifestations of the Welfare State such as the Workmen's (Compensation for Injury) Act 1897 had shown that the traditional court system was

not equipped to deal with disputes arising from such social legislation. When the National Insurance Act 1911 was passed, it was decided that disputes about benefits were to be determined by "umpires and referees rather than by courts" (Thompson 1993). We see here the beginnings of the major development of a court substitute – the administrative tribunal. There are various categories of tribunals but we shall focus on those which are used to settle disputes about entitlement under some government scheme, for example tax, benefits, education and so on.

Tribunals are independent adjudicatory bodies usually established by statute to deal with disputes in a particular area of law. They are seen as having several advantages over the traditional courts. These advantages are cheapness, accessibility, freedom from technicality, speed and expert knowledge of their particular subject. The main reason that tribunals have these advantages are their composition and the procedures they adopt.

Most tribunals will have as their chair someone who is legally qualified, who will be accompanied by others who will have experience of the subject matter of the tribunal and will inject a lay element into the proceedings. This experience will mean that cases can be considered speedily which in turn will reduce costs. Procedure is designed to be as informal as possible. The aggrieved applicant should be encouraged by this informal atmosphere to present his own case. The chairs are usually paid a daily fee (some are full-time and other members are usually only paid expenses). This obviously reduces costs. There are currently proposals to have the chair of industrial tribunals sit more frequently without lay members to save £5 million per year. If this is seen as a success it could be extended to other tribunals (these might however be seen as akin to Diplock courts in Northern Ireland and therefore subject to similar criticisms).

It may be useful to examine the workings of one particular tribunal to gauge how well the system works. Baldwin, Wikely and Young (Baldwin, Wikely and Young, 1992) examined the operation of Social Security Appeal Tribunals to see how efficiently they operated. SSATs were formed by combining national insurance tribunals with supplementary benefit appeal tribunals. This arose because it had become evident that while national insurance tribunals were working effectively this was not true of supplementary benefit appeal tribunals where decisions were inconsistent, issues of law and policy were confused and applicants felt demeaned by the process. Inconsistency was reduced by reducing the discretion available and by improving the quality of tribunal members and by appointing legally qualified chairs. This was felt to be essential as the rules concerning entitlement had become increasingly complex.

One of the disadvantages of the tribunal system is that it adopts the adversarial system which, as we saw earlier, places the burden of establishing a case on the claimant. SSATs began to move away from this by asking questions of applicants. Hopefully this would make them feel at ease. The adversarial system was not, however, replaced by an inquisitorial one; the two merely existed together. However, it seems that this desire to help was not indulged in by the respondent, (the DSS) whose written submissions to the tribunal are seen not as aids to reaching a decision but as justification of their decisions and an attempt to set the agenda. The great majority of chairs competently carry out their roles and the standard of lay membership has generally improved.

There are, however, problems. Legal advice is not always easily available for what are complex legal issues. This absence of legal advice may be the reason that only 50% of appellants attend hearings. This may also be because the documents they receive are technical in nature or because they are not told that attendance is advisable. Research would seem to indicate that another reason for non-attendance is the average 23 weeks between the lodging and the hearing of the appeal. A result of non-attendance is that the appeal will not be dealt with as thoroughly as might otherwise be the case. Representation is accompanied by a higher success rate. This is not surprising given the complexity of the benefit rules and the formal nature of the tribunal procedure. Arguments that there should be representation in tribunals are vintage but would not seem to be a government priority, and with cuts in the traditional legal aid budget. Representation is, however, no guarantee of success. If the representative is not particularly competent, it seems many tribunals will not seek to draw out information, on the basis that as there is representation, there is no reason form them to move away from the inquisitorial approach. It is obviously crucial to have as a representative someone (whether legally qualified or not) who fully understands the issues.

The research concludes that the SSATs are a considerable improvement on what went before. A higher standard of decision-making has resulted from better trained and qualified tribunal members. Those applying for benefits believe they are treated well. The major problem is that tribunals still largely adopt the adversarial approach which is, by its very nature, not user-friendly, particularly to the non-represented applicant.

Most textbooks on administrative law discuss tribunals and inquiries together. This would perhaps suggest that they share a similar function. This is not the case. Public inquiries are held for one of two main purposes. They are held to enable information to be gathered and views canvassed for some future proposal (a motorway, a power station), or they are held to investigate and discover information about some past event (e.g. arms to Iraq, prison riots).

Environmental matters feature largely in public inquiries. Examples would be the route of a motorway, the siting of a quarry, coal mine, or a power station. The authority putting forward the proposal will invite comments from interested parties. These will almost certainly follow, and will consist largely of objections. The current public inquiry into the proposed super-quarry at Lingerbay in Harris has attracted objections from local people and from Scottish National Heritage. This mix of those directly affected and those objecting on wider public interest grounds would be quite normal. A public inquiry will be proposed and an inspector appointed. Both promoters and objectors will make representations. Based upon these the inspector will make his report which he will then submit to the relevant minister who may confirm, modify or reject the proposal.

Where complex technical matters are concerned, expert assessors will be appointed to evaluate representations. Additionally, a counsel to the inquiry will be appointed whose task it will be to test the evidence through cross-examination, as would happen in a traditional court. The structure of the inquiry would seem, therefore, to follow the adversarial method of dispute resolution. There is one major differences: the inspector does not decide the matter. This decision will be taken by the minister who has played no part in the inquiry. The inquisitorial nature of the inquiry will depend a great deal on the individual inspector. The basic function of the inquiry is to allow individuals the right to be heard before a decision is made. It could be argued that inquiries have more to do with the appearance of open government than with accountability.

The Parliamentary Commissioner

For many years Scandinavian countries have had an official known as the ombudsman whose function it is to investigate complaints of maladministration. The first ombudsman appeared in Sweden in 1809 although the powers of the Swedish ombudsman, which included the right to initiate prosecutions, including prosecutions against judges, have not been adopted by other countries which have instituted "ombudsmen". There is no satisfactory translation of the word. It means "complaints office" or "grievance man". The first twentieth-century ombudsman was in Denmark followed by Finland and Norway. New Zealand instituted the office in 1962. The Whyatt Report of 1961 recommended the establishment of a Parliamentary commissioner based on the Danish ombudsman. There was initial rejection of Report largely because it was felt that the office would cut across the age-old doctrine of ministerial responsibility to Parliament and, anyway, complaints could be raised through MPs. These objections were seen to lack substance and the Parliamentary Commissioner Act 1967 established the first British ombudsman who was essentially the officer suggested in 1961. Parliament shied away from the use of such an un-English term as ombudsman but it has been informally adopted by most people, including the British Parliamentary commissioner himself.

The Parliamentary Commissioner Act 1967 (PCA) created the office of Parliamentary Commissioner for Administration with a jurisdiction running throughout Great Britain (except Northern Ireland). It got its own ombudsman in 1969. The commissioner is appointed by the Crown and holds office till the age of 65. He can only be removed following an address from both Houses of Parliament so his tenure is protected in much the same way as superior judges. He is an ex-officio member of the Council or Tribunals and he may investigate any action taken by or on behalf of the government department or certain other listed authorities, so long as there is no court or tribunal in which such an action may reasonably be challenged. He cannot act until a complaint has been received by him that there has been maladministration (see below). The Act provided that the commissioner shall not investigate cases where the complainant has a remedy in a court or tribunal. However, under section 5(2) of the Act, if the commissioner feels that it is unreasonable for the complainant to have resorted to a legal remedy then he can investigate. The factors the commissioner will take into account in undertaking an investigation include the cumbersome and slow nature of the legal process, and the expense involved, relative to the desired objective (Parliamentary Commissioner for Administration 1981). This would, it seems, introduce some calculation of the proportionality of the effort to the objective (Thompson: 330).

COMPLAINTS PROCEDURE

All complaints must be in writing and must be made by someone resident in the United Kingdom who claims to have suffered injustice as a result of maladministration. The complaint must be made in the first instance to an MP within 12 months of the alleged maladministration. It will be up to the MP to refer the complaint to the commissioner with the complainant's consent, requesting that the commissioner investigate. The reason that complaints are through MPs is to prevent the commissioner being swamped and to remove eccentric or worthless complaints. This may be justified as Britain was the first country with a large population to have an ombudsman. This restrictive access has been frequently criticised (see *Justice Our Fettered Ombudsman* 1977) and commissioners themselves have argued for a right of direct access (1993 Report). Direct access would almost certainly increase the level of complaints which would have a financial impact for the Treasury (and of course the taxpayer). Initially commissioners rejected complaints sent directly to them but the more recently they have adopted the practice of sending such complaints to the constituency MP with a request that he decide whether or not to officially refer the complaint back to the commissioner.

Investigations must be conducted in private and procedure is at the discretion of the commissioner. He has the right under Section 8 of the PCA to require any minister, officer or member of a department or authority concerned, or indeed anyone else, to give information or produce documents relevant to the investigation. He has the same power as a court to compel the attendance and examination of witnesses. The Crown is not permitted to shelter behind any claim of Crown privilege in respect of producing documents or giving evidence. He has no jurisdiction over Cabinet meetings. At the conclusion of the investigation he sends to the MP involved a report of his investigation or the reason why he has not conducted the investigation. A similar report must go to the original complainant and to the principal officer of the department or authority concerned. The average investigation takes 13.53 months (1993 Annual Report). This lengthy period for an investigation is frequently referred to as the "Rolls Royce Method", and is one major reason why relatively few MPs refer cases to the commissioner (Leyland, Woods and Harden 1994: 56). He can if he wishes make a special report to Parliament each year but he must make an annual report to Parliament upon his work. Such reports are referred to a select committee for consideration and comment.

The Act lists a large number of departments which are subject to the commissioner's investigation, but there are also a lot of subjects which are exempt from investigation within these departments. A large slice of the power of, for example, the Foreign and Home Office is immune from investigation by the commissioner. Areas of exemption are kept under constant review by the House of Commons. The select committee has eight members and has over the years made suggestions that led to the improvement and efficiency of the commissioner's work.

One major difficulty is that the 1967 Act does not define "maladministration". This has the advantage of giving a commissioner a broad sweep but it also means of course that he may, if he is so inclined, confine his investigations to a very narrow range and indeed this was the case with some of the early incumbents of the office. Happily, it would not seem to be the case today. Over the years 1984–1993 an average of 880 complaints were dealt with by the commissioner. The Department of Social Security and its agencies account for the most significant single part of his workload (Annual Report 1993). He rejected 70% because they were outside his jurisdiction (maybe no central government department was involved or it involved a personnel matter from the Civil Service or Armed Forces). Instances of maladministration were found to be fully justified in 40% of the cases investigated, and partly justified in another 23%. The remedies which departments provide include ex gratia compensation; the remission of tax where under payment has arisen through official error; the payment of arrears of pensions and benefits that have been wrongly withheld; the revised procedures to prevent the repetition of mistakes. If one complainant is granted a remedy this may lead to others being similarly treated. The commissioner cannot compel a department to provide a remedy, but where an injustice caused by maladministration has not been remedied he may lay a report before Parliament and the first time this happened the government introduced legislation enabling the injustice to be remedied.

Early on it was recognised that the creation of the office of commissioner might be only the first step in creating more extra-judicial remedies against the administration and this has lead to the commissioner experiment being adopted in other areas of government. The National Health Service was included from the commissioner's jurisdiction but on the reorganization of the Health Service in 1977 a scheme of Health Service Commissioners was adopted, one for each of England, Scotland and Wales. The procedure to be followed is similar to that laid down for the Parliamentary Commissioner but for the fact that a complaint may be made directly to the commissioner concerned. He will not investigate any action which he feels was based on a clinical judgement.

As pressure built up in the wake of the 1967 Act for extension and improvement of the ombudsman principle, there was a move for the idea to be applied to the field of local government. Reorganization of local government provided the opportunity in 1974/1975. One commission was established for England, one for Wales and one for Scotland (by the Local Government (Scotland) Act 1975). An individual may approach the commissioner for local administration for area in connection with allegations of maladministration by local authorities, joint boards, police authorities (although not the Home Secretary) and water authorities. Procedurally complaints are through a member of the authority made in question, but the commissioner can investigate a complaint if he feels such a member has refused to refer a request. Public transport, entertainments markets and the management and discipline of local authority schools are excluded. The commissioner reports to the local authority and the complainant. Most of the complaints relate to housing and town planning. The commissioner cannot force a local authority to remedy an injustice caused by maladministration, but if his report is not accepted by the local authority he can issue a further report saying so. It can be strongly argued that a local authority should be legally obliged to provide a remedy. One of the main criticisms with regard to the system of local commissioners is the provision that any matter in which all or most of the inhabitants of an authority area are affected is outside the commissioner's jurisdiction.

Further discussion of the Commissioner, for Local Administration and the Health Service Commission follows in Chapter 4.

In practice, there is no end to the implementation of the ombudsman principle if professional and other organizations choose to adopt it within their own spheres. Ombudsmen have been established in professions as diverse as banking, building societies, insurance and the provision of funeral services. The origins of the ombudsman lie in the desire to control the power of state agencies (Bell and Vaughan, 1989). The growth of ombudsmen in other fields is a recognition that there are non-state agencies that have equal if not greater power over the lives of citizens. These ombudsmen although important do not concern us here.

CRITICISMS OF THE PARLIAMENTARY COMMISSIONER

The operation of the PCA system has been subject to criticism from academics, select committees and indeed commissioners themselves. These complaints relate to four broad areas: procedures, jurisdiction, enforcement and the fact that the public are not aware of their existence. The continued existence of the "MP filter" has been subject to criticism. It is seen as distancing the Commissioner from the public. As we saw above, it would seem to be the case that the commissioner will not reject "direct mail" but send it to the relevant MP for resubmission. The commissioner is very much a "fire fighter"; he can only respond to complaints. There have been suggestions that the PCA be allowed to initiate investigations. The Swedish and Danish ombudsmen initiate investigations and receive complaints direct. Their role has a much higher profile than its British counterpart.

The jurisdiction of the PCA is seen as being too narrow. It has been suggested that he should be allowed to investigate the preparation and making of delegated legislation, in addition to investigating administrative functions. He should, moreover, be allowed to investigate complaints regarding personnel matters in the civil service and the making of government contracts.

Criticism is also levelled at the PCA's lack of power to enforce his recommendations. The reality would seem to be that a mutually agreed settlement is reached between the PCA and the minister. In Northern Ireland, if a finding of maladministration has been made, the complainant has the right to apply to the county court for an award of damages or an order against the authority which was found to have caused injustice through maladministration. The government has rejected proposals to extend such judicial enforcement to other commissioners. The commissioner has been criticised on the ground that the public is insufficiently aware of his existence. In his 1988 Report, the Commissioner devoted a paragraph to the issue of publicity pointing out his use of press releases and media interviews and publicity material. One of the main publicising events was the Commissioner's investigation into the failed investment group Barlow Clowes in 1988 which generated hundreds of complaints and made headline news when the Commissioner's Report was published. Northern Ireland commissioners have been more innovatory as regards publicity. They travel round the province "setting up their stall" (Thompson: 337) to advertise their existence to the public. They will, moreover, deal with minor complaints by telephone.

ADVANTAGES OF THE PARLIAMENTARY COMMISSIONER FOR ADMINISTRATION
The PCA system has several advantages over the process of judicial review (which is discussed below).

- The PCA can deal with those form of maladministration which are not amenable to judicial review, for example delay, incompetence, rudeness, losing files and so on. In advertising language, the PCA reaches parts that others do not reach!

- Maladministration may, while being too minor to warrant court action still have an impact on those concerned. Examples might be incomprehensible application forms, or unnecessary complicated procedures.
- Complaining to the PCA costs at the most the price of a stamp. Even this could be avoided by handing in the complaint direct to the MP. In addition the PCA has the power to award complainant's expenses.
- The PCA will undertake the investigation. This is not the case with judicial review where the onus (and expense) is on the complainant.
- There is a twelve-month time limit for bringing a complaint compared with three months under judicial review.
- PCA procedure is not adversarial but conciliatory. This is seen by many as producing a better result because everyone concerned is more at ease.
- Those called to give evidence to the PCA are assured anonymity. This, it is felt, allows for more frankness and honesty.
- The PCA seeks to effect an amicable settlement. This is not the result of an application for judicial review. Remedies granted include an ex-gratia payment, reversal of a decision or the alteration of an administrative process.
- PCA investigations produce what is known as the "Ripple effect". The finding in one individual's complaint of maladministration may affect many others who have not complained. Applications for judicial review, on the other hand, only affect the individuals concerned.

Judicial Review

We have in the United Kingdom a system whereby courts (and other bodies such as tribunals) exercise some monitoring jurisdiction over the acts of administrative authorities. This system is often referred to under the generic title of "judicial review". This however is misleading. Judicial review refers only to a specific form of control exercised by the superior courts and stems from the traditional authority assumed by these courts to subject the acts and decisions of the executive (in all its forms) to examination, in order to ascertain the legality, rationality and procedural propriety of the exercise of power (see *Council of Civil Service Unions v Minister for Civil Service* (1984). Judicial review, which we shall discuss below, is only part of the mechanism by which the courts may call authorities to account. It is in the field of public law that judicial review most frequently arises. The distinction between issues of private law and those of public law is not always easy to define and has been discussed in *West v Secretary of State*, (1992) *Jobeen v University of Stirling*, (1995) *Naik v University of Stirling* (1994). In these cases the court tried to establish guidelines to ascertain whether its supervisory jurisdiction is being sought as a matter of course in the regulation of contract (within the Prison Service in *West, or in university students contracts in Jobeen* and *Naik*, or in respect of the regulation of a relationship between public authority and citizen. Bradley maintains that in Scotland the distinction is almost irrelevant, (Bradley and Ewing, 1993) but it can be argued that it is a matter of some moment in attempting to outline the role of the courts in calling public authorities to account, particularly when it is further complicated by questions of "justiciability" and "proportionality". It would probably suffice to say here that the jurisdiction of the courts to ensure the accountability of public authorities may be exercised regardless of the particular role being played by the authority, whether in the private or public interest. Therefore, we can say that, in addition to the jurisdiction of the courts to regulate the relationship between public authorities and individual citizens in respect of private rights, as seen earlier, an arguably more significant role is played by the courts in calling such authorities to account for the exercise of power in the public interest. The courts have long cherished their traditional right to ensure that the exercise of executive power is subject to constraints related to the extent of the power exercised and the method of its exercise. This was, for example, articulately and clearly laid down in the words of Lord Shaw of Dunfermline in the case of *Moss Empires Limited v Assessor for Glasgow* (1917) 1 where he says:

> I would put my view as to jurisdiction thus: It is within the inherent jurisdiction of the Court of Session to keep inferior judicatories and administrative bodies right in the sense of compelling them to keep within the limits of their statutory powers or of compelling them to obey those conditions without the fulfilment of which they have no power whatso-ever.

This is the area of jurisdiction known as "judicial review".

Judicial review is primarily concerned with the provision of remedies against administrative authorities and bodies on the traditional grounds of *ultra vires* and/or a breach of natural justice as outlined in Lord Shaw's dictum (above). There is a much more modern statement of these grounds by Lord Diplock in the case of the *Council for Civil Service Association v The Minister for the Civil Service* (see above) [The Cheltenham – GCHQ case] where he maintains that the basis on which the courts are entitled to review administrative action and decisionmaking are "illegality, irrationality and procedural irregularity". This is a restatement in the sense that all of these above grounds are reflected in the traditional concepts of *ultra vires* and natural justice examined in this chapter.

Vires, in administrative law, is the term given to power or authority handed down to public authorities through the agency of legislation or the Royal Prerogative. Any action which goes beyond such power or authority or is an abuse or irrational use of such power or authority is termed to be *ultra vires* and, in any case properly brought before the courts where such a finding is made the action or decision complained of will be regarded as invalid and ineffective. This rule of the law extends throughout the whole area of executive or administrative action or decisionmaking – including the area of delegated legislation. The *ultra vires* doctrine is a general and common law concept and, therefore, is not necessarily conducive to compartmentalisation – but for the sake of convenience, it can be broken down into a number of categories which reflect the findings of the courts.

Firstly, a distinction can be made between substantive *ultra vires* relating to the extent of the power and procedural *ultra vires* relating to the method by which the power is exercised. Substantive *ultra vires* comprises the following types of action or decision:

- Exceeding powers given: (*Laker Airways v S of S* DTI) (1977). In Laker the Secretary of State had attempted to give British Airways a monopoly on long-distance flights from the UK contrary to earlier legislation. He could not do this as he was exceeding his powers, therefore acting *ultra vires*.
- Abusing powers given: (*Congreve v Home Office*) (1953). Although the Minister had the power to withdraw TV licences the power had not been meant to be used in these circumstances (see above) and its exercise was *ultra vires*.
- Unauthorised delegation of powers given: (*Barnard v National Dock Labour Board*) (1968) In Barnard, the Dock Labour Board had statutory authority to discipline dockers. They had delegated this authority to the port manager. There was no mention of such delegation in the statute. The manager could not exercise disciplinary powers, and his attempt to do so was *ultra vires*.
- Unreasonable use of discretionary powers given: *Padfield v Minister for*

Agriculture In Padfield, the Minister had made discretionary powers as to whether he would order an investigation into complaints about the operation of a milk marketing scheme. The House of Lords said that such discretion must be exercised properly to promote the policy and objects of the Agriculture Marketing Act 1958. If it appeared that a refusal to order an investigation was to frustrate the purpose of the Act then the courts would interfere, on the grounds that the discretion had been abused and it was, therefore, an *ultra vires* use of power.

- Failure to comply with a statutory duty: *Meade v Haringey BC* (1979). In *Meade,* Lord Denning said that a local authority who had closed schools during a strike of ancillary workers were under a statutory duty to keep them open. Alternative arrangements could have been made and since they were not the Local Authority had acted *ultra vires.*

In these cases, which are but singular examples of a whole series of cases raising the same issues, the courts decided that in exceeding, abusing misusing or wrongfully interpreting the power granted the respective authorities had acted *ultra vires.* Their actions and decisions were therefore declared to be unlawful.

The second aspect of the *ultra vires* doctrine is the concept of procedural *ultra vires.* The standard rule of procedural *ultra vires* is that the powers of the administration may only be exercised in accordance with any procedural requirements laid down by the authoritative source of the power. If such procedural requirements are not adhered to then the exercise is invalid as being *ultra vires.* (cf *Moss Empires*). This fundamental standard has however been qualified by the courts themselves by the making of a distinction between mandatory and regulatory procedures (*Coney v Choyce*) (1975) whereby failure to comply with mandatory procedures renders the exercise of power *ultra vires* while failure to comply with directory procedures does not affect the validity of such an exercise. The decision of the courts as to whether there has been failure to observe the mandatory or directory procedures in a particular case is purely discretionary and tends to depend on whether prejudice has been caused (*London & Clyde Estates v Aberdeen DC* (1979)). If, however, the courts are satisfied that failure to observe mandatory procedures has caused prejudice they will declare any actions or decisions *ultra vires* and therefore unlawful. A recent example was the decision that the Home Secretary had acted illegally in introducing changes to the Criminal Injuries Compensation Scheme.

The second ground of the operation of judicial review is commonly called the rules of natural justice or the principles of natural justice. Before examining the actual content of these rules or principles in so far as they relate to administrative law and consequently to accountability, it is necessary to address two areas of difficulty. The twentieth century has seen a great deal of conflict about the status of natural justice as a legal concept. While many cases can be cited, as below, where judges have been heard to apply the phrase to specific cases and well defined circumstances, it cannot be denied that in other cases there has been criticism of its use and disparaging comment about its meaning. To see but a few examples of the latter position we need only look at the judgement of Lord Shaw in *L. G. Board v Alridge* (1915) where he describes the phrase as "high sounding but harmless". Lord Justice Scrutton's view in *Holt v Mackham* (1923) was that it suggested well-meaning sloppiness of thought. *Norwest Holst v Dept. of Trade* (1978) indicated that the word "natural" in relation to "justice" adds nothing except perhaps a "hint of nostalgia for the good old days when nasty things did not happen" and Lord Roskill's comment in *Council of Civil Service Unions v Minister for the Civil Service* (1985) that the phrase "be allowed to find a permanent resting place and be better replaced by speaking of a duty to act fairly". It can, and has been, compellingly argued by many including Bradley (Bradley and Ewing 1993 above cite 690–99) that the rules and principles of natural justice relate to a great deal more than merely a general requirement to act fairly. The rules are clear and their application in modern administrative law indicates that they constitute minimum standards of fair and lawful decision making and action. In the particular situations in which they apply, a breach of these rules will entitle the court to hold such actions or decisions invalid or ineffective. If we accept as established the fact that, despite difficulties in interpreting, the rules of natural justice set out a minimum standard of judicial requirement for administrative action or decisionmaking, the second problem is to determine where they apply.

Unlike the doctrine of *ultra vires* referred to above the rules of natural justice do not apply to all forms of administrative action or decisions. The rules, for example, have been declared by the courts not to apply to exercises of delegated legislation. As far as any other acts or decisions are concerned, they do not apply where these are purely administrative in character; where there is no direct conflict of interest between state and citizen or between citizen and citizen. But where such conflicts do occur then the rules will apply and where the rights of individuals are involved then the action-taker or decision-maker will not only be expected to observe the rules but will be required to do so. Where there is a failure to observe, the action or decision will be rendered invalid and ineffective. It is not a simple matter to determine where the rules apply and it is a matter for any court to decide in respect of any action raised before it. A review of the standard cases in this area however would seem to suggest that any action or decision by an administrative authority which involves a conflict of interest and relates to an individuals right to earn a living (for example any form of licensing or entry to a disbarment from professional associations or educational establishments), an individual's right to a good reputation (for example dismissal from employment especially on the grounds of improper conduct; an individual's right to keep, use or dispose of property; planning or compulsory purchase) will be required to be dealt with according to the rules of natural justice. This is not, however, exhaustive and other circumstances have been adjudged by the courts to require adherence to the rules, for example decisions by University authorities to refuse students the rights to continue with their courses or to refuse to grant degrees for reasons other than failure to satisfy examiners. Administrative law has endorsed the general concept of natural justice with the status of a precise and potent principle especially related to any interference by authorities with individual rights and the rules themselves have been explicitly referred to in a number of statutes (for example The Tribunals and Inquiries Acts).

The actual content of the rules and the minimum standards required by the courts have been adapted from the traditional and fundamental principles observed by the courts themselves in respect of their own procedures. They are generally referred to as "the rule against bias" (sometimes described by the legal maxim – *Nemo index in causa sua* – let no man be a judge in his own case), and "the right to be heard" (*Audi alteram partem*: hear the other side).

The rule against bias requires a decision-maker or action-taker to be neutral and totally impartial. This very precise rule applies in all court procedures and a judge is required to disqualify him or herself from deciding in any matter in which he or she has any interest which could cause bias, or a real likelihood of bias, or a reasonable suspicion of bias. In administrative matters, however, the interest will usually require to be either a personal financial interest, or a business connection or a family relationship with one of the parties whose interests are affected by the decision or action. In the case of *Metropolitan Properties v Lennon* (1969), for example, the chairman of a rent assessment committee was a member of a firm of solicitors which was negotiating rents with one of the groups of tenants of the property being assessed. It was decided that his position was thus compromised and his decision as Chairman was in breach of this first rule of natural justice.

The right to be heard requires that each party whose rights may be infringed is given an opportunity to state his or her view of the facts in issue. In the courts this amounts to a personal right to be informed of any case to answer, the right to be given reasonable time to prepare such answers, the right to attend a formal hearing, the right to give evidence at such a hearing, the right to be given reasons for the judge's decision and the right, where relevant, to appeal against the decision. In administrative law, however, the right to be heard is not always so clear cut or extensive. It may amount to such an extensive right in certain cases (e.g. *Ridge v Baldwin* (1964) (a Chief Constable dismissed by a local Watch Committee denied the opportunity of presenting his own view before the Committee) and *Malloch v Aberdeen Corporation* (1971) 1971 2A11 ER 1278 (a school teacher dismissed without a hearing by local authority). In other cases, however, "the right to be heard" may merely be a requirement that an interested party be given an opportunity to lodge written objections before a decision is made or action is taken.

Despite all of the complexities surrounding the meaning, operation and extent of the rules of natural justice, it is incontrovertible that, in certain circumstances, the courts will insist and have insisted that in certain actions or decisions a failure to observe the requirements of the rule against bias or the right to be heard will render the action or decision unlawful and ineffective.

In summation it can be said that the grounds for the exercise of judicial review as expressed by Lord Diplock in *Council of Civil Service Unions v Minister for the Civil Service* (above) namely "illegality, irrationality and procedural impropriety", reflect the traditional doctrines of *ultra vires* and natural justice.

Remedies

One of the major differences between Scotland and England lies in the remedies available to applicants for judicial review. It is not thought necessary to go into the remedies in detail here, but the main points will be highlighted. Texts which cover remedies in detail include Clayton and Thomas (1993) *Judicial Review: A Practical Guide* and (for Scotland) St. Clair and Thomas (1986) *Judicial Review in Scotland*. In England, claims can be made for six main remedies: the first three are known as "prerogative orders" and can only be granted against public bodies. They evolved from special types of writs which were only available to the Crown (as one of its prerogatives).

- Certiorari. This is a court order that quashes an unlawful decision of government or public authority. It is the primary remedy in judicial review decision as it allows the courts to control such unlawful decisions. There are some restrictions on the availability of certiorari.
- Mandamus. An order of mandamus is used to compel a public body to carry out its duty. A common use is to compel such bodies to exercise discretion to hear a case or to exercise a discretionary power. Refusal to obey an order of mandamus constitutes contempt of court. Both certiorari and mandamus will frequently be sought simultaneously. Mandamus will of course only be available where the public body is under a duty to act in a particular way. As with certiorari there are some restrictions on the availability of mandamus.
- Prohibition. The remedy of prohibition is used to prevent public bodies from acting unlawfully in the future and is complimentary to certiorari. Prohibition is not available where a decision has already been taken. Failure to comply with an order of prohibition is a contempt of court.
- Injunction. This is a court order directing an individual to act or stop acting in a particular way. Failure to comply is a contempt of court.
- Declaration. This is an order of the court whereby it states the legal position based on the facts available to it. Unlike the preceding remedies, failure to comply is not a contempt of court, that is the order has no coercive force. A declaration will usually be sought when the law is unclear. There are some restrictions on the availability of the remedy.
- Damages. This is the award of a sum of money to compensate for loss suffered.

Scottish Remedies

The prerogative orders (above) have, with one exception, never been part of Scotish Law. Administrative law remedies in Scotland are generally no different from those that apply in private law generally. The most important of these are reduction, declarator, interdict, damages, and specific implement. It will be useful to examine these briefly.

- Reduction. This is a remedy whereby decisions of tribunals, local byelaws, dismissals or public servants may be quashed as being in excess of jurisdiction in breach of natural justice, or otherwise contrary to law.

- Declarator. This is the equivalent of the English declaration of right and is an action whereby an interested party seeks to have a legal right declared but without any claim on the defender to do anything.
- Interdict. This is an judicial prohibition, comparable to the English injunction and prohibition.
- An action for damages. This is for monetary compensation for loss suffered and specific implement is a remedy to enforce performance of statutory duties. It is similar to but not identical with the English mandamus.

The Effectiveness of Judicial Review

In *Judicial Review: A Possible Programme for Reform* (1992) *Public Law*, Lord Woolf expressed his deep concern as to the state and future of judicial review. He quotes Lord Lane who

> had compared (judicial review) with a motorway, and pointed out that if you provide a motorway it will become an invitation for the public to respond by using it. This has proved to be all too true. There is a danger of it becoming as overcrowded as the M25. The tailback, or backlogs, are becoming more and more disturbing. The use of judicial review has grown and is continuing to grow at a pace with which the present structure cannot cope. I believe the rate of increase is going to accelerate.

It is certainly true that the last 15 years has seen what seems like an explosion in judicial review of administrative action. Between 1980 and 1992 judicial review applications rose from 500 to 2500 (Law Commission 1993). Research, however, shows that the growth has been largely confined to three areas: immigration, homelessness and criminal proceedings (Sunkin, Bridges and Meszaros, 1993). Together these three areas accounted for more than half of all applications. The only other two areas of significance are town and country planning and education. This would suggest that there are many administrative agencies untouched by judicial review. This is particularly true of government departments as 75% of all applications are directed against local government. Of the applications against central government, 75% are against the Home Office. Most applications were instituted in the names of individuals. Somewhat unexpectedly, pressure groups made little use of judicial review. One problem highlighted by the research was the problem of access. This arose for two main reasons: first the limited availability of legal aid, and secondly the fact that only a small minority of solicitors had experience of processing a judicial review case (Sunkin, Bridges and Meszaros, 1993).

Another area highlighted was the poor "survival" rate for actions; only a third reached a final hearing. This average hid some very poor "survival" rates, for example only 11% of immigration actions reached a final hearing. For those applications that lasted the course there was only a one in six chance of getting a ruling against the body challenged. The research shows that there are two main reasons for this poor "survival" rate. The first and most worrying is the discrepancy in granting leave to apply for judicial review between the judges. One judge was found to grant 82% of applications, whereas another granted leave to apply in only 21%. It is difficult to believe that the variance can be accounted for by the merits of the caseload before the two. Sunkin and his colleagues say: "The result for applicants is that leave is somewhat of a lottery".

The second reason is that many of the bodies challenged agree to a settlement once leave has been granted. Obviously if leave is not granted there would be no need for a settlement. Kate Morris says that the Law Commission should:

> expand the scope of judicial review and (promote) measures to ensure that ordinary people have even better access to the protection of the courts against the abuses of power by public officials.
> (Morris 1993).

This research also argues that one straightforward solution would be that public authorities should be under an obligation to make known the reasons for their decisions to applicants, their legal advisers and judges at a much earlier state. This view has been echoed by Lord Woolf who says that this would be the most beneficial improvement that could be made to administrative law. In *Padfield v Minister of Agriculture* (1968), the court said that in the absence of express reasons the court could infer that the minister had no good reasons for his decision. Some recent decisions would suggest that there is a move towards establishing a general duty to give reasons.

Both the government and public authorities are wary of giving information and will use a variety of chances to avoid doing so. *Matrix Churchill* would but one recent example. A culture change in this area would assist the process of accountability immeasurably. Do not hold your breath.

Conclusion

Does our existing system of controlling the actions of public authority (both central and local) work effectively? There are obviously major problems. Foremost among these are issues such as the cost to the complainant coupled with the non-availability of legal aid. The very nature of the legal system with its emphasis on adversarial procedures is another major drawback. There may be a move away from such procedures if the views of Lord Mackay of Clashfern, the Lord Chancellor, on increasing access to justice come to fruition. The analysis of judicial review outlined above is disturbing. The research discussed certainly seems to indicate that the system of judicial review is not working effectively, for the reasons discussed. The same lack of effectiveness also seems to apply to tribunals and inquiries. As indicated above, the Parliamentary Commissioner may have advantages over judicial review, and tribunals and inquiries, but it is, at least theoretically, fatally wounded because of lack of powers of enforcement (although this may be less important in practice). Another disadvantage that applies to the PCA and judicial review is that they only come into force after the event. They do not play a preventative role, although they may prevent abuse of power, maladministration and so on from happening in subsequent cases. (This is truer of the PCA).

We shall leave the last word to S. A. de Smith's epic work on judicial review of administrative action which begins with a ringing and oft quoted disclaimer:

> Judicial review of administrative action is inevitably sporadic and peripheral. The administrative process is not and cannot be a succession of justiciable controversies. Public authorities are set up to govern and administer, and if their every act or decision were to be reviewable on unrestricted grounds by an independent judicial body the business of administration could be brought to a standstill.

Harlow and Rawlings observed that: "the number of judicial review decisions is infinitesimal compared with the millions of decisions taken daily by public authorities". Although these writers were speaking specifically about judicial review, what they say would have relevance to the Parliamentary Commissioner.

Accountability should perhaps be seen as a recipe with many ingredients. The effectiveness of the completed dish will depend on a mixture of ingredients, in correct measure. Judicial review, tribunals and inquiries and the PCA are but three ingredients. The effectiveness of the completed dish will depend on the presence of other ingredients, such as popular accountability, parliamentary accountability, consumerism and so on. Unless all of these are present we will end up with a tasteless dish that fails to rise to the occasion.

References

Baldwin, Wikely and Young (1992), *Judging Social Security: The Adjudication of Claims for Benefit in Britain*, Oxford: Clarendon Press.

Barnard v National Dock Labour Board [1953] 2 QB 18.

Bell and Vaughan (1989), "The Building Societies Ombudsman: A Customer's Champion", *Solicitors Journal* 132 1478–80.

Bradley and Ewing (1993), *Constitutional and Administrative Law*, London: Longman.

Burmah Oil v Lord Advocate [1965] AC 75.

Churchward v Regina [1865], 1QB 173.

Commissioner of Crown Lands v Page [1960] 2 QB 274.

Coney v Choyce [1975] 1 ALL ER 979.

Congrieve v Home Office [1968] AC 997.

Conway v Rimmer [1968] AC 1910.

Costa v Enel [1964] CMLR 425.

Council of Civil Service Unions v Minister for Civil Service [1984] 3 ALL ER 935.

de Smith (1980), *Judicial Review of Administrative Action* (4th Edition), London: Stevens.

Dicey (1959, 10th Edition), *An Introduction to the Law of the Constitution*.

First Report from the Select Committee on Procedure HC 588 of 1977–78.

Glasgow Corporation v Central Land Board [1956] SC. HL1.

HMA v Khaliq [1983] SCCR 483.

Hogg (1971), *Liability of the Crown in Australia, New Zealand and the United Kingdom*, Melbourne: Law Book Co.

Holt v Mackham [1923] 1KB 504.

Home Office v Dorset Yacht Company [1980] AC 1004.

Kodeeswaran v Attorney General of Ceylon [1970] AC 1111.

Krylenko Av. Sudi i pravo v SSSR, (1927–30) Moscow and Leningrad.

Laker Airways v Secretary of State DTI [1971], QB 643.

Leyland, Woods and Harden (1994), *Administrative Law*, London: Blackstone

L. G. Board v Alridge [1915] AC 120.

Locke (1690), *Second Treatise on Civil Government*.

London and Clyde Estates v Aberdeen DC [1979] 3 ALL ER 876.

Malloch v Aberdeen Corporation [1971] 2 ALL ER 1278.

Meade v Haringey BC [1979] 2 ALL ER 1016.

Mersey Docks and Harbour Board Trustees v Gibbs (1866) LR 1 HL.

Metropolitan Properties v Lennon [1969] 1 QR 577.

Mitchell v Regina [1896] 1 QB 121.

Montesquieu, *De L'esprit Des Lois*, Book XI, Chapter 6.

Moss Empires v Assessor for Glasgow [1917], SC HL 1.

Morris (1993), *Judicial Review in Perspective: An Investigation of Trends in the Use and Operation of the Judicial Review Procedure in England and Wales*, Public Law Project.

New South Wales v Bardolph [1934] 52 CLR 455.

Norwest Holst v Department of Trade [1978] Ch. 20.

Parliamentary Commissioner for Administration, Annual Report for 1993 HL 290 of 1993–94

Padfield v Minister for Agriculture [1968] AC 997.

Rederiaktiebolaget Amphritite v Rex [1921] 3 KB 500.

Regina v Civil Service Appeal Board, ex parte Bruce [1984] 3 ALL ER 395.

Regina v Lord Chancellor's Department, ex parte Nangle [1991] IRLR 343.

Reilly v Rex [1934] AC 176.

Ridge v Baldwin [1964] AC 40.

Ridley (1988), "There is no British Constitution: A Dangerous Case of the Emperors Clothes", 41 *Parliamentary Affairs*, 340.

Shaw v DPP [1962] AC 220.

Stoke-on-Trent County Council v B&Q [1991] 2 WLR 42.

Sunkin, Bridges and Mesmoros (1993), "Trends in Judicial Review", *Public Law* 443.

Thompson (1993), *Constitutional and Administrative Law*, London: Blackstone Press.

Van Gend en Lous v Nederlandse Administratie der Belastingen [1963] ECR 1.

Wade, HNR (1988), *Administrative Law* (6th Edition), Oxford: Clarendon Press.

Whitehall v Whitehall (1957) SC 30.

4

ACCOUNTABILITY IN LOCAL GOVERNMENT AND THE NHS

Allan Bruce and Allan McConnell

Introduction

The importance of local government and the National Health Service (NHS) within the context of the modern-day state cannot be overlooked. In total, these institutions spend something in the order of £115 billion per annum, representing some 40% of all public expenditure. Coupled to this, there is also a sense in which local government and the NHS represent an important interface between the state and its citizens, in that they are both responsible for delivering services to the populations that they serve. With the rise of alternative delivery systems, however, emphasis has switched from direct service delivery to an enabling role of ensuring that individuals have access to services. Nevertheless, these important aspects of decentralised government have tended to be analysed quite separately. Specialists in local government and the NHS abound, but with a few notable exceptions substantially less effort has been devoted to comparing and contrasting their mode of operations and the means by which they are held to account.

Students of decentralised government may find that the analysis of accountability has a stronger tradition within the local government literature when compared to the NHS. Local government operates under the auspices of elected representatives who are, notionally at least, accountable to the local population. On the other hand, the NHS is constitutionally accountable to the centre, but must also derive a degree of local autonomy to meet locally-defined needs, wants and demands. The means by which this local autonomy is derived differs. This analysis, therefore, invests some effort in developing a perspective of the NHS which alerts us to the nature of this autonomy and facilitates a comparison with local government.

The environment in which local government and the NHS is now operating has changed in recent years and both have been exposed to a considerable amount of upheaval. The analysis presented here, identifies and discusses the "traditional regimes" of accountability which existed from the post-war period until the economic crisis of the mid 1970s. Subsequently the emphasis of central government's approach to accountability has changed. Indeed, with the election of the Thatcher Government in 1979, it has taken on a more intense ideological flavour.

The main thrust of our analysis is to indicate that while local government and the NHS exhibit important differences, there are also commonalities which have a significant bearing upon the way in which accountability has been redefined. A principal means of achieving this is to draw upon Rhodes' (1994) analysis of the "hollowing out of the state". In this analysis Rhodes addresses four key issues: privatisation; the rise of alternative delivery systems; Europeanisation and; the new public management, all of which imply a weakening of the state. The experience of decentralised government is incorporated into this framework in terms of centralisation, inflexibility, complexity and a reformulation of the concept of accountability. In essence, the analysis points not so much to a weakening of the state but a transfer of power within the hollowed out state, wherein there has been a strengthening of accountability to the centre.

The Concept of Accountability
In many respects, it is easy to become distracted by the general concept of accountability. In the first instance, as already indicated in the Introduction to this book, it appears to have a multitude of component parts. Lawton and Rose (1991: 19–24), for example, point to the existence of political accountability, managerial accountability, legal accountability, consumer accountability and professional accountability. Furthermore, as identified in Chapter One, much of the literature approaches it as something of an enigma. Day and Klein (1987: 1) describe it as a "chameleon word"; Hinton and Wilson (1993: 123) suggest that it is "intriguing", whilst Lawton and Rose (1991: 17) call it a "complex phenomenon", operating in different ways under different circumstances. This is undoubtedly so, but it nevertheless masks the fact that, beneath the surface, it actually has very clear roots. Stewart (1993: 4), therefore, suggests that "those who exercise public power in society should be answerable for the exercise of that power. On that simple proposition rests the concept of accountability".

This clearly delineates the two main sets of actors involved in accountability relationships. On the one hand, there are the people, acting as "stewards" who entrust their powers to those in government and the governmental system. On the other hand, the latter are "accountees", responsible for their actions and use of resources. In terms of the relationship between these, Stewart (1993: 4) does in fact indicate that being "answerable" extends beyond "giving an account for actions taken", and also includes "being held to account" for those actions. Thus, Oliver (1991: 22), drawing on the work of Turpin, suggests that:

> Accountability has been said to entail being liable to be required to give an account or explanation of actions and, where appropriate, to suffer the consequences, take the blame or undertake to put matters right if it should appear that errors have been made. In other words, it is explanatory and amendatory.

As we will see shortly, the way in which this operates in local government and the NHS is substantially different. The very fact that local government is elected is a central feature of public authorities both explaining and being restrained by the populace. In the unelected NHS, there is the absence of such a clear steward / accountee relationship, and instead the focus is on the accountability of the locality to the centre, using its national electoral mandate in an attempt to hold the NHS responsible for the delivery of public services. Despite such differences, however, we will see how in both local government and the NHS an increasingly strident centre has, *inter alia*, used the powers at its disposal in an attempt to reformulate the concept of accountability. In effect, it has attempted to redefine the interests of those who entrust their powers to those in government and the governmental system.

Accountability in Local Government

Local government in the UK is big business. It spends in the region of £80 billion per annum; it employs nearly three million people (Wilson and Game, 1994: 228), and it is under the charge of roughly 25,000 councillors, (Byrne, 1994: 181). In one sense, the position of local government within the British system of government is abundantly clear. Parliament is sovereign and local government is a creature of Parliament, in that it owes its very existence to statute, and its activities must be *intra vires*. Despite this apparent clarity, however, a number of commentators have recognised, as Elcock (1994: 1) suggests, that the "place of local government in the British Constitution is ambiguous and ambivalent".

This is rooted in the absence of a written constitution, and the existence of two sets of elected governments in the country – central and local – each legitimately claiming a democratic mandate. Yet this does not stop us delineating what might be called the "traditional" and main characteristics of local government. Thus, Hampton (1991: 3) identifies local government as being contained within clearly defined territorial boundaries; multi-purpose in its functions; directly elected and possessing independent although limited tax-raising powers. No sooner have we identified these, however, than we find ourselves forced to concede that the defining characteristics of local government are changing. For example, with the growth of joint boards, urban development corporations and other similar bodies, there is the rapid growth of "non-elected local government". Similarly, independent tax-raising powers are now severely restricted with the advent of the centre's capacity (through the legal right to limit revenue spending), to effectively "cap" local taxes.

Throughout these changes, there has been a persistence in one form or another of the idea that local government is accountable to the centre. This is particularly the case as a result of the locality's legal obligations and its strong financial dependence upon the centre. In parallel, however, there has also been a persistent belief in the necessity for local government to be accountable to local people. Given the aforementioned changes in the nature and activities of local government (stemming from an increasingly strident centre), then the mechanisms to facilitate accountability have also undergone change. It is this change which needs to be identified in more detail, by setting-out the "traditional" regime of accountability, and then the way in which it has been supplemented (and indeed partially supplanted) in recent years by a host of new measures.

``TRADITIONAL´´ ACCOUNTABILITY IN LOCAL GOVERNMENT

In broad terms, most aspects of this traditional system operated in the 1950s and 1960s before peaking in 1976, just prior to the period of fiscal retrenchment as a consequence of the conditions imposed by the International Monetary Fund on the then Labour Government. Although not exhaustive, the following list summarises the main components of this "traditional" system which was designed to ensure that local government is held accountable to local people.

Political Representation: Elections can be described as the hallmark of a liberal-democratic system which prides itself on producing government which represents and which is responsive to the people. In local government, elections take place at the level of community/parish councils, but it is the mainstream authorities which lie at the forefront of this political representation. The right of citizens to vote and to choose between competing candidates places at their disposal a potential sanction over incumbent representatives. T. H. Marshall's (1950) classic work *Citizenship and Social Class*, for example, refers to this as political citizenship, complementing entitlements in the civil and social spheres. Councillors, once they are elected, also adopt the role of ombudsmen, available to pursue individual grievances against the council. It must be recognised, of course, that councillors vary in their interpretation of their roles, and Newton's (1976) study of Birmingham, for example, identifies variation in six different dimensions of councillors' roles. Nevertheless, all councillors perform this grievance-chasing role to some extent, and indeed Newton's (1976: 128) case study found 73% of councillors preferring to focus on dealing with constituents' problems as opposed to broad policy.

The Officer as Public Servant: The Maud Committee (1967: 39) clearly reflects the traditional and constitutional wisdom, when it recognised that officers have a role in terms of responsiveness to the public.

> If the officers are responsible for day-to-day administration and the many sensitive decisions involved, they must be alive to the difficult case, the instance which is likely to cause an outcry, the hard case for which no precedent exists, and they must be prompt in bringing any such cases to the members for decision.

Leaving ultimate control with members, therefore, officers deal with cases in accordance with traditional administrative values of trust, neutrality, probity and professional honour (Lawton and Rose, 1991: 10–11).

Public Finances: For most of the post-war period, the principal form of local taxation was the rating system, where domestic property owners were taxed on the basis of the notional annual rental value of their property. Whilst the 1986 Green paper (Cmnd 9714) was the starkest exposition of the fact that the rates burden fell largely on the one-third of the population who paid full rates, previous examinations of the rating system found it difficult to avoid the conclusion that the rates helped promote local accountability. The Layfield Committee (Cmnd 6453, 1976: 154), for example, suggested that "[t]he wide coverage of rating and its perceptibility ensure that the consequences of local decisions are brought home to electors in a way which makes councillors answerable for their actions".

Moving away from taxation matters in the financial sphere, there is the more specific matter of the traditional audit as a vehicle for attempting to ensure the probity, openness and legality of financial accounts and activities. Until the early 1970s, external audit by the district auditor was the only statutory requirement, although in the wake of the Poulson scandal, a series of reforms imposed a duty on authorities to operate an internal audit function. There is some overlap between the external and internal audit functions, however in general they deal with such matters as adherence to the law, detection of fraud and effectiveness of financial control systems (see Hepworth, 1984: 226–227).

Ombudsmen: The Commissioners for Local Administration (as they are formally titled) were created by Acts of Parliament in 1974 and 1975. This followed in the wake of legislation in the late 1960s and early 1970s which established commissioners for central government and the NHS. Their remit is to investigate complaints from members of the public who feel that they have suffered injustice as a result of maladministration. This latter term is not defined in law, although Richard Crossman, Housing and Local Government Minister, provided in 1967 a rough point of reference when he depicted it at as "bias, neglect, inattention, delay, incompetence, ineptitude, perversity, turpitude, arbitrariness and so on" (quoted in Stacey, 1971: 75).

The sum of the foregoing parts, therefore, is a political system where accountability accords closely with constitutional characteristics of public administration. Elcock (1991: 2) encapsulates the spirit of this age when he suggests that:

> public accountability is supposed to be assured by the requirements that all local authority officers and employees report to the elected members of the council. In consequence, public servants are expected to record their activities meticulously. Unconventional or unduly speedy actions tend to be frowned upon. Compliance with appropriate laws and regulations is of paramount importance, together with acceptance of the policies and decisions of elected representatives.

THE ``NEW'' ACCOUNTABILITY IN LOCAL GOVERNMENT

In a recent book, Allan Cochrane (1993) asks the question. "Whatever Happened to Local Government?" He rightly avoids seeing the pre-mid 1970s period as a "golden age" which was devoid of conflict and tensions, but does recognise the impetus for change as rooted in the crisis of Keynesianism and resultant public spending restrictions. This was accelerated in 1979 by the Thatcher Government, which, although partly pragmatic in its approach (particularly in its attack on the "left" in local government), adopted policies which accord substantially with public choice theory (Midwinter and Monaghan, 1993: 31). This attacked the self-interest of politicians and bureaucrats, and offered in its a place a solution based on cost-cutting, promoting competition, expanding consumer choice, and reducing functions. This in turn has had a crucial impact on accountability, because it has led to specific reforms which supplement the traditional structures, and essentially reconstitute the way in which local authorities are intended to be accountable to local people. A detailed analysis of these changes will be undertaken later on. For the moment, however, we can identify four main changes.

Compulsory Competitive Tendering: Competitive tendering in local government has existed for many years, but legislation in 1980, 1988 and 1992 introduced and then extended a compulsory element in services ranging from construction and building maintenance, through to a number of professional, financial and technical services. Local authorities are, or will be, required to bid alongside private contractors for the bulk of work in these areas, although as Wilson and Game (1994: 324) rightly note, "it is the competitive tendering – the cost comparison – that is compulsory, not the contracting out of the service, which may or may not result". The impact of this on accountability is primarily two-fold. On the one hand, it downgrades accountability through elected members because as Mallabar (1991: 159) suggests, there is "less opportunity for councillors to vary either service policy or the levels of service provision during the period a contract is in force". On the other hand, it reconstructs accountability by couching it in terms of the provision of cheap, efficiently produced, high-quality services. This can be expanded upon in considering the next reform category of value for money.

Value For Money: This is an umbrella term which covers a wide range of reforms. Although used in complex and often conflicting ways (McSweeney, 1988: 32), its now generally accepted components are economy (minimum resource inputs), efficiency (maximum outputs for a given set of resource inputs) and effectiveness (the achievement of service goals). The Commission for Local Authority Accounts (now the Accounts

Commission for Scotland) was established in 1975, and the Audit Commission (for England and Wales) was set-up in 1983. Both now have a statutory duty to produce value for money audits and to produce national studies of selected local government activities. Both are also required, as per the Accounts Commission (1993: 4), to ensure the "effectiveness of management arrangements to secure economy, efficiency and effectiveness in the use of resources". Linked to this is the growth of performance indicators. Some authorities initially embraced these as "tangible" evidence of value for money pursuits, although the Government took this a stage further with the Local Government Act 1992 which required that the Audit Commission and the Accounts Commission publish league tables of performance indicators in order to allow inter-authority comparisons to be made. This is also linked to the Citizen's Charter (Cm 1599, 1991) and its main themes of improving quality, promoting competitive choice, providing information on standards, and producing value for money in the provision of public services (see Chapter Six). The common denominator in all these value for money reforms is a reconstituting of accountability. In essence, it assumes at the very crudest level that people want little more than cheap, high quality services, and that if mechanisms to ensure this are in place and work well, then local authorities will be held accountable to local people.

Non-Elected Local Government: This is a burgeoning and complex area. Stoker (1991: 59), identifies six types of organizations in this field, although for present purposes we need focus only on those areas where a number of activities have been removed from local government and transferred to other bodies. In its most extreme form, local authority functions have been completely severed from the council. This, for example, is the case with police, fire and transport functions transferred to joint boards in the wake of the abolition of the GLC (Travers, 1990), and also in the creation of joint boards to take over responsibilities for water, police, fire, valuation services and the Strathclyde Passenger Transport Executive as part of the local government reorganisation process in Scotland. In all such cases, members of joint boards are appointed by the appropriate Secretary of State. In a more diluted form of non-elected local government, the local authority retains a functional role (partly as an "enabler"), but certain components of service provision are passed to other bodies whose members are appointed by the appropriate Secretary of State. This, for example, has occurred particularly in the areas of planning and urban development with the emergence of Urban Development Corporations, Training and Enterprise Councils, Scottish Enterprise and Local Enterprise Companies.

When we add to these the plethora of bodies such as School Boards, Housing Action Trusts, Scottish Homes, boards of governors of grant-maintained schools and further education colleges, then the sheer scale of non-elected local government is formidable. A report produced in May 1994 by Democratic Audit and Charter 88 found about 60,000 "quangocrats" (a "new magistracy" in the words of John Stewart) running local services, and outnumbering elected councillors by about three to one (Stott, 1994: 79). As Gray (1994: 66) observes, this further complicates existing patterns of accountability, although it does correspond closely with the argument that value for money brings accountability. Stott (1994: 80) sums up the ministerial argument when he states that

> Accountability has been strengthened by making services responsive to their customers and this is better than giving citizens a distant and diffuse voice over the make-up of services to be provided.

Whatever the merits of this argument (and we will return to it later), it is obvious that accountability is once again reconstituted.

Centralisation: Andrew Gamble's (1988) depiction of the "free economy and the strong state" is of relevance here, because it is obvious that all of the aforementioned reforms were initiated by a "strong" government intent on restructuring local government in its own image. We can add to these a multitude of acts of centralisation such as tax capping, centralising of business rates, centralised power over fees and charges, the power to impose model standing orders on local authority meetings and the creation of "politically restricted" posts for senior officials. Certainly, the persistent logic behind such reforms has been that the local authorities cannot be trusted to be accountable to local people, and therefore central government has been forced to intervene. Most commentators, however, would not be so sanguine in terms of this reconstituting of accountability. To paraphrase Jones and Stewart (in Midwinter and Mair, 1987: 117), the government believes that local accountability is acceptable, only when it is in accordance with the wishes of the centre.

In total, therefore, the traditional regime of accountability in local government (although still in existence) has been partially supplanted. A fuller analysis of this will be undertaken later in this chapter. In the meantime, it should be recognised that it is not only local government that has faced changes in the system of accountability. The NHS brings with it considerable scope for an analysis of similar themes and issues.

Accountability in the NHS

The NHS became an operational reality on the 5th of July 1948 and was part of a post-war welfare state which aspired to provide a range of services to the British population from the cradle to the grave. For its part, the NHS sought to make comprehensive provision of medical services freely available to the entire population, regardless of income and wealth. Entitlement to these services was to be based upon clinically defined need and paid for mainly out of general taxation.

The NHS currently employs in excess of one million people (Johnson, 1990: 69) and as such, health care expenditure in Britain is dominated by the NHS. Only around 13 percent of expenditure upon health care in Britain today is accounted for by private provision (Holliday, 1992: 38). Financing the NHS accounts for something in the order of 5.2 percent of Gross Domestic Product (GDP), or to put it another way, some 12 percent of public expenditure (Bailey and Bruce, 1994: 489–90). In monetary terms, expenditure on the NHS for financial year 1993–94 was in the region of £35 billion (Cm 2519, 1994: 10). General taxation represents the largest single source of income available to the NHS at around 78 percent. National Insurance Contributions (NICs) account for a further 15.5 percent, user charges 5 percent and miscellaneous sources, including income generation, account for the remaining 1.5 percent (Ensor, 1993: 9).

Other than its capacity to raise a small amount of money from income generation at a local level, the NHS is centrally financed, and in this respect at least it differs from local government. This reliance upon central government finance, in addition to the non-elected nature of the NHS, has had an important bearing upon the concept of NHS accountability. Yet, accountability by the locality to the centre has never been cut and dried. In consequence, there have been a number of contradictions and tensions evident within the system over the years.

The NHS is at face value at least an agency system and Hunter (1984: 41), for example, has identified the NHS as belonging to that species of public institution known as the quango. However, in addition to paying heed to directives and exhortations from the centre, the NHS must also pay attention to meeting locally defined needs and demands for professional autonomy. According to Klein (1982: 387), the NHS has been faced with the prospect of having to square two circles:

First, it is an attempt to reconcile central government responsibility for financing the service with the delegation of responsibility for service delivery to peripheral authorities. Second, it is an attempt to combine the doctrine of public accountability with the doctrine of professional autonomy.

The fortunes of the NHS at a local level have waxed and waned over the years with the centre tightening and subsequently loosening its grip upon the locality. Since the early 1980s, however, there has been a more pronounced move on the part of the centre to assert its control over the locality (Hunter, 1983). This position is echoed in Gamble's (1988) view of the strengthening of the state and is very ably supported by Klein (1989: 198).

> If the scope of government was reduced in some respects, as by privatisation, its tread became heavier. In a sense, the Conservative Government can be seen as the equivalent of the Tudor Monarchy asserting the power of the state in order to modernise a country previously dominated by feudal barons and corporate interests like the Church.

A corollary of this, therefore, is that changes are detectable in terms of the guiding principles that have more recently underpinned the concept of accountability within the NHS. What might be termed "traditional strategies" have been challenged through a process of re-evaluation and of the development of new ideas. Many of these ideas, it will be shown, have been driven by a potent combination of ideology and financial pressures.

THE ``TRADITIONAL APPROACH´´: CONTRADICTIONS AND TENSIONS

Centralist influences relating to accountability within the health sector were evident from the inception of the NHS with a "hierarchy of accountability running from the coal-face of health service delivery to parliament" (Day and Klein, 1987: 76). The reality, however, was that this concept of direct accountability to the centre was flawed, or at least undermined to some degree, in that the nature of central-local relations contained a conundrum. The relationship between the centre and the locality was articulated by Richard Crossman on the basis of his experience as Secretary of State at the DHSS thus:

> You don't have in the Regional Hospital Boards a number of obedient

civil servants carrying out central orders . . . You have a number of powerful, semi-autonomous Boards whose relation to me was much more like the relations of a Persian satrap to a weak Persian Emperor. If the Emperor tried to enforce his authority too far he lost his throne or at least lost his resources or something broke down.
(cited in Klein, 1989: 79).

The nature of this conundrum was brought into sharp relief following a major reorganization of the NHS in 1974. The 1974 reorganization had enshrined the belief that a sound management structure ought to be created at all levels in order to ensure that maximum delegation downwards was matched by accountability upwards (Watkin, 1978: 145). Over the years, however, a substantial body of literature has recognised the difficulties associated with achieving the compliance of lower level participants. Elmore (1979: 602), for example, has argued that "the notion that policy makers exercise – or ought to exercise – some kind of determinant control over policy implementation might be called the 'noble lie' of conventional public administration". Thus the position adopted by Hunter (1984: 42) regarding the NHS in the post-1974 period closely resembles that articulated earlier by Crossman when he suggests that:

in practice, health authorities exercise more discretion over resource allocation and priority-setting than is often acknowledged. Contrary to received wisdom, policy rarely emanates from the centre in order to be faithfully implemented, without distortion, by agents in the field.

In some senses, explanations for the difficulties that the centre experienced in calling the locality to account for its actions can be derived from notions of organizational complexity and a reluctance to become embroiled in matters of detail. In addition, however, it must be remembered that the NHS at a local level exhibits evidence of considerable diversity in terms of geography, social circumstances and medical need. Therefore, some legitimacy on the part of key participants at a local level has been derived from the necessity to match available resources to locally defined needs. In this respect, accountability to the centre was framed largely in broad brush financial terms, so that the locality was effectively responsible for working within resources that were made available each year.

In the same way as local government, the NHS has also been exposed to mechanisms which are intended to promote financial probity and administrative integrity. In the contemporary sphere, external audit is now conducted by the Audit Commission in England and Wales and the Accounts Commission in Scotland. This was previously the responsibility of the National Audit Office until the Audit Commission assumed this responsibility in England and Wales in October 1990. Changes in Scotland were somewhat later with the Accounts Commission assuming responsibility as of December 1994. With reference to administrative integrity, an NHS Ombudsman (formally the Health Service Commissioner) was established in 1973. Its remit was and is to investigate cases of maladministration, although this remit falls short of investigating matters of clinical judgement.

This concept of local autonomy, nevertheless, has rested rather uncomfortably upon the contradictory role of appointed members who, unlike their counterparts in local government, do not enjoy the legitimacy of being elected by the local population (Regan and Stewart, 1982). Members of health authorities were and remain appointees, appointed by the minister to whom they are ultimately accountable while at the same time expected to make resource allocation decisions at a local level which are essentially political in character. It is hardly surprising, therefore, that many appointed members found themselves between a rock and a hard place. On the one hand, they were formally accountable to the minister for the implementation of policies which were characteristically vague and imprecise. On the other hand, they experienced difficulties in asserting a degree of legitimate authority over the allocation of resources at a local level. In some senses, therefore, the accountability conundrum of the traditional approach can be distilled into two sets of relationships: central-local and intra-local.

Looking first at the central-local axis, the centre had traditionally taken an arm's length approach to its dealings with the locality. Over the years, however, some efforts had been made on the part of the centre to develop general guidelines. The purpose of these guidelines was to instil within the locality a sense of direction while simultaneously permitting some measure of local autonomy. The Hospital Plan of 1962 (Cmnd 1604, 1962) was the first of these initiatives and was, amongst other things, aimed at a gradual redirection of resources from the acute hospital sector into what are described as the "Cinderella services".

The Hospital Plan of 1962 was followed in the 1970s and the early 1980s with a clutch of initiatives produced by the centre with a view to encouraging the locality to prioritise its activities within the more hostile financial environment which then prevailed. In England and Wales these initiatives took the form of *The Way Forward* (DHSS, 1977) and *Care in Action* (DHSS, 1981). In Scotland the necessity to provide expression to centrally prescribed priorities was contained within *The Way Ahead* (SHHD, 1976) and *Scottish Health Authorities Priorities for the Eighties (SHAPE)* (SHHD, 1980). While differences of detail existed between each of these documents and their contextual settings in the health service both north and south of the border, two common elements were evident. First, there was a continuing recognition of the need to secure some expansion of the relatively underfinanced "Cinderella services". Second, in the light of a reduction in growth money available to the NHS in the 1970s, any expansion of the "Cinderella services" may have to be financed, in part at least, from savings achieved in the acute hospital sector.

Central priorities, however, had at best only a marginal influence upon the behaviour of the locality and Klein (1989: 128) has clearly indicated that "in practice the language of norms and objectives turned out merely to be a vocabulary of exhortation". This nationwide picture is supported by research carried out in Scotland into the implementation of the *SHAPE* initiative. Bruce (1990) has indicated that serious weaknesses existed in terms of the centre holding the locality to account for its performance. To all intents and purposes, the existence of centrally-inspired guidelines did little to influence the nature of policy making at a local level. In short, the centre's flirtation with strategic planning had experienced a number of fairly rudimentary problems.

Objectives contained in *SHAPE* were of a general nature and did little to hold the locality to account for performance, or alternatively, non-performance. There was also the notable absence of attempts by the centre to review the progress that had been made at a local level in terms of albeit vague and imprecise guidelines. This, coupled with a general absence of good quality information, casts doubts upon the ability and/or willingness of the centre to hold the locality to account. Indeed, this rather nebulous relationship between the centre and the locality had the effect of blurring the machinery of accountability to the advantage of the centre. In this way the centre maintained its arm's length relationship with the locality and, in the process, had been able to side-step the necessity to take the flack for much of what went on at a local level.

The net effect of all this was that the "Cinderella services" which the centre had been exhorting the locality to prioritise remained relatively under resourced, asphyxiated it seems by the momentum of the more powerful acute hospital sector. Recalcitrance on the part of the centre, however, extended beyond the framework of its priorities documents to reveal a nebulous relationship between the centre and the locality concerning *specific* policy issues. Bruce (1990) has identified a situation in which the centre had issued a specific instruction that a defined range of cardiac surgery should only be carried out in three nationally funded centres in Scotland. Nevertheless, this type of cardiac surgery was being carried out quite openly elsewhere against the expressed wishes of the centre.

Turning then to the situation that pertained within the locality. In addition to a lack of legitimacy derived from not being democratically elected, appointed members were also expected to square this with the expectation that they should exert some degree of control over the formulation, implementation and evaluation of policy. Therefore, members need to do more than feel that they are accountable:

> . . . to be fully accountable implies the ability to exercise control. If service providers are not accountable to authority members, that is if the links in the chain are broken, then how can authority members be accountable, be it to voters or a secretary of state?
> (Day and Klein, 1987: 227).

The prospect of members asserting themselves fully over the policy-making process had always been fairly remote. The nature of decision making was all too often concerned with "putting out fires" (Hunter, 1980a) rather than adopting a more strategic or visionary role. There was also a tendency for members to become something of a rubber stamp for decisions which had been taken elsewhere (Hunter, 1980b: 167). Decisions tended to be precipitated largely on the basis of demands which emanated from the medical profession and legitimised on the basis of professional autonomy and expertise.

This is not unusual in that ministers are often highly dependent upon a permanent staff of senior civil servants. Similarly, in local government part-time councillors have experienced difficulties in controlling the behaviour of experts. In the NHS, however, the relative weakness of appointed members was exacerbated by the strength of the medical profession. Held in high esteem by members of the public (Harrison, 1988: 88), the medical profession had been able to draw considerable support from the health care population on the basis of its life-saving activities. In addition, the medical profession have traditionally domi-nated the bureaucratic machinery of the NHS, which tended to encourage a situation whereby issues were defined as belonging to the medical domain. Members of the medical profession, therefore, were content with an approach to policy making which depended heavily upon the application of their medical expertise.

In its traditional mode, therefore, accountability was dominated largely by financial probity and the necessity for the locality to work within the context of global budgets which were allocated by the centre. Thus, the locality would be in a position to avoid closer scrutiny by the centre, so long as it did not overspend. With reference to matters of policy, the centre lacked both the willingness and the ability to challenge the locality. As far as the centre was concerned, this allowed ministers to insulate themselves from local difficulties. Crucially, the traditional approach was founded largely on the expectation that growth money would continue to be made available. Retrenchment in the 1970s then brought with it a variety of pressures which had the effect of initiating some movement towards strengthening the hand of the centre.

THE STRENGTHENING OF THE CENTRE

The 1980s and 1990s was a somewhat turbulent period for the NHS during which much more strident efforts were made to bring the locality to account for its performance. Key themes which emerged during the 1980s included increased central control, a new management style, and the prospect of influencing the behaviour of the medical profession. Binding these issues together was the need to pay due regard to the virtues of economy, efficiency and effectiveness.

This is not to say that the incoming Conservative Government had from the outset elected to expose the NHS to its own brand of ideological fervour. Early pronouncements were indicative of an approach which continued to recognise the importance of local autonomy and professional freedom (DHSS, 1979). No doubt the widespread popularity of the NHS had blunted the zeal of "would-be reformers", so that swift and relatively radical reforms were less evident in the health sector than in other areas of social welfare, such as housing and social security.

This "hands off" approach, nevertheless, was incompatible with the economic circumstances that Britain had experienced from the mid-1970s onwards. Attempts had already been made to contain expenditure on the part of local government (Glennerster, 1992). With reference to the NHS, Harrison (1988: 108) has demonstrated how the DHSS had come under increasing pressure in the early 1980s from the Social Services Select Committee and the Public Accounts Committee to assert a greater degree of central control over what went on at a local level. Unlike local government, with its own tax-raising powers, the key issue for the DHSS was not so much about containing local expenditure. Global budgets were already contained in that they were allocated by the centre to the locality. Crucially, however, the centre had no real means of ensuring that resources were being deployed in an efficient manner. Nor did it have any real means of calling the locality to account for its performance.

As the 1980s progressed, the NHS began to exhibit increasingly stronger centralist tendencies which had also taken on an ideological flavour. Armed with a battery of new initiatives, central control had become much tighter. In spite of this, however, the organizational conundrum of centralization versus localism was still in evidence. A key theme of the 1980s which found expression in the Griffiths Report (Department of Health and Social Security, 1983), was to encourage a situation in which decisions were taken at the lowest effective point. Yet the main thrust of many of these initiatives, as Paton has indicated, was "centralism masquerading as its opposite, devolution" (Paton, 1993: 105).

The sentiments expressed here regarding centralization are important but some clarification is needed in terms of the question of "devolution" and of the constitutional position of the NHS. Quite importantly, Brown has argued that accountability within the NHS is the obverse of delegation. He continues by stating that:

It is not, however, a concomitant of devolution, which means shedding both responsibility and accountability to some other body; it is unfortunate that the word "devolution" has been used in the context of examining the delegation of functions within the NHS.
(Brown, 1977: B9).

The need for brevity does not permit a "nuts and bolts" analysis of the flock of initiatives which have emanated from the centre during the 1980s and 1990s. This is dealt with quite admirably elsewhere – see for example, Baggott (1994), Harrison (1988), Harrison *et al* (1990), Harrison *et al* (1992), Klein (1989), Ranade (1994). Suffice to say that the drift towards a centralist philosophy has been facilitated by the introduction of general management, resource management, performance indicators, league tables and a general strengthening of the centre's capacity to exercise its influence through the Policy Board and NHS Executive.

More recent developments point to a strengthening of the role of the NHS Executive with the abolition of the regional tier. Under these new arrangements, the eight new regions will effectively be an extension of the centre, with each of the regional directors accountable to the NHS Executive (Millar, 1993). Scotland does not have a regional tier so that any moves towards a more direct relationship between the centre and locality would not require elaborate structural upheaval.

In addition, there is also a sense in which, far from creating local responsibility and a greater responsiveness to the health care needs of the local population, the market-based approach outlined in *Working for Patients* (Cm 555, 1989) has been accompanied by increased central interference and managerial control. Harrison *et al* (1992) have identified some merit in conceptualising the reformed NHS, characterised by the purchaser/provider split in terms of "post-Fordism". In this respect the centre is able to avoid detailed managerial control and the development of an all-embracing plan. They go on to argue that:

> The centre would be concerned with maintaining and, where necessary, revising the "rules of the game". The aim would be to keep both purchasers and producers on their toes, to keep the playing field level and visible to all the potential players. There might also be a need to set, or to ensure that someone else set, some quality and access standards. (Harrison *et al*, 1992: 121).

The other side to this is whether the centre is content to maintain a "hands off" approach in the face of mounting public and political concern about the fortunes of the NHS. After all, the White Paper *Working for Patients* was itself a reaction to crises and mounting public concern over the NHS (Butler, 1992). It is unlikely, therefore, that the centre is willing to entrust an initiative of this magnitude to the locality without some degree of central control. Thus, the rhetoric of delegation and decentralization cloaks the prominence of the centre in the scheme of things.

The means by which the centre has elected to strengthen its grip over the organization and delivery of the major welfare services is indicative of important differences that exist between local government and the NHS. Thus, while local government and the NHS have both been exposed to an imperative for competitive tendering, organizational change within the NHS runs deeper than in local government. The main thrust of the White Paper *Working for Patients* and subsequent legislation in the form of the National Health Service and Community Care Act (1990) was the creation of a planned market, characterised by a purchaser/provider split. The NHS is now typified by a constellation of providers (hospitals) vying with one another to secure contracts for the delivery of services from purchasers. These purchasers take the form of District Health Authorities (DHAs), their Scottish equivalents, Area Health Boards (AHBs), and General Practitioner Fund Holders (GPFHs).

The essence of the purchaser/provider split is that DHAs and AHBs are divested of the necessity to provide services to the local population directly. Their role is now principally concerned with assessing the health care needs of the local population and ensuring that local people have access to appropriate services. Access to these services is organized by way of block contracts, cost and volume contracts, and extra contractual referrals. GPFHs are able to purchase a limited range of relatively minor services on behalf of their patients, although financial responsibility for more expensive services still rests with DHAs and AHBs (Bruce 1994).

So far, therefore, the conundrum of central control versus local autonomy has yet to be resolved. Of course, this is not to say that there is a neat and tidy solution to the issue. After all, much will depend upon the vagaries of the political process as it is played out on the national stage. Hunter, however, is scathing of the type of politics that has been practised with regard to the NHS in recent years. He accepts, it seems, that questions such as accountability and the relationship between the centre and locality will, as ever, provide a "perplexing paradox". Nevertheless, he argues that the NHS has been "subjected to a daily diet of tactical politics without any reference to strategy or purpose" (Hunter, 1994). The time may now be ripe for injecting a stronger measure of accountability into a system that has sacrificed policy at the altar of manipulation, strategy and tactics.

Governing the Locality: Trends in Local Government and the NHS
During the time in which ideas for the present analysis were being formulated, the authors were musing over the differences that existed between local government and the NHS. It was like comparing apples and oranges; the two it seemed were different species entirely. Yet in spite of their obvious differences, apples and oranges share some common characteristics. If nothing else, both are spherical and can be eaten! As a point of comparison, Rhodes (1987: 67), for example, makes use of the idea of citizenship to delineate the public service orientation. This orientation he argues, has a noble element and is not "equated with any

one activity (voting) [and] is not restricted to any one institution (local government)". In consequence, many of the differences between local government and the NHS may be more apparent than real and this has important implications for the analysis of accountability. These common trends must now be identified.

On the surface, as indicated, one of the more obvious differences between local government and the NHS is to be found in the comparison that has been drawn between the election versus appointment of councillors and members. Nonetheless, there is a sense in which these key participants, whether elected or appointed, are operating increasingly within a deterministic policy frame, where decisions represent a compromise between what is desirable and what seems feasible. Room for manoeuvre will vary and is influenced, amongst other things, by the legal framework, circumstances prevailing within the locality, the passage of time, availability of resources, issue salience and the disposition of key participants. These key participants include the centre, senior officers or managers and professional opinion. Notions of accountability, therefore, will tend to be woven into a fabric of pragmatism, compromise, and the perceptions that individuals (whether elected or appointed) have of accountability. These points are worthy of expansion.

The evidence unearthed by Day and Klein (1987: 228) is illuminating in this regard. They make use of the need to recognize accountability both in terms of legitimacy and control, with the latter proving problematic for both elected representatives and appointed members. Put plainly, the very fact that councillors enjoy the legitimacy associated with being democratically elected does not eliminate the difficulties associated with a lack of control. As Wilson and Game (1994: 269–277) suggest, power relationships within local authorities should be seen as a series of shifting alliances, and will vary depending on the roles of the ruling party, backbench councillors, inter-departmental battles, intra-departmental divisions, and whether the council is "hung" or "balanced".

This general absence of determinant control over those who are charged with the task of providing services, has the effect of casting councillors and appointed members increasingly in the role of "decision takers" rather than "decision makers". The latter refers to individuals who are able to exercise a considerable amount of influence over the decision-making process while the former will tend to give their approval to decisions that have been precipitated elsewhere. Such a distinction may be criticised for being simplistic in that due regard has to be paid to the specific circumstances in which elected or appointed representatives might wish to exercise their resolve. It nevertheless highlights, among other things, the dependency relationship that exists between part-time representatives and full-time officials. Moreover, full-time officials may be part of, or at the very least exposed to, a fairly potent professional culture in which professional judgement and technical expertise are influential factors. There are no shortage of examples to be drawn from the NHS as regards the potency of professional power and the ability of doctors to impose their priorities upon the NHS. Similarly, while local government may not be dominated to the same extent by a single professional group, officials have the potential for substantial influence, even taking into account the increased presence and intensity of political parties since the mid-1970s (Gyford *et al*, 1989). As Elcock *et al* (1988: 92) suggest, for example, local budgetary processes are still influenced significantly by professionals who man the various service departments and are able at times to use their professional knowledge and expertise in order to resist demands for spending reductions.

The situation is further complicated because accountability is a concept which is often perceived differently by the various individuals involved. Appointed members, though not usually chairmen, do not feel as though they are directly accountable to the minister. Similarly, councillors do not usually see themselves simply as being directly accountable to voters or, in many instances, their party. Instead, perceptions of accountability tend to be permeated with their own interpretations of civic duty and common good (Day and Klein, 1987: 229). Inter-party differences then compound the matter even further. As evidence to the Widdicombe Committee shows, Labour and Conservative councillors were less enthusiastic about consultation with ordinary citizens when their party was in control (see Barron *et al*, 1991: 162–165).

There may of course be good reason why a more detached approach to accountability is justifiable. Not all decisions are likely to be popular, either with the electorate or for that matter, the appropriate minister. There is a danger in interpreting accountability as the slavish pursuit of demands that are articulated by those to whom elected or appointed representatives are held to account, leastwise without good reason for doing so. Competing and conflicting needs, wants and demands are difficult, if not impossible, to satisfy within the context of limited financial resources. Therefore, unpopular decisions about who gets what, how much and when, may need to be made on behalf of the local community with an eye for the common good. This should not of course obscure the necessity for decision makers to account publicly for their actions. As Oliver (1991: 22–23) suggests:

> Decision makers must be obliged to justify their acts and not be allowed to rely on claims that their rightness is to be assumed. Alternative policies must be permitted to be advanced to highlight the fact that claims that "there is no alternative" may be flawed. There must be provision for matters to be put right when things have gone wrong.

A further trend in both local government and the NHS has been a pronounced move away from a locally-based focus to developments on the national stage. Cochrane (1993) sees local government as part of the welfare state, and this allows us to view this centralist shift in terms of the "crisis" of the Keynesian welfare state and the Conservative Party's reaction to this. The political salience of these major welfare services has increased in recent years with successive governments under the leadership of Margaret Thatcher and John Major, initiating and orchestrating a process of change. The rationale for change has been a heady mixture of ideology and pragmatism. The outcome of change, however, has been to encourage a situation in which community issues have been obscured. The delivery of these services is now taking place against a backcloth of nationally-expressed concern about creeping privatisation, lower standards and a reduction in services for the most vulnerable groups in society. Indicative of this concern was the breadth and depth of dissent within society which Butler (1992) identifies as having accompanied the publication of the White Paper *Working for Patients*.

It must be understood, of course, that these centralist tendencies are seldom universal in nature. Instead, the centre has exhibited a tendency to be selective. The drift towards centralism has been most pronounced in the major welfare services such as education, housing and health care. It is here that the locality derives some strength from political vision and professional values. These imbue the locality with ideas and practices which have the potential to drive "political" and "economic" wedges into the heart of the government's broader strategies. As Duncan and Goodwin (1988: 72–73), suggest:

> State systems need to be developed at a local, subnational level if dominant groups are to confront fully the problems of uneven development of society and of nature. If this subnational response is to make any sense, then this local level must have some sort of autonomy in

implementing policy or even in formulating it ... [but] this local autonomy will, by the same token, become a hostage to fortune.

Local Government and the NHS: Assessing the New Regimes of Accountability
One way of conceptualising the foregoing commonalities (and attendant differences) is in terms of the "hollowing out of the state" (Rhodes, 1994). The concept of "hollowing out" is not unproblematic, since the language tends to imply a weakening of the role of the state, when in many respects (as we have seen) the opposite is the case. Nevertheless, it does provide a useful framework which we can build upon in order to assess the changing nature of accountability in local government and the NHS.

As Rhodes (1994: 151) suggests, to "talk of the hollowing out of the state is to signal there are potentially dramatic changes underway in British government". These are the combined impact of four interconnected trends. First, there has been a redefinition of public intervention. Certainly, this pertains particularly to matters of "privatisation", but there is also the more general matter of a changing philosophy at the centre. Rhodes cites a number of quotations from Mrs Thatcher's memoirs, amply illustrating her distaste for centralization, bureaucracy and interventionism. In many respects, these undoubtedly fit with the language deployed by the centre to buttress changes in local government and the NHS. In local government, the buzz words have been "enabling" (where government has an oversight role, thus allowing other agencies and contractors to get on with the business of effective service provision) and "value for money" (where public intervention is redefined as justifiable only on the basis of cheap, efficiently produced and effective services). In the NHS, the talk has been similar, with the centre expounding, leastwise at face value, the philosophies of "delegation", "decentralization" and "value for money".

Second, a further aspect of the hollowed-out state which reinforces the above is the rise of alternative delivery systems. In local government, the previous local authority monopoly of service provision has been broken by the introduction of the quasi-market of CCT, and the expansion of non-elected local government in education, housing, planning and a host of other services. In the NHS, the alternative delivery systems are more extensively market-based, through the introduction of a purchaser/provider split into healthcare provision, and through fragmenting the NHS via the promotion of largely free-standing Self Governing Trusts (SGTs).

Third, and another aspect of hollowing out although the least important area to present concerns, is a loss of functions to the European Union (EU). Neither local government nor the NHS has had functions wrenched from it and appropriated at the EU level. Indeed, opponents of the present government and its philosophies often look for "protection" to the European level – ranging from local government lobbying of the Committee of the Regions, through to public sector unions in local government and the NHS attempting to utilize the EC's 1977 "Acquired Rights Directive" to combat changes in employment rights under CCT.

Fourth and finally, a key feature of the hollowed-out state is that there is a limiting of the discretion of public servants through the rise of the new public management. As we have seen, the impact of this on both local government and the NHS has been pervasive. In local government, officers are constrained not only because of the creation of politically restricted posts, but also because the watchwords of value for money have been accompanied by a variety of "policing" factors, such as the Audit and Accounts Commission, VFM audits, performance indicators and the Citizen's Charter. In the NHS, there has been a similar drift, with the introduction of general management, resource management, the Audit Commission, performance indicators, medical audit and the Patient's Charter (Department of Health, 1991). More generally, however, officials are constrained because they have to work within the confines of a quasi-competitive environment, the purchaser/provider split, and the contracts which flow from this.

If all of this amounts to a "hollowing out" of local government and the NHS, therefore, then we must ask ourselves how accountability fares under this new regime. Although not exhaustive, we can approach this in a number of different ways, remembering throughout that both local government and the NHS are the providers of *public* services, and that accountability rests on comprehending the link between the public and those entrusted to provide services on their behalf.

CENTRALISATION

In the first instance, hollowing out has been accompanied by a transfer of power *within* the hollowed-out state. More specifically in terms of both ideas and concrete practices, there has been a centralization of power and a consequent diminishing in power of the locality in both local government and the NHS.

In local government, this has happened in a number of ways. Most straightforward is the reduction in local autonomy through the centralization of decisions such as business rating, the upper limit for local revenue spending, capital spending limits and the school curriculum. In simple terms, this limits the freedom of local authorities to be held to account by local people. But decisions need not be directly in the hands of the centre to warrant the label of "centralization". As we have seen, local government is further restricted by performance indicators, charters, competition with contractors and a plethora of other factors. As a consequence, the centre has in effect been able to "ring fence" the locality's freedom of movement in being held accountable to local people. Yet it does not stop at this. There has also been the growth of non-elected local provision, under the charge of central appointees and within guidelines set by the centre. The impact of this, in clear and precise terms, is that there is less local government that is directly accountable to local people via the traditional notions of representational and bureaucratic channels. But what of accountability in this unelected sphere? In many senses, it is becoming more and more like the NHS. As Stewart (1993: 7) suggests:

> There is no sense in which those appointed can be regarded as locally accountable. Indeed the membership of these bodies is largely unknown locally. Nor are they necessarily subject to the same requirements for open meetings, access to information and external scrutiny that local authorities are subject to. Accountability such as it is rests upon the accountability of these bodies to central government.

This centralization is reinforced further when we consider the personal background of appointees. Many accusations have been anecdotal, and the evidence is by no means overhwhelming, but it is difficult to deny some form of link between support for the Conservative Party and quango appointments. For example, research for the BBC's *Here and Now* programme revealed that directors of companies donating to the Conservative Party were three times as likely to be appointed to a quango than those who did not make any such donations (BBC1, 1994). In total, therefore, all this supports the view identified earlier, whereby in local government the centre accepts the idea of local accountability, provided that this operates essentially within the context of central *fiat*.

A similar process has been occurring in the NHS. Local managers have increasingly found themselves with agendas that are cramped and largely dictated by the centre (Harrison *et al*, 1992). Added to this, the medical profession has come under considerable pressure to relinquish its tradition of independence and become incorporated into the managerial structure (Harrison and Pollitt, 1994). There has also been some containment and politicization of the role of appointed members.

With specific reference to appointed members, important changes have accompanied the creation of the purchaser/provider split. The logic for these changes was expressed in *Working for Patients* (Cm 555, 1989: 64–65) in terms of the need to:

- reduce the representative role of appointed members in favour of developing a stronger managerial orientation.
- develop a leaner and more effective focus for decision making.

Since these changes, however, there has been a considerable amount of criticism regarding the operation of the appointed member system, the means by which individuals are appointed, and the political sympathies that these individuals possess. The use of appointments of this nature as a means of extending political patronage or rewarding individuals for loyalty is hardly innovative. There are, however, worries about the extent to which political patronage is being used as a means of securing a greater degree of central control. A recent editorial in the *Health Service Journal* put the issue plainly. It argued that:

> There is a figure fast gaining credibility in NHS folklore. It is that of the over mighty chair who resembles a baron of old, acting in an arbitrary, inconsistent and occasionally reckless manner. Invariably this person is guided predominantly by their political allegiances, and they are too full of their own experience in commerce and industry to sit back and let their chief executives manage. Such figures may still be caricatures from mythology with no counterparts in reality. Concerns may still be exaggerated. But they are sufficiently widespread among long serving career NHS managers to warrant serious attention.
> (Anon, 1993: 15).

As more and more evidence is published pointing to the rise to power of "Westminster placemen" (Cohen *et al*, 1993) and of individuals appointed to boards who live outside the district they serve (Brindle, 1994), serious questions are being asked about the accountability of these individuals. Moreover, managerial and commercial experience is one thing but the public sector orientation requires more than an ability to understand the contractual process. For example, assessing the health-care needs of a local community has never been straightforward and there is little evidence to suggest that the proliferation of business management techniques has made this task any easier.

What impact does all this have on accountability in the NHS? Certainly, the accountability link between local people and local health provision has always been ambiguous. In essence, successive national governments have been given mandates to continue with NHS provision, and the matter of popular restraint only really came into play alongside the multiplicity of concerns that electors had to come to terms with when voting in a general election. In the new hollowed-out regime of the 1980s and beyond, however, the conundrum of central-local relations still exists, but it has been transformed by a clear drift towards central government's prescription of competition, and imposition of value for money constraints. Once again, therefore, accountability is framed in terms of equating with the predilections of the centre.

INFLEXIBILITY

Following on from the above, service provision in both local government and NHS is becoming more inflexible because of the growth of contracts, the necessity to justify value for money and other such factors. Whether it is local government or the NHS, this culture introduces rigidities which can undermine responsiveness to changing local demands, needs and circumstances. The fact that the NHS is not elected has always diluted this to a degree, but for those desirous of local government being held accountable and restrained by local people, then it is a powerful blow. As Leach *et al* (1994: 164–165) note, the removal of services to arm's length DSOs and private contractors

> has made it much more difficult for councillors whose preferred specialism is the constituency role to operate in the way to which they are accustomed. It is now much more difficult for a councillor to affect directly the detailed operation of many services.

There are similarities here with the situation in which GPs now find themselves. GPs are gatekeepers to the NHS, with the result that their referral decisions have a crucial bearing upon an individual's access to specialist services. Prior to the purchaser/provider split, GPs were able to exercise professional judgement in respect of their referral decisions. GPFHs by virtue of the funds at their disposal are free to enter into contractual agreements with their chosen providers, but only for relatively minor procedures – usually elective surgery and diagnostic tests. Financial responsibility for more expensive procedures rests with the appropriate DHA or AHB. Therefore, GPs who do not have fundholding status must depend entirely upon the contractual agreements that are negotiated by DHAs or AHBs and their chosen providers. GPs may of course exert pressure upon DHAs and AHBs in an effort to influence their purchasing decisions, but ultimately their referral patterns are constrained by contractual agreements. In short, other than the autonomy that GPFHs enjoy to freely negotiate contractual agreements for minor procedures, the patient must follow the money. This is at odds with the consumerist-style rhetoric that accompanied *Working for Patients*, which boasted of responsiveness to individual needs and of money following the patient.

COMPLEXITY

A further feature in the transformation of local government and NHS accountability in the hollowed-out state, is that it is becoming more complex and less transparent. This is not, however, to hark back to some mythical golden age of comprehensibility and transparency. In local government, the Layfield Committee (Cmnd 6453, 1976: 35) rightly perceived the absence of a coherent system which made clear where the real responsibility lay, whilst in the NHS there has consistently been a mismatch between the supposed "hierarchy of accountability" and the realities of a conundrum in central-local relations. The point to be made here is that the process of hollowing-out has exacerbated all this. In local government, the hiving-off of functions to private contractors and unelected bodies not only confuses responsibility, but it also creates what Stewart (1993: 7) describes as a "vacuum" because there is no single agency with overall responsibility.

In the NHS, a similar effect has been achieved through persistent restructuring and the growth of SGTs, with some dilution of strategic vision at a local level. There is a sense in which SGTs provide a buffer between the local population and the main purchaser of healthcare in the form of DHAs and AHBs. SGTs, therefore, will tend to take the flak for unpopular decisions, if people identify with their local hospitals rather than purchasers. In this regard, one objective of *Working for Patients* was to bring hospitals closer to the population they serve and encourage a sense of local ownership. If SGTs are successful here, then they must inevitably put some distance between the local population and the DHA or AHB, which is responsible for making the crucial purchasing decisions.

REFORMULATION

The concept of accountability has itself been reformulated. Under the traditional systems, notions of "democratic" restraint of public authorities were most evident in elected local government, although democracy of a different form did exist in the NHS, with local clinical and managerial discretion operating within the centre's broad brush financial frame. In the hollowed-out state, however, accountability has been redefined. Gray (1994: 65) suggests that the

> underlying theme of this revolutionary process . . . [is] a shift in emphasis from *democratic* accountability to *economic* accountability: a concern with the public as economic actors rather than as "citizens".

The logic of this is that provision of public services in local government and the NHS can only be accountable to the populace if they are provided in accordance with the centre's dictats of broad value for money provisions. Paradoxically, therefore, "local" responses which cater for changing local demands, needs and circumstances (rooted in elections or otherwise) are considered as having the potential to drive a wedge into the heart of the relationship between the people and the providers of public services.

A BALANCE SHEET

It is important to recognise that this restructuring of accountability should not be viewed from a one-dimensional perspective. There are two points to be made in this regard. In the first instance, if the hollowed-out state in local government and the NHS increases efficiency and so leads to less pressure on taxation, maintains service levels, provides the public with more information through Charters and performance indicators and puts more pressure on public authorities to meet public expectations, then we must be prepared to concede that there are some positive benefits accruing from this new regime. If, even to some degree, people want cheap, high quality services, then the new system of accountability (coupled with the noble efforts of public employees) will act on their behalf in an attempt to ensure that they obtain this.

One must, of course, recognise that the efforts of public employees and professionals are now being put under a considerable amount of strain. In local government, for example, officers are having to cope with "permanent revolution" in the form of such matters as three different local tax systems within three years, the introduction of performance indicators, the accruing of community care responsibilities, structural reorganization, and the extension of compulsory competitive tendering.

In the NHS, witness, for example, recent efforts to bring doctors into management. This strategy no doubt stems from a desire by central government to control the activities of professionals, who have hitherto been characteristically independent of managerial structures but at the same time are engaging in activities which have huge resource consequences. This position rests uncomfortably with the new public management and a desire for efficiency, effectiveness and economy in the use of scarce resources. This is not to say that doctors ought to have a free hand in the allocation of resources. Nevertheless, the managerialization of doctors on the scale currently being promoted may be inappropriate, not least because they lack the necessary managerial skills. More importantly, serious questions must be asked about whether doctors have the capacity to maintain clinical credibility at the same time as they are expected to deal with increasing managerial pressures. For example, in their study of eight acute hospital providers, Bruce and Hill (1994) identify a situation in which managers are burdening experienced consultants with managerial responsibilities in addition to their already substantial clinical responsibilities.

The second point can be derived from Elcock's (1994: 189) observation that an "accountability relationship is also a power relationship but contrary to common belief, it is not necessarily a simple superior – subordinate one". Despite the centre's restructuring of accountability in accordance with its own values, the locality is not dead. We need look no further than Rhodes' (1988) delineation of the authoritative, financial, political, informational and organizational resources at the disposal of the centre and the various sub-central governments of Britain. The centre undoubtedly dominates in this relationship, but this domination is not absolute. In the NHS, for example, Maxwell, himself an appointed non-executive member of a SGT, has this to say about his generic role. It includes:

helping the institution to take an honest view of itself, warts and all; advising and counselling the chair and executives; deciding any matters on which the executives cannot be impartial; and satisfying themselves that the institution and its officers are behaving competently and with integrity.

Indeed, he goes on to suggest that: "When (if ever) waters are tranquil, the board can afford to sleep. Even then it should do so with at least one eye open". (Maxwell, 1993: 22).

The role that is being alluded to here is of "oversight" rather than "hands on" interference, where the integrity, probity and smooth running of the organization is being subject to scrutiny, rather than being tightly controlled. Importantly, however, the nature of political patronage which has been amplified earlier with respect to the NHS, demands that this perception of the situation is approached with a degree of caution.

Perhaps the situation in local government is more clearly delineated, because as Cochrane (1993) rightly points out, there has in many respects been a "failure" of centralization. For example, local spending throughout the 1980s maintained its share of domestic spending; employment in local government rose; local authorities were able to circumvent many central restrictions through creative accounting; the opposition parties have enjoyed increased success in local elections and the Conservatives have gradually lost control of local councils. Thus, as Cochrane (1993: 44) notes:

> Every change from above seems to have been met by adjustments elsewhere in the system first to take account of and then to evade the intended consequences of the central legislation . . . If the relationship between central and local government is a hierarchical one, it is certainly a complex hierarchy. It looks rather more like a constant process of negotiation in which the ground rules are not always clear and may be changed by the centre with often unpredictable consequences.

Overall, therefore, the ambiguous and ambivalent role of local government, and the conundrum of central-local relations in the NHS, will continue to persist – thus leaving some freedom of movement for those contesting the centre's reformulation of the ideas and practices of public accountability.

Conclusion

The analysis presented herein has represented an attempt to bring together the key features of local government and the NHS, which are shared within a changing political and economic environment. In particular, it has attempted to fill an important gap in our understanding of public accountability in two key areas of decentralized government. Quite clearly, what the analysis has demonstrated is that each of these components of the public sector possess features which delineate one from the other. The sum of the parts, which includes important similarities, allows us to paint a wider picture of the way in which the focus of accountability has been reconstituted.

When considering the nature of accountability within local government and the NHS, the authors were keen to avoid the danger of retreating to a "comfort zone" in which ideas of accountability were expressed simply in terms of such matters as legal, managerial, political, professional and financial accountability. A failure to move beyond this conventional approach to accountability brings with it the danger that analyses fail to comprehend fully the political dynamics and consequence of change. This does not mean to say that the components of the conventional approach are unimportant – they are. Consequently, these conventional components were supplemented by an analysis which took into account key policy and ideological changes which have emerged in recent years.

A key feature of the analysis has been the observation of trends within local government and the NHS. More specifically, there has been a clear indication of the way in which the regimes of accountability in local government and the NHS have been exposed to substantial change. In essence, the "traditional" regimes have been supplemented, and indeed supplanted, by a multitude of mechanisms which have their roots in a heady mixture of ideology and pragmatism.

The nature of the analytical framework that has been adopted here gave expression to the ideas developed by Rhodes which were based upon the notion of a "hollowing out of the state". The ideas contained in this "hollowing out" approach are significant in that they point to a new regime for the delivery of public services. Its main elements are privatization, the rise of alternative delivery systems, Europeanization and the rise of the "new public management". If a common thread is to be identified from these themes, then it must surely be the centre's prescriptions for achieving value for money in one form or another. The authors, however, have not been uncritical of Rhodes' use of the concept of the hollowed-out state, since the language tends to imply a weakening of the state. Instead, the analytical framework has been developed in such a manner as to recognize that, far from there being a weakening of the state, there has in fact been a transfer of power within the state. Thus the centre has become more powerful.

While the net effect of all this has been an increase in the power of the centre, there has been room here for the centre to be selective. Thus the drift towards centralism has been more pronounced in the major welfare services. It is within the context of these services that the locality has been exposed to more political control, because it has the potential to undermine the centre's broader political and economic strategies.

This has had a crucial impact on accountability. In terms of the public services which are delivered under the auspices of local government and the NHS, it has meant that the centre has been attempting in effect to reconstitute the concept of accountability in accordance with its own predilections. The focus of attention that has come to dominate the centre's activities is part and parcel of a clear shift away from traditional "political" mechanisms of accountability towards mechanisms which are primarily "economic" in their nature. Whilst this is not without its contradictions and tensions, for a society based partly on ideas of pluralism and diversity the consequences are plain to see.

References

Accounts Commission (1993), *Reports and Accounts 1993*, Edinburgh: Accounts Commission.

Anon (1993), "Fair Play", *Health Service Journal*, 22nd April, 15.

Baggott, Rob (1994), *Health and Health Care in Britain*, Houndmills: MacMillan.

Bailey, Stephen J. and Bruce, Allan (1994), "Financing the National Health Service: The Continuing Search for Alternatives", *Journal of Social Policy*, Volume 23, Number 4, 489–516.

Barron, J. Crawley, G. and Wood, T. (1991), *Councillors in Crisis: The Public and Private Worlds of Local Councillors*. Houndmills: MacMillan.

BBC1 (1994), *Here and Now*, 30th November.

Brindle, David (1994), "Labour Points to 'Gulf' as Figures Show One in Four NHS Trust Board Members Live Outside Area", *Guardian*, 16th August.

Brown, R.G.S. (1977), "Accountability and Control in the National

Health Service", *Health and Social Service Journal*, Centre Eight Papers, October, B9-B16.

Bruce, Allan (1990), *Policy Implementation and the Health Service in Scotland*, Unpublished Ph.D. thesis, CNAA.

Bruce, Allan (1994), "Finance and Delivery of Health Care", *Teaching Public Administration*, Volume XIV, Number 1, 49–63.

Bruce, Allan and Hill, Sandra (1994), "Relationships Between Doctors and Managers: The Scottish Experience", *Journal of Management and Medicine*, Volume 8, Number 5, 49–57.

Butler, John (1992), *Patients, Policies and Politics: Before and After Working for Patients*, Buckingham: Open University Press.

Byrne, Tony (1994), *Local Government in Britain*, London: Penguin, 6th Edition.

Cm 555 (1989), *Working for Patients*, Department of Health, London: HMSO.

Cm 1599 (1991), *The Citizen's Charter*, London: HMSO.

Cm 2519 (1994), *Public Expenditure Statistical Supplement to the Financial Statement and Budget Report 1994–95*, Department of Health, London: HMSO.

Cmnd 1604 (1962), *A Hospital Plan for England and Wales*, Ministry of Health, London: HMSO.

Cmnd 6453 (1976), *Local Government Finance: Report of the Committee of Enquiry* (Chair: Frank Layfield), Department of the Environment, London: HMSO.

Cmnd 9714 (1986), *Paying for Local Government*, Department of the Environment, London: HMSO.

Cochrane, Allan (1993), *Whatever Happened to Local Government?*, Buckingham: Open University Press.

Cohen, Nick, Judd, Judith, Jones, Judy and Clement, Barrie (1993), "What Happened to Democracy?", *The Independent on Sunday*, 29th March, 19.

Day, Patricia and Klein, Rudolf (1987), *Accountabilities: Five Public Services*, London: Tavistock.

Department of Health and Social Security (1977), *The Way Forward*, London: HMSO.

Department of Health and Social Security (1979), *Patients First*, London: HMSO.

Department of Health and Social Security (1981), *Care In Action*, London: HMSO.

Department of Health and Social Security (1983), *NHS Management Inquiry*, (Chairman: Roy Griffiths), London: DHSS.

Department of Health (1991), *The Patient's Charter*, London: HMSO.

Duncan, Simon and Goodwin, Mark (1988), *The Local State and Uneven Development*, Cambridge: Polity Press.

Elcock, Howard. Jordan, Grant and Midwinter, Arthur (1989), *Budgeting in Local Government: Managing the Margins*, London: Longman.

Elcock, Howard (1994), *Local Government: Policy and Management in Local Authorities*, London: Routledge, 3rd Edition.

Elcock, Howard (1991), *Change and Decay? Public Administration in the 1990's*, London: Longman.

Elmore, Richard F. (1979), "Backward Mapping: Implementation Research and Policy Decisions", *Political Science Quarterly*, Volume 94, Number 4, 601–614.

Ensor, T. (1993), *Future Health Care Options: Funding Health Care*, London: Institute of Health Services Management.

Gamble, Andrew (1988), *The Free Economy and the Strong State*, Houndmills: MacMillan.

Glennerster, Howard (1992), *Paying for Welfare: The 1990s*, London: Harvester Wheatsheaf.

Gray, Clive (1994), *Government Beyond the Centre*, Houndmills: MacMillan.

Hampton, William (1991), *Local Government and Urban Politics*, London: Longman, 2nd Edition.

Harrison, Stephen (1988), *Managing the National Health Service: Shifting the Frontier*, London: Chapman and Hall.

Harrison, Stephen, Hunter, David J. and Pollitt, Christopher (1990), *The Dynamics of British Health Policy*, London: Unwin Hyman.

Harrison, Stephen, Hunter, David J., Marnoch, Gordon and Pollitt, Christopher (1992), *Just Managing: Power and Culture in the National Health Service*, Houndmills: MacMillan.

Harrison, Stephen and Pollitt, Christopher (1994), *Controlling Health Professionals: The Future of Work and Organisation in the NHS*, Buckingham: Open University Press.

Hepworth, Noel P. (1984), *The Finance of Local Government*, London: Unwin Hyman, 7th Edition.

Hinton, Peter and Wilson, Elizabeth (1993), "Accountability" in Wilson, J. and Hinton, P. (eds), *Public Services in the 1990s*, Eastham: Tudor.

Holliday, Ian (1992), *The NHS Transformed*, Manchester: Baseline Books.

Hunter, David J. (1980a), *Coping with Uncertainty: Policy and Politics in the National Health Service*, Chichester: Research Studies Press.

Hunter, David J. (1980b), "Policy Making in Area Health Boards: The Role of the Board Member", in Drucker, H. M. and Drucker, N. L. (eds), *The Scottish Government Yearbook 1981*, Edinburgh: Paul Harris, 156–186.

Hunter, David J. (1983), "Centre Periphery Relations in the National Health Service: Facilitators or Inhibitors of Innovation?" in Young, Ken (ed), *National Interests and Local Government*, London: Heinneman, 133–161.

Hunter, David J. (1984), "Managing Health Care", *Social Policy and Administration*, Volume 18, Number 1, 41–67.

Hunter, David (1994), "Perplexing Perpetual Paradox", *Health Service Journal*, 12th May, 21.

Johnson, Norman (1990), *Reconstructing the Welfare State: A Decade of Change*, London: Harvester Wheatsheaf.

Klein, Rudolf (1982), "Performance Evaluation and the NHS: A Case Study in Conceptual Perplexity and Organisational Complexity", *Public Administration*, Volume 60, Winter, 385–407.

Klein, Rudolf (1989), *The Politics of the NHS*, London: Longman, 2nd Edition.

Lawton, Alan and Rose, Aidan (1991), *Organisation and Management in the Public Sector*, London: Pitman.

Leach, Steve, Stewart, John and Walsh, Kieron (1994), *The Changing Organisation and Management of Local Government*, Houndmills: MacMillan.

Mallabar, Norman (1991), *Local Government Administration – In A Time of Change*, Sunderland: Business Education Publishers.

Marshall, T. H. (1950), *Citizenship and Social Class*, Cambridge: Cambridge University Press.

Maud, Sir John (Chairman) (1967), *Management of Local Government: Volume 1: Report of the Committee*, London: HMSO.

Maxwell, Robert J. (1993), "Sleeping with One Eye Open", *Health Service Journal*, 1st April, 22.

McSweeney, Brendan (1988) "Accounting for the Audit Commission", *The Political Quarterly*, Volume 59, 28–43.

Midwinter, Arthur and Mair, Colin (1987), *Rates Reform*, Edinburgh: Mainstream.

Midwinter, Arthur and Monaghan, Claire (1993), *From Rates to the Poll Tax*, Edinburgh: Edinburgh University Press.

Miller, Barbara (1993), "Shedding a Tier: How Regions will be Restructured", *Health Service Journal*, 29th October, 11–14.

National Health Service and Community Care Act 1990, London: HMSO.

Newton, Kenneth (1976), *Second City Politics*, Oxford: Clarendon Press.

Oliver, Dawn (1991), *Government in the United Kingdom: The Search for Accountability, Effectiveness and Citizenship*, Milton Keynes: Open University Press.

Paton, Calum (1993), "Devolution and Centralism in the National Health Service", *Social Policy and Administration*, Volume 27, Number 2, 83–108.

Ranade, Wendy (1994), *A Future for the NHS: Health Care in the 1990s*, London: Longman.

Regan, D. E. and Stewart, John (1982), "An Essay in the Government of Health: A Case for Local Authority Control", *Social Policy and Administration*, Volume 16, Number 1, 19–43.

Rhodes, R.A.W. (1987), "Developing the Public Service Orientation: Or Let's Add a Soupcon of Political Theory", *Local Government Studies*, May/June, 63–73.

Rhodes, R. A. W. (1988), *Beyond Westminster and Whitehall*, London: Routledge.

Rhodes, R.A.W. (1994), "The Hollowing Out of the State: The Changing Nature of the Public Services in Britain", *The Political Quarterly*, April-June, Volume 65, Number 2, 138–151.

Scottish Home and Health Department (1976), *The Way Ahead*, Edinburgh: HMSO.

Scottish Home and Health Department (1980), *Scottish Health Authorities Priorities for the Eighties*, Edinburgh: HMSO.

Stacey, Frank (1971), *The British Ombudsman*, Oxford: Oxford University Press.

Stewart, John (1993), *The Rebuilding of Public Accountability*, Unpublished Paper.

Stoker, Gerry (1991), *The Politics of Local Government*, Houndmills: MacMillan, 2nd Edition.

Stott, Tony (1994), "Local Government: Why Quangos Must Come Out Into The Light", *Parliamentary Brief*, October, 79–80.

Travers, Tony (1990), "London After Abolition", *Local Government Studies*, May / June, 105–116.

Watkin, Brian (1978), *The National Health Service: The First Phase 1948 – 1974 and After*, London: George Allen & Unwin.

Wilson, David and Game, Chris (1994), *Local Government in the United Kingdom*, Houndmills: MacMillan.

5

ACCOUNTABILITY IN THE UTILITIES

Robert Pyper

Introduction

This chapter's primary purpose is to set out the arrangements for, and the key debates surrounding, the accountability of former public utilities in Britain. A range of regulatory agencies have been established in the wake of the privatization of these utilities, and the functioning of these new bodies has raised a number of important issues relating to accountability in this strange territory, this world of meso-government where public services are provided by private organizations.

In order to understand the systems of accountability which operate in the privatized utilities, we must first set out the arrangements for accountability which existed in the publicly-owned utilities.

Before Privatization: Public Utilities and the Problem of Accountability

For the purposes of the discussions in this chapter, the "public utilities" shall be considered to be those spheres of the public service charged with the supply of gas, water, electricity, and telecommunications facilities. One might argue whether or not telecommunications truly represents a utility service, and there could be a case for including transport, in its myriad forms, as a utility. It is no part of this book's purpose to engage in theoretical debates about the most accurate definition of a utility. The selection of gas, water, electricity and telecommunications is designed to illustrate the fundamental issues surrounding accountability in this sphere, where previously publicly-owned, basic services have been privatized in a more or less straightforward fashion (the exception being the water utility in Scotland, which remains in the public sector), and comparisons between the regimes of accountability before and after privatization are possible.

By the 1970s, public ownership of these utilities had evolved in distinct forms. Water supply and sewage disposal was managed by local authorities in Scotland and Regional Water Authorities in England and Wales, while the gas, electricity and telecommunications utilities took the form of public corporations associated with sponsoring departments in central government. Thus, two quite separate regimes of accountability were in operation. These can be examined in turn.

WATER

A distinction has to be drawn between the management and accountability of the water utilities in Scotland and those in England and Wales. In some senses, by the 1970s the trends north and south of the border were running in quite different directions.

One consequence of the Local Government (Scotland) Act of 1973 was the abolition of thirteen Regional Water Boards, and the return of their functions to local government. Thus, the new Regional Councils assumed responsibility for water and sewerage services, and these were delivered through conventional local authority departments. In terms of accountability, therefore, matters were relatively clear and straightforward. Internal lines of accountability ran from officers to members, and the latter were externally accountable in the fashion described in Chapter Four.

The Water Act of 1973 established nine Regional Water Authorities in England, plus the Welsh Water Authority. These new bodies assumed responsibility for the full range of water services, which had previously been managed by a large number of public and private organizations, including local authorities, water undertakings and river authorities (Greenwood and Wilson, 1989: 257). A majority of the members on each Regional Water Authority (RWA) were nominated by local authorities, while the chairman and other members were appointed by the Secretary of State for the Environment (or the Secretary of State for Wales in the case of the Welsh Water Authority). The ministerial appointees were meant to secure representation for particular consumer groups, as well as provide the necessary expertise for the efficient management of the industry. This resulted in a curious hybrid of accountability. Ministerial involvement in appointments was similar to that which applied in the case of the nationalised industries' Boards, and, accordingly, one line of accountability ran from the RWAs to central government ministers. This type of accountability presented problems of its own, as we shall see. However, at the same time, another line of accountability ran from the RWAs to local authorities. In each RWA a number of different local

authorities would have representation, since the geographical boundaries of the RWAs did not correspond to local government boundaries. In
addition, there was a rather oblique accountability to the consumers,
supposedly secured in part through the ministerial appointees. It was all
rather confusing. The precise demarcation lines between those matters of
policy and management which were the responsibility of the centre, and
those which were the responsibility of the localities, was never entirely
clear. Indeed, the fact of local government involvement seemed to be at
odds with the original thinking behind the 1973 reform, which had been
to managerialize the industry through the creation of technocratic
agencies (Keating, 1985; Gray, 1982). Matters were further complicated
by the existence of another body which had been established under the
terms of the 1973 Water Act, the National Water Council, which had a
vague advisory and liaison function. This body was abolished ten years
later.

A partial managerial rationalization took place, albeit without
enhancing accountability, as a consequence of the 1983 Water Act,
which ended the automatic right of local authorities to representation on
the RWAs, and vested full appointing powers in ministers. The rights of
the press and public to attend meetings of the RWAs were severely
curtailed. Consumer representation was to be secured, in the style of the
nationalized industries, through consultative committees. In practice,
these had no significant power or influence (Greenwood and Wilson,
1989: 259–60).

We can summarise by saying that the regime of accountability in the
pre-privatized water utilities varied significantly. In Scotland, water
services were fully integrated with the local authorities, and the system of
accountability was characterized by the strengths and weaknesses of local
government accountability. In England and Wales, the hybrid nature of
the RWAs, at least until 1983, produced a rather disparate regime of
accountability which proved to be highly unsatisfactory.

TELECOMMUNICATIONS, GAS AND ELECTRICITY

In the cases of telecommunications, gas and electricity, the public
corporation regime of accountability applied. Telecommunications, as
part of the Post Office, was the last of this group of utilities to come under
the umbrella of a public corporation. Until 1969, the Post Office was a
government department, headed by a cabinet minister, the Postmaster
General. Conventional Parliamentary mechanisms of accountability
applied until that date (see Chapter Two). From 1969, the postal and

telecommunications services of the Post Office were managed in the context of a public corporation, with the Department of Trade and Industry as the "sponsoring department".

The gas and electricity utilities had become public corporations at an earlier stage, in the 1940s. Each was characterized by a federal structure. The Gas Council co-ordinated the activities of Area Gas Boards, covering the whole of Great Britain. The Electricity Council had general supervisory duties, and in addition there was a Central Electricity Generating Board and twelve Area Electricity Boards. Two further corporations existed in Scotland, the North of Scotland Hydro-Electricity Board and the South of Scotland Electricity Board (Tivey, 1973: 11–12).

In theory, the public corporation regime of accountability was clear and straightforward. Ministers were accountable to Parliament for the activities of their departments, and if a given department happened to be a "sponsoring department" for a nationalized industry or a public corporation (as was the case with the Department of Energy in relation to gas and electricity, and the Department of Trade and Industry in relation to telecommunications), then the ministers would be accountable to Parliament for the functioning of these bodies. Provision for the representation of consumers or service users existed in the form of consultative or consumer councils, which were based in statute, and had roles in relation to redress of grievances and policy advice (Greenwood and Wilson, 1989: 240; Tivey, 1973: 284).

In practice, the functioning of this regime of accountability was far from simple, and distinctly problematic. One of the fundamental flaws which lay at the very heart of the "Morrisonian" concept of public ownership (Herbert Morrison had established the basic parameters of nationalization adhered to by the Attlee Government) was the unclear division of responsibilities between ministers in the sponsoring departments and the boards of the industries and corporations. In general terms, ministers were to establish the policy framework, while the boards had responsibility for day-to-day operational matters. The nationalized industries and public corporations were meant to become financially self-sufficient at an early stage. However, the fact that financial self-sufficiency was elusive combined with a (perhaps understandable) reluctance on the part of many ministers to leave operational matters solely in the hands of the boards. Informal pressures were used by ministers to overcome the restrictions inherent in their statutory powers (Greenwood and Wilson, 1989: 240). "Lunchtable directives" and "backstairs manoeuvring" became increasingly common ministerial methods of influencing the functioning of the boards. This would not have presented serious problems in relation to accountability had it not been for the fact that ministers and board members became skilled at buck-passing, with each claiming that particular problems were in the province of the other. The familiar, problematic distinction between policy and administration provided a convenient smokescreen, behind which both ministers and board members could hide. In the face of tangled internal lines of accountability, convoluted and largely unsuccessful attempts were made to clarify the rules regarding the legitimacy or otherwise of Parliamentary Questions on aspects of the public corporations (Tivey, 1973: 163–76). Ultimately, ministerial power without adequate accountability became the order of the day.

What of accountability to consumers and service users? The consumer councils and consultative bodies enjoyed occasional successes, but suffered from three major failings (Greenwood and Wilson, 1989: 241). The first was that the complex apparatus of committees functioned in relative obscurity. Tivey noted that "few consumers" were even aware of their existence (Tivey, 1973: 284). The second failing was the perceived close proximity, in policy, personnel and sometimes even physical terms, of the consumer "watchdogs" to the bodies they were supposedly supervising. Thirdly, the consumer and consultative bodies were poorly funded, had few staff and often lacked the expertise to make an impact.

Within this general haze, there were specific gaps in the system of Parliamentary accountability, to which we should make reference. The nationalized industries and public corporations were not subject to scrutiny under the established system of state financial audit. The Comptroller and Auditor General and the Public Accounts Committee of the House of Commons had no remit to examine the accounts of these bodies, on the grounds that, under the Morrisonian theory, financial independence from the Treasury would be the norm (in practice, it became the exception). The annual reports of the nationalized industries and public corporations were debated in Parliament, but these debates tended to be very generalized and superficial.

In the initial period after the Attlee Government's nationalization programme, limitations placed on MPs wishing to question ministers about the operation of the nationalized industries and public corporations, and the deliberate exclusion of these bodies from the remit of the PAC, led to increasing frustration in Parliament. As a result of this, backbenchers succeeded in getting an *ad hoc* committee of inquiry set up in 1951, to look into the general problem of accountability. The outcome of this was a recommendation in 1953 that a new Committee on Nationalized Industries (also covering the public corporations) should be set up. This body was finally established in 1955.

The committee obtained an early review of its rather restrictive original terms of reference. In these, there had been an attempt to draw strict dividing lines between matters of policy which were seen to be the preserve of ministers and could not be subject to scrutiny by the committee, matters of day-to-day administration which were the preserve of the Boards and similarly could not be subject to scrutiny by the committee, and matters pertaining to reports and accounts which were seen as the sole legitimate sphere of concern for the committee (Coombes, 1966: 55–57).

When the new Select Committee on Nationalised Industries was set up in 1956, it had no restrictions within its terms of reference, either in relation to ministerial responsibility for policy or the responsibility of the Boards for day-to-day management.

During the period 1956–79, the Select Committee on Nationalized Industries worked away in the sphere it had carved out for itself. Although understaffed and starved of facilities, the committee won the right to appoint sub-committees (eventually up to three of these) in order to enable two or more inquiries to be carried out simultaneously.

Although the committee's work was generally respected, especially during the 1960s, when it conducted a series of investigations into the main nationalized industries and public corporations, in addition to an analysis of ministerial powers, it faced a huge task.

> Though it used specialist advisers it continued to lack anything in the nature of a staff trained in industrial performance evaluation . . . By the end of the seventies it was doubtful whether it was any longer achieving the impact which it undoubtedly had in the sixties . . .
> (Johnson, 1981: 219).

In 1979, despite the protestations of past and present members of the committee, it was abolished as part of the general reform which created the new system of departmentally-related select committees (see Chapter Two). In order to fill the gap, allowance was made for a sub-committee, drawn from the membership of a number of specified new select committees, to consider any matter affecting two or more nationalized industries or public corporations. Not surprisingly, this cumbersome procedure was not invoked, and serious doubts were expressed regarding the appropriateness of this arrangement (Liaison Committee, 1983). Instead, sporadic scrutiny of particular industries or corporations or general issues was carried out by individual select committees from time to time (see, for example, the Transport Committee, 1980, and the Treasury and Civil Service Committee, 1981).

By this time the Thatcher Government's privatization programme was starting to get into its stride, and new questions were arising regarding the accountability of the utilities. While addressing these, we should not lose sight of the fact that the arrangements for securing the accountability of the old nationalized industries and public corporations to Parliament and the public were distinctly problematic. In particular, Parliament had at its disposal few mechanisms for scrutinising ministers and Board members, and even the most widely respected of these, the Select Committee on Nationalised Industries, was severely flawed.

Privatization and the Question of Accountability
In the course of a five year period during the 1980s, the utilities passed from the public to the private sector (with the sole exception of the water utility in Scotland, to which we shall return in due course).

Telecommunications services were disaggregated from the postal services, becoming British Telecom in the process, before being privatized in 1984. British Gas moved from the public to the private sector in 1986, while the electricity generation and supply industry, as well as the water utility (in England and Wales) were privatized in 1989.

The forms of privatization differed. For example, from the outset British Telecom faced a form of limited competition from Mercury. The statutory duopoly was ended by the government in 1991, and new telecommunications licences began to be issued. Despite this, BT "retains an effective monopoly of the local network as virtually all of its competitors' calls have to originate or terminate on it" (Vass, 1994: 158).

British Gas remained virtually a monopoly supplier for an extended period following privatization, and was only facing the prospect of serious competition as the end of the century approached.

In the electricity utility, a system of regulated competition emerged in both generation and supply. In England and Wales, the generators (initially National Power and PowerGen) and suppliers (twelve Regional Electricity Companies, as well as National Power and PowerGen themselves) participated in a wholesale electricity market. In Scotland, three major companies emerged: Scottish Nuclear was licensed to generate electricity, while Scottish Power and Hydro-Electric were licensed to generate, transmit and supply (Office of Electricity Regulation, 1991).

Under the terms of the Water Act, 1989, ten regionally-based water companies were established throughout England and Wales. No competitive market was possible in this sphere. The water utility in Scotland was to remain within the ambit of local authorities, until April 1996, when the old two-tier structure of local government was abolished. At that time, three new water and sewerage authorities covering the east, west and north of Scotland were to come into being. The members of these new authorities were to be appointed by the Secretary of State for Scotland. Thus, in Scotland at least, the water utility remained in the public sector, albeit with a new regime of accountability, directed to the centre rather than to local authorities.

It is not our purpose here to examine the rationale for or the broad political and economic consequences of, privatization. Our sole concern is accountability. Improving accountability *per se*, did not figure as one of the major imperatives which lay behind the Thatcher Government's privatization programme, but it was important for the Government that this issue should be seen to have been addressed. This was done, in part, by giving emphasis to the rights of consumers, and in this sense the Government was effectively stressing the primacy of a narrowly economic strain of accountability. Beyond this, the vacuum created by the loss of public "control" over key utilities (however attenuated this might have been in practice) had to be filled in some fashion. The solution was apparently to be found through the appointment of regulatory agencies.

The Public Utility Regulators in Context

Regulatory agencies can broadly be defined as bodies which, although entrusted with public duties of scrutiny, and although often set up by Parliament, exist outside the normal framework of elected central and local government, and possess a degree of independence from it. These agencies are not new: in the 18th century, boards and commissioners dealt with the regulation of many matters of central and local administration. However, regulatory agencies declined in importance during the 19th century, as the scope of government widened and Parliament came to demand more direct control (through the medium of responsible ministers) over state activities.

As the scope and scale of public administration increased in the course of the twentieth century, pragmatism and political expediency led governments to turn increasingly to regulatory agencies. Ministerial workloads could be lightened, disinterested expertise could be developed in complex policy areas, speedier and more expert decisions could be obtained than would be the case if matters were referred to the courts. In addition to these advantages, agencies could, in some circumstances, supplement, enhance or even replace extant modes of accountability.

Normally, the staffs of regulatory agencies were not civil servants, although their pay and conditions of service were broadly similar to those found in the civil service. Most of the agencies had a statutory basis, although the specific powers granted might differ. Some agencies would be given quasi-legislative powers to issue rules and guidelines. Some would be allocated quasi-judicial powers to investigate breaches of rules, and enforce rules. Some would be given administrative powers to conduct business operations. A broad typology of regulatory agencies would include the following.

- *State Audit*: the Audit Commission and the Accounts Commission.

- *National Lottery*: the activities of the lottery operator, Camelot, are regulated by the Office of Lottery Regulation (OFLOT).

- *Housing*: the voluntary housing associations which provide homes for those who cannot afford market rents have their standards set and monitored by the Housing Corporation.

- *Education*: inspections of schools in England and Wales are coordinated by the Office of Standards in Education (OFSTED).

- *The City and the Financial Sector*: agencies in this sphere may be classified as part of the self-regulatory framework (a plethora of agencies operate under the auspices of the Securities and Investment Board, including the Personal Investment Authority (PIA) and the Financial Intermediaries and Brokers Association (FIMBRA)), or the field of state regulation (including the Office of Fair Trading (OFT), the Monopolies and Mergers Commission (MMC) and the Serious Fraud Office (SFO)).

- *The Press and Broadcasting*: the BBC Board of Governors has a multifaceted role, part of which includes regulatory functions. In addition, a range of regulators, with widely varying powers, operates in this sphere, including the Independent Television Commission, the Radio Authority, the Broadcasting Complaints Commission, the Broadcasting Standards Council and the Press Complaints Commission.

- *Employment*: agencies with regulatory functions in this realm would include the Health and Safety Council, the Health and Safety Executive (the former has a policy role, the latter a monitoring function), the Advisory Conciliation and Arbitration Service (ACAS), the Equal Opportunities Commission (EOC) and the Commission for Racial Equality (CRE).

- *Discrimination*: the last two agencies cited in the preceding category (EOC and CRE), have a remit which extends beyond the sphere of employment.

- *Environment*: the 1990 Environmental Protection Act introduced a new system of regulation in this sphere, and allocated a key role to Her Majesty's Inspectorate of Pollution (HMIP). Under the terms of the 1994 Environment Agencies Bill, which was still making its way through Parliament in the summer of 1995, a new Environment Agency would be established, combining the functions of HMIP, numerous locally-based waste regulation authorities and the National Rivers Authority (the latter had been created at the time of the privatization of the water utility in England and Wales). The new agency was expected to become operational in April 1996. This Bill also made provision for a new Scottish Environmental Protection Agency, which would replace the River Purification Boards.

- *Civil Aviation*: powerful policy, executive and judicial functions were allocated to the Civil Aviation Authority under the terms of the 1971 Civil Aviation Act.

This typology makes no claims to be exhaustive. It is offered here in an attempt to locate within a broader perspective the regulatory agencies operating in the sphere of the former public utilities. It is the category which includes these regulators, the Office of Telecommunications (OFTEL), the Office of Gas Supply (OFGAS), the Office of Electricity Supply (OFFER) and the Office of Water Services (OFWAT), which is our concern, and to which we will now turn our attention.

Regulation of Utilities: Agencies' Remits and Records
A complex regulatory framework has emerged in the wake of privatization of the public utilities. Although our main focus will be on the utility
regulators *per se*, it should be noted that certain regulatory roles are also
played by other regulators, and by ministers.

The competition regulators, the Office of Fair Trading and the
Monopolies and Mergers Commission, may have particular issues
referred to them from time to time. For example, during the summer of
1992, OFGAS referred British Gas to the MMC twice, and the Secretary
of State for Trade and Industry made another two referrals, and these
episodes culminated in a report from the MMC which recommended
that British Gas be split into two companies (one covering gas trading and
the other transportation and storage). While rejecting the need for the
company to be divided in this way, the government proposed that British
Gas should be stripped of its monopoly in supplying tariff users (Beavis
and Weston, 1993; Monopolies and Mergers Commission, 1993; Vass,
1994: 155–56). Referrals may emanate from the other side of the fence
too, and this was illustrated in 1994, when South West Water
(unsuccessfully) challenged the new price formula set by OFWAT by
appealing to the MMC (Lorenz and Waples, 1994). In broad terms, the
OFT and the MMC are meant to pursue general competitive objectives,
but the utility regulators also have some responsibility for encouraging
competition. The result of this has been a degree of confusion.

> The inter-relation between the regulators, not always obvious at
> privatisation, became increasingly complex and significant as regulation
> developed.
> (Price, 1994: 86).

To add to the confusion, ministers also have a regulatory function, in
the sense that they license the utility operators, and, on advice from the
MMC, make decisions about proposed mergers. Thus, the utility
regulators do not operate in isolation. Nonetheless, it is to these bodies
that the day-to-day task of regulation falls.

TENSIONS AND CONTRADICTIONS
From the outset, it was clear that the work of the utility regulators was
going to be complicated by an inherent imprecision in relation to their
fundamental roles and responsibilities. This imprecision produced a
number of tensions and contradictions.

There was a basic tension between two functions, as overseers and guarantors of quasi-markets, and as agents of accountability and control. For new right idealists within the Thatcher Government, privatization would lead to the creation of free markets, and the open competition which followed would, in turn, secure the best form of accountability (economic accountability, to the consumers). The problem associated with privatization of public utilities was that true free markets and full open competition could not be created at the outset. For a time at least, and perhaps for an indefinite period in the case of some utilities, the best hope of the government was to create quasi-markets, with the regulators performing a key role in maintaining "competitive" prices. This objective was summarised by Ian Byatt, the Director General of OFWAT, when he argued that his fundamental task as a regulator was: ". . . to achieve through regulation the same balance as would otherwise have been achieved by competitive markets." (cited by Maloney and Richardson, 1992: 15).

At the same time, however, it was clearly intended that the regulatory agencies should function as agents of accountability, doing more than "holding the ring" in the interests of maintaining a quasi-market, but also obliging the utilities to answer for their policies and actions and provide redress of grievances where necessary. Thus, Sir James McKinnon, the first Director General of OFGAS, saw his job in terms of: ". . . making sure British Gas has the interests of its customers in mind at all times . . ." (Office of Gas Supply, 1990: 4).

We should note, in passing, that the prominence McKinnon gave to the "customer watchdog" role was slightly confusing, in the sense that OFGAS, unlike OFTEL, for example, has only limited powers to deal with customer complaints!

These basic roles, of securing quasi-markets and accountability to the consumers, were not necessarily contradictory, but the fact that the relative weighting attached to each was never made entirely clear, did serve to produce a tension at the heart of the regulatory regime.

The issue of accountability raised further questions. In particular, to whom should the newly-privatized utilities be held accountable? Clearly, since the utilities remained providers of public services, the concept of accountability to service users or consumers was important. In this context, the regulatory agencies came to be widely (if somewhat inaccurately, as we shall see) perceived to be consumer "watchdogs", charged with the task of enforcing the accountability of the utilities. There was an obvious tension, and arguably even a contradiction, between this concept of accountability and the more conventional mores

of corporate governance, within which primacy is attached to accountability to shareholders. Peter Vass has neatly summarized this tension:

> An increase in profits from one point of view is seen as an unwarranted use
> of monopoly power; from another it is simply productivity improvements
> or the contribution from diversification of the business into competitive
> sectors that are not subject to regulation.
> (Vass, 1992: 211).

As we shall see, regulators differed in terms of the relative importance
they attached to the accountability of utilities to consumers and the desire
of boards of directors to protect the interests of shareholders.

ECONOMIC FRAMEWORK OF THE REGULATORY REGIME

Despite these tensions and apparent contradictions, it is possible to
identify at least one relatively clear and straightforward element of the
regulatory regime. The cornerstone of utility regulation in the UK is the
Littlechild formula.

The economic aspect of regulation was to be characterised by price
control. When the Thatcher Government was devising the ground rules
for regulation of the utilities, at the time of BT's privatization, it accepted
the recommendation of Professor Stephen Littlechild that the type of
economic regulation favoured in the United States, which involved
limiting profits, be rejected in favour of a price-cap mechanism (Jackson
and Price, 1994: 12). The Littlechild formula was RPI-X. Thus, the
maximum price increases in the utilities would be determined by the
annual changes in the Retail Price Index (RPI) minus an amount set by
the regulator (X), normally for a four or five year period. The X factor is
designed to reflect particular features of the utility, and incorporate
efficiency savings as well as special investment requirements. The net
effect of this formula is to place the utilities under pressure to reduce the
price of their products, cut costs and improve efficiency.

Littlechild, who moved from academia to become Director General of
OFFER, saw the price-cap mechanism, and indeed regulation *per se*, as a
temporary requirement, which could be dispensed with once proper
competitive markets had become established.

> Regulation is essentially a means of preventing the worst excesses of
> monopoly; it is not a substitute for competition. It is a means of "holding
> the fort" until competition arrives.
> (cited by Veljanovski, 1991: 20).

Additional formulae apply in some of the utilities (for example, RPI+Y in gas and RPI+K in water) to allow some categories of costs to effectively by-pass the price-cap (Price, 1994: 92; Maloney and Richardson, 1992: 15). Thus, allowance is made for the fact that certain costs (such as the price of gas purchased from the North Sea companies under long-term contracts, or additional investment required in the water sector due to EU environmental regulations) are beyond the control of the utilities, and can legitimately be passed on to the consumers.

The economic framework of the regulatory regime in each utility, and, indeed, the whole form and level of regulation in each sphere, are subject to periodic review. However, there are significant variations between the utilities in this respect. For example, the regulation of British Telecom was initially subject to five-yearly review, and this was latter shortened to four years plus interim reviews. British Gas, or OFGAS could apply for changes to the regulatory framework after five years. Electricity transmission prices were reviewed at the time of privatization, while the price-caps applied to the supply companies were re-examined after three years. A fundamental review of the regulatory regime in the water utilities will take place after ten years, but there will be an interim review in five years, and specific variations to individual targets more frequently (Price, 1994: 93–94).

Let us now move beyond the broad framework of the regulatory regime, to look in slightly more detail at the remit and records of specific regulators.

TELECOMMUNICATIONS

As the first regulatory agency in the sphere of the former public utilities, OFTEL established the basic model for the others. In fact, OFTEL was itself partially modelled on the Office of Fair Trading.

OFTEL is a non-ministerial government department, with approximately 160 staff, some of whom come from the civil service, with others having backgrounds in consumer affairs, business and industry (Office of Telecommunications, 1994). Three Directors General of Telecommunications have held office since OFTEL was established under the Telecommunications Act of 1984. Sir Bryan Carsberg held the post between 1984 and 1992, and there was a brief interregnum under Bill Wiggleworth before Don Cruikshank took office in 1993. Under the terms of the 1984 Act, the broad remit of OFTEL is to:

- ensure that the licensed telecommunications operators (including BT, Mercury, local cable companies and mobile network operators) comply with their licence conditions. The operating licences set out in detail what the operators can and cannot do, and, in the case of BT, the licence contains the price-cap formula in relation to the main network services;
- initiate modifications to licence conditions by agreement with licensees or through reference to the MMC;
- enforce competition legislation in relation to telecommunications (in conjunction with the OFT);
- advise the Secretary of State for Trade and Industry on all telecommunications matters, including the granting of new licences;
- obtain and publish information helpful to service users;
- consider complaints and enquiries about telecommunications services or apparatus.

Two general trends emerge from examinations of OFTEL's record since 1984. The first is the steady tightening of the price cap within the BT licence. In the wake of successive reviews, the formula has changed from RPI-3 (1984), to RPI-4.5 (1989), to RPI-6.25 (1991), to RPI-7.5 (1993) (Vass, 1994: 172). These reductions have not produced total satisfaction on the part of consumers, who continued to complain, in increasing numbers, about excessive profits (*The Guardian*, 1992). The second trend is the developing struggle between BT on the one side, and the expanding number of operators seeking interconnection with the local network, which BT controls, on the other. OFTEL's role is to impose terms of access, where these cannot be agreed between BT and an operator. However, Mercury and many other operators have argued that BT's interconnection charges are invariably too high, and, despite OFTEL's enforced reduction of access charges at the end of 1993, continued to contest the very basis on which these charges are worked out (Vass, 1994: 158–59).

A marked change in emphasis took place in the general approach adopted by OFTEL following the appointment of Don Cruikshank as the new Director General in 1993. In part, this seems to stem from Cruikshank's personal perspective on public management, developed in the course of his career in the private sector, and then as Chief Executive of the NHS in Scotland. In part, the changing approach may be linked to the changing nature of the telecommunications sphere, in which a more competitive market has slowly developed since 1984. A further factor may be the timing of Cruikshank's appointment: the last price-cap imposed by Carsberg came into effect in 1993, and would remain in place until 1997, leaving Cruikshank with time to focus his attention on other matters.

Whatever the explanation, it is clear that, in some respects at least, Cruikshank's is a less interventionist approach than that of his predecessors. He sees OFTEL's major, overriding, role as being a facilitator of competition. This was illustrated within a few months of his appointment, when he took the first steps towards obliging BT to provide more information about its costs and charges (Bannister, 1993a). The objective here was to give BT's rivals access to comprehensible, disaggregated accounts, as a means of enhancing competition. Cruikshank's priorities became even clearer at the end of 1994, when he published a consultative document which set out a range of possible options for increasing competition in telecommunications (Office of Telecommunications, 1994a). OFTEL's preferred option, the radical Option 4, could only come into effect at the end of the lifespan of the current price-cap, in 1997. This option would involve a substantial freeing-up of the market, by ending BT's subsidy of residential line rentals (currently subsidised by call charges), and, as a consequence, end the requirement for BT's rivals to make contributions towards the cost of maintaining uneconomic lines. Commentators were in no doubt that the net effect of Cruikshank's strategy would be to change the role of OFTEL ". . . from intervention and making detailed decisions on prices to ensuring fair trading, and stamping out anti-competitive behaviour and abuse of market position." (Bannister, 1994). Since the latter activities had fallen within the remit of this regulator from the outset, this shift in emphasis can only be interpreted as a fundamental narrowing of OFTEL's role as an agent of accountability.

GAS

The Office of Gas Supply is, like OFTEL, a non-ministerial government department. Although OFGAS's staffing levels have varied somewhat from year to year, it tends to operate with only approximately 30 full-time officials, most of whom transfer from the Office of Fair Trading (Office of Gas Supply, 1991: 62–63). In the period since OFGAS was set up, within the terms of the 1986 Gas Act, two Directors General of Gas Supply have held office: Sir James McKinnon until 1993, and Clare Spottiswoode thereafter. The 1986 Act conferred upon OFGAS powers to:

- fix maximum charges for the resale of gas;

- authorise suppliers of gas through pipes;
- agree the terms on which suppliers have access to British Gas pipelines, in the event of a dispute;
- review general developments concerning the gas supply industry;
- change the authorisation covering the operations of British Gas, with the agreement of the company. Where agreement is not forthcoming, the Director General can refer the amendments to the MMC;
- publish information and advice for the benefit of tariff customers;
- investigate complaints where legal action may be necessary.

The part played by OFGAS in terms of consumer accountability is more limited than that played by OFTEL. In effect, OFGAS becomes involved in the procedure for redressing grievances only as a last resort. Consumers who have grievances concerning gas supply service have to pursue these matters with the relevant British Gas regional office in the first instance, and, if this does not result in satisfactory redress, the next step is to seek help from the regional office of the Gas Consumers' Council. This body has a duty to investigate complaints, and resolve problems wherever possible. Only if these methods fail will the facts of a case be passed on to OFGAS for further investigation, and, if necessary, enforcement of the decision.

When discussing the development of OFTEL, we noted the change in emphasis which came in the wake of the first Director General's departure. This was even more marked in the case of OFGAS. The tenure of Sir James McKinnon was characterised by a series of running battles between the regulator and the utility. Widely perceived at the outset as a weak regulatory agency, OFGAS lacked the overtly consumerist role of OFTEL, and faced the task of regulating a large monopoly with apparent longevity. However, four years into his post, McKinnon would comment wryly on the changing perceptions of his agency: "In 1986 OFGAS was written off as being 'a toothless watchdog', whereas today we are beginning to be portrayed as savage, dangerous and out of control." (Office of Gas Supply, 1991: 1).

Under McKinnon, OFGAS used its statutory powers to push British Gas into cutting its prices for tariff customers by 20% in real terms during the first five years following privatization (Lorenz, 1993). However, while this reduction was taking place, OFGAS continued to attack various aspects of British Gas management and operations. OFGAS claimed that British Gas had utilized an uneconomic pricing policy to produce a demand for gas for electricity generation, that the company had attempted to recoup price cuts from tariff customers through sharp increases in service charges, and that capital investment had secretly been cut by 10% (Bannister, 1993).

The relationship between OFGAS and British Gas reached its nadir in 1993, when, in reporting upon a year when he had referred British Gas to the Monopolies and Mergers Commission, McKinnon noted that customer complaints reaching OFGAS had almost doubled to 1,624. He speculated that complaints made directly to the company itself may have numbered 100,000. In this context, the regulator accused British Gas of "wriggling", "squirming" and "intransigence", and attacked the "monopoly management culture" of the utility (Office of Gas Supply, 1993). Shortly afterwards, McKinnon openly called for British Gas to be broken up into 17 components (Lorenz, 1993).

Having previously called for McKinnon to be replaced by a committee (Hamilton, 1992), Cedric Brown, the chief executive of British Gas was openly relieved when McKinnon's period in office came to an end. Brown claimed that Clare Spottiswoode, the new Director General of OFGAS, achieved more in her first eight days than her predecessor had in eight years (Hencke, 1994). Where McKinnon had been determined to assert the total independence of OFGAS at every opportunity and avoid "agency-capture" at all costs, the new Director General appeared to be seeking a *modus vivendi* with the utility. The contrast in Spottiswoode's approach was marked, to the point where serious questions began to emerge about OFGAS's capacity to act as a full-blooded regulator.

Spottiswoode's appointment was controversial. Her name was not on the original shortlist recommended by a headhunting agency, but was apparently added to the list by a senior civil servant at the DTI (Hencke, 1994). Her initiatives attracted further controversy. She expressed a desire to employ Ian Greer Associates on behalf of OFGAS, despite the fact that this company already acted as lobbyists for British Gas (Hencke, 1994a). She appeared to be openly hostile to an energy conservation project within the terms of which OFGAS can levy money on gas bills (Prescott, Bethell and Driscoll, 1994), and curbed an annual subsidy of £125 million which was designed to help cut gas bills for pensioners and disabled people (Hencke, 1994b).

Eschewing the broad-ranging, interventionist approach of her predecessor, Spottiswoode declared that the management of British Gas was not her direct concern, and, in this context, she rejected suggestions that she should act to limit the pay rises of senior executives. Instead, she played down the significance of Cedric Brown's 70% pay rise (Harper,

1995). This came only weeks before she launched her own bid for a substantial increase in salary (Hencke, 1995).

Sir James McKinnon and Clare Spottiswoode operated within the same legal framework. The differing emphasis and approach of these two Directors General demonstrate the importance of personality and individual preferences in the sphere of regulatory agencies. That one agency can change, virtually overnight, from being the consumerist scourge of the utility to a utility-friendly body, illustrates the distinct element of volatility within this regime of accountability.

ELECTRICITY

The Office of Electricity Regulation, OFFER, shares the basic constitutional feature of OFTEL and OFGAS in the sense that it is a non-ministerial government department. With headquarters in Birmingham, OFFER has over 200 staff, based in 14 offices throughout Great Britain, corresponding with the regional boundaries of the electricity supply companies. One Director General of Electricity Supply, Professor Stephen Littlechild, has been in post since OFFER became operational in 1990. The 1989 Electricity Act conferred upon OFFER powers to:

- grant licences to those who wish to supply, transmit or generate electricity;
- fix and publish maximum resale prices for electricity;
- monitor and enforce the price control formulae;
- monitor electricity suppliers' performance against Codes of Practice and Standards of Performance;
- settle the terms on which suppliers have access to the transmission and distribution systems operated by licensees;
- protect customers in respect of the price, quality and continuity of the supply of electricity;
- help consumers with complaints against their electricity supplier.

Consumers complaints and issues of concern are handled, in the first instance, by the Electricity Consumers' Committees, which are regionally based. These bodies are appointed by the Director General, and are given secretarial, legal and administrative support by OFFER. The regulatory agency will pursue with the relevant electricity supply company any Consumers' Committees recommendations on compensation or the resolution of complaints which are not accepted or properly implemented.

It could be argued that Stephen Littlechild attempted to be true to his ideal of a regulator whose fundamental role was to "hold the ring" until the true protector of consumer interests, full-blooded competition, arrived in the fullness of time. One of his problems was that competition, as conventionally understood, was going to take a considerable time before arriving in the electricity supply industry. Perhaps as a consequence of this, Littlechild's ability to "hold the ring" came under increasing pressure, and he came to be seen as "a watchdog on Valium" (*The Guardian*, 1995).

Judged by the basic standard of accountability Littlechild established for himself, and all of the regulatory agencies (the determination and enforcement of the RPI-X formula) OFFER suffered an embarrassing setback following its major price review in 1994. After making semi-public hints to the effect that he was about to insist on substantial price cuts and impose a very tight price-cap mechanism for the next five years, Littlechild announced one-off cuts on the electricity supply companies averaging 14%, and a new price-cap of RPI-2 (Beavis, 1994; Beavis and Bannister, 1994). On the day these supposedly stringent controls were announced, the stock market fell by 1%, but the value of the 14 electricity supply companies rose by over £978 million. This seemed to vindicate the views expressed by consumer groups, that OFFER had put forward weak price controls and virtually guaranteed high prices and profits until the end of the century (Beavis and Bannister, 1994).

Proof of the accuracy of this analysis was forthcoming when, following representations from consumer groups and MPs, Littlechild was forced to announce a major review of the new price regime only six months after the 1994 review. While the existing controls would continue for a year, a further tightening of the price-cap, together with a more substantial rebate to customers, would be considered for the remainder of the five-year period. Share prices in the electricity supply companies dropped substantially on this news while the stock of National Power and PowerGen, issued only the day before, almost immediately fell below the issue price (Beavis, 1995). Littlechild's action subsequently resulted in a political row, with the Government being accused of insider trading, in the sense that ministers knew about Littlechild's pending price review but allowed the floatation of National Power and PowerGen to go ahead (Beavis, Confino, Springett and Atkinson, 1995).

This episode epitomised one of the contradictions of this regime of accountability. Regulators in the role of Littlechild and OFFER are, in a sense, caught between the devil and the deep blue sea: their chances of enforcing a regulatory framework which will simultaneously please consumers and shareholders are fairly remote. If they successfully avoid "agency-capture" (the phenomenon detected in the United States, whereby agencies come to see their role primarily in terms of protecting, and even lobbying for, the interests on the regulated industry or utility) they run the risk of being criticised for excessive interventionism and damaging the interests of shareholders.

WATER

In the sphere of the water utility we find the most fragmented regime of accountability. The fragmentation is apparent in both functional and geographical terms.

As we have already noted, geographical differences occur due to the fact that the water utility in Scotland was not privatized, and remains subject to a conventional (albeit changing) public sector regime of accountability. From April 1996, the three new water and sewerage authorities covering the east, west and north of Scotland will be accountable to the Secretary of State for Scotland. The interests of customers and consumers will be represented through a Scottish Water and Sewerage Customers' Council (like the authorities, this will be appointed by the Secretary of State), which will have some power to approve the pricing schemes of the new authorities. However, pricing disputes between the Customers' Council and the authorities will be referred to the Secretary of State for resolution. The numerous small environmental regulators, the River Purification Boards, will become part of a new Scottish Environment Protection Agency.

In England and Wales, functional fragmentation is evidenced by the existence of three separate regulatory bodies; the Office of Water Services (OFWAT), the National Rivers Authority (NRA) and the Drinking Water Inspectorate. Matters are further complicated by the fact the NRA will cease to exist in April 1996, when, along with Her Majesty's Inspectorate of Pollution and the waste regulation authorities, it will become part of a new Environment Agency. Our main concern here is OFWAT, although brief comments should be made about the remit of the other regulatory agencies.

The National Rivers Authority is a quality regulator, with responsibility for "controlled waters", such as rivers, lakes, reservoirs, canals and coastal waters. It is charged with the responsibility of keeping these waters up to prescribed standards, and regulates discharges into them. The NRA can be contacted directly by individuals who have concerns about aspects of the management of controlled waters.

The Drinking Water Inspectorate is also a quality regulator, with authority to investigate complaints about the standard of tap water. Individual complainants are required to approach the relevant water company in the first instance, then, if the problem is not resolved, the local OFWAT Customer Service Committee (CSC) may be asked to look into the matter. If necessary, the CSC will refer the case to the Drinking Water Inspectorate.

Important though the functions of these bodies may be, their powers are distinctly limited, and the major role in the regulation of the water utility falls to OFWAT. Established under the terms of the 1989 Water Act, this non-ministerial government department, based in Birmingham, is headed by a Director General, Ian Byatt, and has a broad remit to:

- monitor the discharge of licence responsibilities by the water companies, giving regard to the need for the companies to finance their functions by securing a reasonable rate of return on their capital;
- set and review the price-cap formulae;
- monitor the performances of the water companies to ensure that they are meeting performance targets and adhering to standards of service;
- ensure that the companies' plans for the maintenance of water mains and sewers are adequate;
- ensure that each company publishes Codes of Practice informing customers about their rights and about company policy in relation to leakages and disconnections;
- establish and coordinate the activities of ten Customer Service Committees, which are charged with the tasks of investigating complaints and advising the Director General on matters of importance to customers.

OFWAT has been, arguably, the most criticised of the regulatory agencies operating in the sphere of the former public utilities. The criticisms would seem to have stemmed from a combination of factors, including the nature of the utility itself and the approach taken by Ian Byatt.

Water and sewerage was privatized in England and Wales on the basis of regional monopolies, and competition was never likely to feature prominently in this sphere. The new water companies faced the task of upgrading the utility's infrastructure while meeting increasingly high UK and EU environmental standards. It was inevitable that prices would rise considerably. Perhaps less predictable were the huge profits secured by the companies and the generous salary increases taken by directors. Against this backdrop, Byatt and OFWAT came to appear increasingly beleaguered during the first five years following privatization.

In the period between privatization in 1989 and the first review of the price controls in 1994, water bills for customers in England and Wales increased by an average of 74%. In the same period, the profit secured by each of the ten water companies increased by 20% a year, share prices rose by between 85% and 135%, while the total share options held by their directors rose to over £13.5 million and the average annual salary earned by their chief executives increased to £206,000 (Vidal, 1994). It appeared to many observers that the major financial burden of capital investment and rising environmental standards was falling on the customers, while the companies were concentrating on reaping the rewards.

To make matters worse, in the early period following privatization, the number of disconnections for non-payment of bills reached record levels: almost 22,000 in 1991–92 alone (Horsnell, 1992). OFWAT received remarkably high numbers of complaints about charges and billing. For example, in 1991, there was a 130% increase in complaints, to 10,635. Of these, 15% were eventually resolved by rebates and compensation, with a total of £841,000 being paid out by the water companies (Office of Water Services, 1992). This represented some measure of success for the regulator, but it is important to retain a sense of perspective. The water companies were not obliged to provide compensation, and there were numerous instances of this being refused. For example, in 1991 Southern Water rejected OFWAT's recommendation that 40 of its customers should be granted a total of £10,000 because of the company's failure to deal efficiently with a leak of sewage into their properties (Millar, 1992).

The image of a regulator whose prime concern seemed to be for the financial well-being of the companies he was regulating, was confirmed by a number of controversial stances Byatt adopted. He staunchly advocated water metering (much favoured by the water companies), in the face of consumer opposition, while opposing some environmental controls emanating from the EU (particularly the 1994 Waste Water Directive) despite criticism from his fellow-regulator, the Chief Inspector of the National Rivers Authority (Vidal, 1994). In 1994, Byatt refused to renew the contract of the Chairwoman of the Yorkshire Customer Service Committee, after she had developed a reputation for being prepared to vigorously criticise both Yorkshire Water and OFWAT (Wainwright, 1994).

The 1994 review of the price-cap mechanism gave Byatt and OFWAT a chance to shift the balance within the water utility back in the direction of the consumers. The new formula would allow the prices levied by the companies to rise on average by RPI+1 over a ten-year period, although there would be some variation across the regions, with, for example, Southern Water applying RPI+3.5 and Severn Trent RPI+0.2 (Lorenz and Waples). The general effect seemed to be that the companies would now have to bear a larger share of the cost of capital investment and environmental improvements. In the face of criticisms to the effect that even more could have been done to get prices down, Byatt argued that he had successfully struck a balance between the need to reduce bills, facilitate improvements in the environment and allow the companies to secure the financial resources they require (Byatt, 1994: 91)

OFWAT and the water companies came under further criticism in the summer of 1995. The juxtaposition of record profits and poor capital investment with cuts to customers' water supply led to sustained attacks upon this regime of accountability.

Having examined the broad remits and records of the utility regulators, let us now conclude the chapter with a survey of the main issues and debates surrounding the question of accountability in this sphere.

Issues and Debates

In the United States of America, where regulatory agencies have long featured prominently in the systems of public administration, there is a well-developed academic literature on the subject. The advent of the utility regulators has sparked off increasing interest amongst academics and informed commentators in Britain, to the point where an embryonic literature is emerging. Within this, some themes are particularly relevant in the context of our area of interest – accountability.

ACCOUNTABILITY ENHANCED?

Arguably the most fundamental question of all is rarely touched upon by the contributors to this literature. While the pros and cons of the regulatory agencies are pored over in considerable detail, few writers are prepared to offer a comparative analysis of the pre- and post-privatization regimes of accountability.

The contents of this chapter offer something of a guide here. Our basic conclusion would be that, flawed though they may be in many respects, these regulatory agencies represent an improvement upon the old system. This has perhaps been one of the unintended consequences of privatization, and one which dismays the free-marketeers, who placed their faith on competition *per se*, rather than regulators. However, the existence of dedicated agencies in the sphere of each utility where before there was at best a single House of Commons select committee and sporadic Parliamentary debates, marks a definite improvement in structural terms at least. The fact that the locus of accountability has shifted away from Parliament has to be placed in the balance against the relative failure of the system of accountability which applied to the nationalized industries. The variable records of the regulators, to which we shall return shortly, should not detract from this fact. Furthermore, although serious problems still exist in respect of accountability, we do well to note the comments of Tony Prosser:

> ... the creation of the regulators has resulted in considerably greater openness than was the case under nationalisation, through imposing a form of external supervision which ... did not exist previously ... individual regulators have been, by the standards of British public bodies, exceptionally open in reaching some of their decisions.
> (Prosser, 1994: 255)

`` WORKING AS ENVISAGED´´?

In allocating credit, however, we must not become complacent. It is difficult to share the view of the effective creator of the British utilities' regulatory regime, Professor Stephen Littlechild, that "regulation is working as envisaged" (Beavis and Weston, 1993). As he originally envisaged it, regulation was to be a temporary phenomenon, which would "hold the fort" until competition arrived. Leaving aside the issue of whether or not competition itself would be a sufficient guarantor of accountability (a sweeping assumption which Littlechild and free-marketeers stretching back to Friedrich Hayek and beyond have been prepared to make), it has to be pointed out that the competition cavalry had not even saddled up, let alone reached the besieged fort in most of the utilities.

In another respect, Littlechild's claim that his regulatory regime was functioning according to plan simply does not ring true. It will be recalled that he disavowed the US style of regulation, which is based on limiting rates of return, in favour of price-capping. In practice, however, some of the British regulators (for example, OFTEL and OFWAT) have tightened the price-cap formulae partly in response to concerns about excessive dividends (Prosser, 1994: 253–54). While this differs from the

US system in the sense that the basic principle in Britain is not the limitation of profits, the indirect effect may be similar.

DOES THE FRAMEWORK NEED TO BE STRENGTHENED, OR WEAKENED?

There are two broad critical analyses of the regime of accountability which has emerged through the work of the utility regulators. The first holds that the existing system is weak in several respects, while the second holds that the regulators are too powerful. Let us examine these arguments in turn.

While prepared to give the regulators a certain amount of credit, a range of analysts, commentators and consumer activists (see, for example, Ayres and Braithwaite, 1994; Hutton, 1994; Institute for Public Policy Research, 1994; National Consumer Council, 1993; Prosser, 1994) have argued that the existing system falls short of guaranteeing an acceptable degree of accountability to the public, broadly defined. Even the additional powers to set guaranteed service standards and secure redress of grievances, which were given to the regulatory agencies under the terms of the 1992 Competition and Service (Utilities) Act, are insufficient for these critics. The fundamental problem which they perceive is the looseness of the regulatory environment.

A number of key variables play a part in determining the style and effectiveness of each agency. Some of these variables are "external" in the sense that the agencies themselves can do little or nothing to influence matters such as the powers they have been allocated, the type of person who is appointed as director general, the scale of the utility which is to be regulated, the prevailing style of the board of directors of the utility, and the extent to which it may be possible to introduce competition in the utility's sphere of operation. Other variables are "internal" in the sense that they are more or less under the control of the agencies themselves. These variables include the quality, expertise and deployment of staff, and the relative importance attached by the director general to the agency's responsibilities. Together with what Prosser (1994: 259) has described as "the lack of a coherent regulatory philosophy", critics argue that the interplay of these variables has contributed to a slack regulatory environment.

Prosser also comments specifically upon one of the variables, which we have already commented upon in this chapter: the importance of individuals in the regulatory regime. In particular, the manner in which a new Director General with a different outlook from his or her predecessor can bring about a basic change in the approach of a regulatory agency has been a striking feature of the framework. We noted this phenomenon in relation to the Carsberg and Cruikshank regimes at OFTEL and, most significantly, the McKinnon and Spottiswoode regimes at OFGAS.

The way forward identified by these critics, in their different fashions, is to redesign the British regulatory agencies, perhaps along American lines. Ayres and Braithwaite (1994) argue the case for a system of tough "republican regulation" predicated on accountability to the public interest in the first instance. Prosser (1994) appeals for a move away from the "highly pragmatic approach" which has developed in Britain, towards a system of regulation which exhibits "a greater concern with procedural and substantive principle". In particular, he cites the US Administrative Procedure Act as an example of the kind of procedural code for regulators which he would like to see established in Britain (Prosser, 1994: 255).

One problem with this approach, alluded to by Prosser himself, is that the regulatory agencies have developed in what might be described as a fashion typical to the British constitution. The emphasis on personalised systems of accountability, typified in another context by the doctrine of individual ministerial responsibility, rather than highly developed concepts of the state and administrative law, tends to produce empirical, pragmatic and evolutionary approaches to problems. In seeking to wrench the regulatory agencies from this *milieu*, and set them down within a highly codified, theoretically rigorous (apparently, at least!) constitutional environment, the would-be reformers perhaps ask for too much. It might also be argued that they minimise the disadvantages inherent in the highly formalised, legalistic, and inflexible US system of regulation.

The second broad critique of the regulators is based on the argument that the agencies need to be restrained. Senior figures from the utilities, shareholders, City institutions and free-market economists argue that the balance struck in the current system leaves the fate of boards and shareholders in the hands of unpredictable Directors General. The Chairman of BT once likened the regulators to boys at Christmas time, whose instinct on Boxing Day was to take their new toys to pieces (Beavis and Weston, 1993). The inconsistencies of the regulatory regime are a theme in this critique too: procedures and practices may vary from one regulatory agency to another, and even between successive Directors General of the same agency. The result has been that utility shares can be subject to sharp vacillations, and an atmosphere of uncertainty surrounds almost any impending statement from a Director General.

Various proposals have been put forward by this camp, with the intention of minimising the disruption caused by the regulators. The Chairman of National Power, John Baker, suggest the establishment of a "college of regulators" which would allow for the development of common standards and consistent practices (Brummer, 1994). A more radical solution has been proposed by Cento Veljanovski. In a report for the European Policy Forum, he argued for limitations to be placed on the power of regulators to amend the licence conditions of the utility companies, and for the MMC to be given the major role in this sphere. He went on to propose a series of mergers which would reduce the number of regulatory agencies (OFGAS and OFFER being amalgamated into a single energy regulator, for example). Finally, Veljanovski favoured curtailing the autonomy of the regulatory agencies by making them subject to monitoring and review by the National Audit Office (he apparently missed the point that they are already subject to NAO review by virtue of their status as non-ministerial government departments) and a new House of Commons select committee (Veljanovski, 1993).

This concern about the accountability of the regulators themselves is shared, for different reasons, by those who favour strengthening and those who wish to weaken, the regulatory regime.

QUIS CUSTODET IPSOS CUSTODES?
It is somehow appropriate that we should end this chapter by turning the question of accountability around, and briefly examining the position of the regulatory agencies themselves in this respect.

Criticism of the apparently unaccountable nature of the utility regulators can be seen in the writings of some of those who wish to see the system toughened up (see, for example, Brummer, 1994; Hain, 1995; and Prosser, 1994) as well as those who favour a loosening of the regulatory reins (see, for example, Veljanovski, 1993). Thus, Brummer (1994) argues that a utility regulator exerts substantial power over the daily lives of most citizens, safe in the understanding that he is effectively "the Tsar of the system". Prosser takes a similar line:

> The regulators are not elected nor are they subject to even that most attenuated form of accountability, ministerial responsibility to Parliament. They therefore lack democratic legitimacy.
> (Prosser, 1994: 254)

In fact, under closer examination it becomes clear that the position is not quite as stark as it at first appears. There are several layers of accountability which apply to the regulators.

The relevant secretaries of state appoint the Directors General of OFTEL, OFGAS, OFFER and OFWAT, normally for periods of up to five years, which may be renewable. Directors General may be removed from office by the minister on grounds of incapacity or misbehaviour. The primary line of accountability therefore runs in the direction of Whitehall. Ministers are not required to report these appointments to Parliament (Garner, 1990: 331), and, in this sense at least, Prosser's argument about ministerial responsibility has some validity.

Nonetheless, there are three strains of Parliamentary accountability above and beyond that which links Directors General to ministers. Contrary to the assertion of Veljanovski (1993), the National Audit Office already conducts annual reviews of the regulatory agencies' accounts: in this sense, there is clear financial accountability to Parliament. The agencies are subject to investigation by the Parliamentary Commissioner for Administration on the same basis as conventional government departments and executive agencies (see Chapter 2). Finally, the regulators may be subject to investigation by House of Commons select committees, as Clare Spottiswoode discovered to her great discomfort in the spring of 1994, when she was called before both the Employment and the Environment committees. Beyond these mechanisms, Directors General can have their decisions subjected to judicial review.

Therefore, while there may not be a single body, such as a National Regulatory Office, with sole responsibility for enforcing the accountability of the regulatory agencies, it is wrong to suggest that they are totally "unaccountable". The forms of accountability which apply may be flawed and inadequate in some respects, but that is another story!

References

Ayres, Ian, and Braithwaite, John (1994), *Responsive Regulation*, Oxford: Oxford University Press.

Bannister, Nicholas (1993), "Regulator in New Row With British Gas Over Secret Cut in Investment", *The Guardian*, 26 January.

Bannister, Nicholas (1993a), "BT in Power Struggle With New Oftel Boss", *The Guardian*, 9 June.

Bannister, Nicholas (1994), "Oftel Suggests Loosening Reins", *The Guardian*, 8 December.

Beavis, Simon and Weston, Celia (1993), "Tories Hold Gas Prices Timebomb", *The Guardian*, 18 August.

Beavis, Simon (1994), "Electricity Charges to be Slashed", *The Guardian*, 11 August.

Beavis, Simon (1995), "Price Cuts to Follow Electricity Review", *The Guardian*, 25 March.

Beavis, Simon and Bannister Nicholas (1994), "Power Shares Soar on 'Weak' Price Controls", *The Guardian*, 12 August.

Beavis, Simon, Confino, Jonathan, Springett, Pauline and Atkinson, Michael (1995), "Insider Deal Inquiry into Power Sale", *The Guardian*, 9 June.

Beavis, Simon and Weston, Celia (1993), "Regulators Paper Over Policy Cracks", *The Guardian*, 24 April.

Brummer, Alex (1994), "Minding Whose Business?", *The Guardian*, 26 May.

Byatt, Ian (1994), "A New Financial Climate for Customers", *Parliamentary Brief*, Volume 3, Number 1.

Coombes, David (1966), *The Member of Parliament and the Administration. The Case of the Select Committee on Nationalised Industries*, London: Allen and Unwin.

Garner, J. F. (1990), "After Privatisation: Quis Custodet Ipsos Custodes?", *Public Law*, Autumn.

Gray, Clive (1982), "Regional Water Authorities", in Hogwood, Brian and Keating, Michael, *Regional Government in England*, Oxford: Clarendon.

Greenwood, John and Wilson, David (1989), *Public Administration in Britain Today*, London: Unwin Hyman 2nd Edition.

The Guardian (1992), "BT and the Busy Life of Sir Bryan", 10 June.

The Guardian (1995), "Crossed Wires", 9 March.

Hain, Peter (1995), *Regulating for the Common Good*, London: GMB.

Hamilton, Kirstie (1992), "Gas Demands New Regulator", *The Sunday Times*, 20 December.

Harper, Keith (1995), "Watchdog Refuses to Bite Gasman", *The Guardian*, 26 April.

Hencke, David (1994), "Pressure Mounts on 'Laughing Regulator' ", *The Guardian*, 24 May.

Hencke, David (1994a), "MPs Call For Spottiswoode's Suspension", *The Guardian*, 25 May.

Hencke, David (1994b), "MPs Put Ofgas Chief On Defensive", *The Guardian*, 26 May.

Hencke, David (1995), "Ofgas Chief Seeks 65pc Pay Rise", *The Guardian*, 31 May.

Horsnell, Michael (1992), "Water Companies Cut Off 22,000 For Non-Payment", *The Observer*, 5 June.

Hutton, Will (1994), "Inconsistent Regulators Allow Utilities to Run Out of Control", *The Guardian*, 12 December.

Institute for Public Policy Research (1994), *Regulating Our Utilities*, London: IPPR.

Jackson, Peter M. and Price, Catherine (1994), "Privatisation and Regulation: A Review of the Issues", in Jackson, Peter M. and Price, Catherine M. (eds), *Privatisation and Regulation: A Review of the Issues*, Burnt Mill: Longman.

Johnson, Nevil (1981), "Select Committees as Tools of Parliamentary Reform: Some Further Reflections" in Walkland, S.A. and Ryle, Michael, *The Commons Today*, Glasgow: Fontana.

Keating, Michael (1985), "Whatever Happened To Regional Government?", *Local Government Studies*, Volume 2, Number 6.

Liaison Committee (1983), 1st Report, HC 92 1982–83.

Lorenz, Andrew (1993), "Gas Feud Flares Up Into Final Showdown", *The Sunday Times*, 7 March.

Lorenz, Andrew, and Waples, John (1994), "Watershed", *The Sunday Times*, 31 July.

Maloney, William A., and Richardson, Jeremy J. (1992), "Post-Privatisation Regulation in Britain", *Politics*, Volume 12, Number 2.

Monopolies and Mergers Commission (1993), *Gas*, Cmnd 2314.

Millar, Robert (1992), "Byatt Faces Trial By Water", *The Observer*, 14 June.

National Consumer Council (1993), *Paying the Price: A Consumer View of Water, Gas and Telephone Regulation*, London: NCC.

Office of Electricity Regulation (1991), *Annual Report 1990*, Birmingham: OFFER.

Office of Gas Supply (1990), *OFGAS, Protecting the Rights of the Consumer*, London: OFGAS.

Office of Gas Supply (1991), *Annual Report 1990*, London: OFGAS.

Office of Gas Supply (1993), *Annual Report 1992*, London: OFGAS.

Office of Telecommunications (1994), *A Guide to the Office Of Telecommunications*, London: OFTEL.

Office of Telecommunications (1994a), *Framework for Effective Competition*, London: OFTEL.

Office of Water Services (1992), *Annual Report 1991*, Birmingham: OFWAT.

Prescott, Michael, Bethell, James and Driscoll, Margarette (1994), "Watchdog Who Got Bitten", *The Sunday Times*, 29 May.

Price, Catherine (1994), "Economic Regulation of Privatised Monopolies", in Jackson, Peter M. and Price, Catherine M. (eds), *Privatisation and Regulation: A Review of the Issues*, Burnt Mill: Longman.

Prosser, Tony (1994), "Regulation, Markets and Legitimacy", in Jowell, Jeffrey and Oliver, Dawn, *The Changing Constitution*, Oxford: Clarendon 2nd Edition.

Tivey, Leonard (ed) (1973), *The Nationalised Industries Since 1960. A Book of Readings*, London: Allen and Unwin.

Transport Committee (1980), 3rd Report: "The Form of Nationalised Industries' Reports and Accounts", HC 390 1980–81.

Treasury and Civil Service Committee (1981), 8th Report: "Financing of the Nationalised Industries", HC 348 1980–81.

Vass, Peter (1993), "Regulated Public Service Industries", in Terry, Francis and Jackson, Peter, *Public Domain 1992. The Public Services Yearbook*, London: Chapman and Hall.

Vass, Peter (1994), "Regulated Public Service Industries" in Jackson, Peter and Lavender, Michaela, *The Public Services Yearbook 1994*, London: Chapman and Hall.

Vidal, John (1994), "A Twist of the Tap", *The Guardian*, 28 July.

Veljanovski, Cento (1991), "The Regulation Game", in Veljanovski, Cento (ed), *Regulators and the Market*, London: Institute of Economic Affairs.

Veljanovski, Cento (1993), *The Future for Industry Regulation in the UK*, London: European Policy Forum.

Wainwright, Martin (1994), "Water Watchdog Sinks Chairwoman", *The Guardian*, 17 March.

6

CHARTERISM AND CONSUMERISM

Peter Falconer

Introduction
Since the early 1980s, public administration in Britain has revolved around an emerging public management ethos which locates the quest for quality, efficiency and value for money in public service delivery squarely in the realm of management practice within the public sector. A central feature of this shift in emphasis toward public sector management has been an apparent shift in power from those responsible for providing public services to those who "consume" these services. Public sector reforms introduced by successive Conservative governments since 1979 have been founded upon the ideological desire to subject the public sector to the disciplines and rigours of the private sector, introducing competitive business practices and market forces wherever possible into public service delivery.

A key element of this market-oriented reform effort has been the inculcation of a consumerist ethos into the public sector. The term "consumer" has come to pervade the language of the public sector in recent years. This definition of users and recipients of public services as consumers is an attempt to "connect public sector practices and ethos with those of the private sector" (Isaac-Henry et al, 1993: 9). It stresses the importance of members of the public coming to be treated as, and to view themselves as, customers with rights and expectations within the public sector marketplace similar to those they enjoy in their relation with the private sector. Moreover, the treatment of public service recipients as consumers implies a more direct form of accountability within the public sector, with the establishment of a clear link between the provider of a service and the expectations of its customers.

The policy embodiment of consumerism within public sector reform has been the Citizen's Charter (Prime Minister, 1991) which establishes the parameters of rights and standards for the relationship between providers and consumers in the public sector. In its aims and principles, members of the public are advised of what they are entitled to expect of public services and how they might seek redress should their experience of public services fall below these expectations. This chapter considers the consumerist ethos as it has developed in the public sector since the early 1980s, its encapsulation within the Citizen's Charter and its implications for accountability in public service delivery.

The Rise of Consumerism in the Public Sector

Since 1979, all parts of the public sector in Britain have been subjected to significant change. This change has been the product of an ideologically-driven reform agenda for the public sector implemented by post-1979 Conservative administrations. The fundamental principles underpinning this agenda, simply stated, were that the market is the most efficient mechanism for the allocation of resources in society; that the post-1945 collectivist ethos in welfare provision should be replaced by an individualist ethos; and that the public sector should be more directly accountable to the public it serves (Isaac-Henry *et al*, 1993). Founded on these principles, beginning in the early 1980s, a series of sweeping reforms have been introduced in the public sector through a variety of distinct yet interconnected reform mechanisms.

The "shift to consumerism" lies at the heart of the public sector reform effort and is inextricably linked to the wider reform agenda. As such, a review of these wider reform themes is useful in order to place consumerism within its broader context. These themes can be summarized under the following headings: the separation of purchasers and providers in the public sector; the growth of "contractualism" in public service delivery; accountability for performance; the establishment of market or quasi-market relationships; and the separation of political processes from managerial processes (Stewart and Walsh, 1992).

THE SEPARATION OF PURCHASERS AND PROVIDERS

Across the public sector, a separation has been instituted between the role of deciding what to provide and the role of actually providing it. This distinction is an essential precondition for the establishment of market relationships in the public sector. In its application, the language of purchaser-provider separation differs from institution to institution within the public sector and local government. For example,

the framework document for Next Steps agencies constitutes a contract

for performance by the agencies, establishing a principal-agent relationships with ministers; the purchaser-provider split in the National Health
service and in community care, and the client-contractor divide in local
authorities, create trading relationships.
(Stewart and Walsh, 1992: 504).

In the case of the National Health Service, for example, the purchaser-
provider split is crucial to the possibility of an internal market. It is from
this distinction that "much else in the new National Health Service flows"
(Holliday, 1992: 48). Within the health service, we can identify three
types of purchaser and provider. Purchasers consist of district health
authorities, GP fundholders and private patients, while providers are
directly managed units (those hospitals still under the auspices of district
health authorities), NHS Trusts and private hospitals or clinics. Linking
these two sets of actors is a system of contracts. On both sides, under the
internal market, the consumer is to benefit, since funding "follows the
patient" in accordance with purchasing decisions made on the patient's
behalf. Since the establishment of the internal market in health care in
1991, however, the separation of purchasers and providers has been less
clear than it is eventually desired to be. This has been due to the
anomalous status of district health authorities, in that they have been
responsible for both purchasing and providing health care. As purchasers, they have operated on behalf of those GP practices which have not
taken the opportunity to move to fundholding status, while as providers
they are managerially responsible for those hospitals which have not yet
acquired trust status. This anomaly, it is hoped by reformers, is
temporary, given the assumption that more and more GPs and hospitals
will opt out of health authority control and assume positions as
independent units within the internal market in healthcare delivery
(Holliday, 1992: 53).

THE GROWTH OF CONTRACTUALISM

The establishment of purchaser-provider splits has promoted a movement toward contracts as the basis for public service delivery. Through
contracts, public sector managers or local authorities act as agents for the
definitive client, namely the public. As an important element in the desire
of the Thatcher Government in the early 1980s to reduce the level of
public expenditure, the decision was taken to first encourage then compel
public sector bodies to open many of their services to competitive
tendering. Moreover, the introduction of contracts in public service

delivery was consistent with a second objective of the Conservative Government, namely to separate the process of service provision from politics (Mather, 1989; Walsh, 1995: 112).

The Code of Practice for Compulsory Competition in local government was first published in 1981, following the passage of the Local Government Planning and Land Act of 1980. A number of amendments were made to the code in subsequent years, culminating in the extension of compulsory competition under the terms of the Local Government Act of 1988. Under this Act, local authorities were required to put out to tender contracts in relation to the following services: refuse collection, catering, ground maintenance, internal cleaning of buildings, street cleaning and vehicle repair and maintenance.

According to a 1993 report, prepared for the Department of the Environment by Kieron Walsh and Howard Davis, on the impact of the 1988 Act (Walsh and Davis, 1993), the introduction of compulsory competition in local government had a number of important implications for service provision. First among its main effects was the way in which competition provided an impetus for service review, in the sense that local authorities were now more concerned with monitoring the management of services. According to one local government officer, competition "sharpens people up and shakes old practices out of the system. People had to take a long hard look at what they do" (Walsh and Davis, 1993: 165). Second, competition facilitated an improvement in the level of knowledge within local authorities of the cost of service provision (Lawton and Rose, 1991: 145–6; Walsh and Davis, 1993: 165). Third, local authorities now have clearer statements of performance targets to be achieved. Indeed, these targets have become something of a "justification and a rationale for action" within local authorities (Walsh and Davis, 1993: 165). Finally, the introduction of competition highlights the issue of accountability, both to elected members and the public:

> elected members were having to learn to operate new approaches, for example with more concern for strategic issues. Questions were raised about the appropriate form of local democracy in a competitive system, for example whether existing reporting systems are adapted to the new circumstances. The public had had little involvement in the process of compulsory competitive tendering in the early stages, for example in the definition of specifications.
> (Walsh and Davis, 1993: 166).

The Department of the Environment report did indicate that a number of local authorities were in the process of developing mechanisms for greater public participation, but that such initiatives were at a very early stage (Walsh and Davis, 1993: 167).

The scope of compulsory competitive tendering in local government was taken a step further with the Local Government Act of 1992. Under the terms of the 1992 Act, the Audit Commission was empowered to publish performance indicators for local authorities and to monitor performance in regard to these indicators. As such, local authorities were required for the first time to publish information on their performance. This requirement was specified by the Audit Commission in December 1992 as part of its role under the Act and as part of the Citizen's Charter initiative (Audit Commission, 1994). The main legal requirements were that the information must be:

- published between 1st April and 31st December 1994;
- placed in a newspaper or published by the local authority itself;
- accurate, as far as is practicable;
- published in a comprehensible form without reference to other material (Audit Commission, 1994: 7).

The first report of the Audit Commission on local government performance was published on 30th March 1995 (Audit Commission, 1995). Not surprisingly, the information provided by local authorities for 1993/94 demonstrated wide discrepancies in the standard of service delivery across local authorities. Andrew Foster, Controller of the Audit Commission responded thus:

> the idea of the all-competent, all-conquering council that runs everything efficiently is tosh. There is a substantial variation, and if some councils are breathtakingly bad, we don't have any that are even competent all round. (Murray, 1995).

The next Audit Commission report for 1994/95 is expected in 1996. On the possible impact of the Audit Commission's oversight role, Andrew Foster states, "it will, I think, bring great pressure to bear. If you are in the bottom two or three of some of the indicators this year, you do not want to be there next year" (Timmons, 1995).

In the National Health Service, compulsory competitive tendering was first introduced in September 1983. Under its terms, National Health Service units were compelled to put out to competitive tender specified ancillary services, such as portering, security, catering, the organization and maintenance of medical records and non-emergency ambulance services (National Audit Office, 1987; Milne, 1987). Overall, across the range of public services, compulsory competitive tendering has developed into an established approach to service provision (Walsh, 1994; 1995).

In terms of accountability, the increasing shift to service on the basis of contract has significant implications. Under contractualism, we have two sets of actors: the public sector body or local authority which puts the contract out to tender, and the contractor who physically provides the service. As such, the basis of their relationship is the contract. The public sector agency responsible for drawing up the contract is required to specify the standard of performance required in service delivery and thus becomes acutely aware of the true cost of service provision. As such, the process of accountability is sharpened. The contract becomes the focus and the increased concern with performance standards embodied within contracts makes public sector agencies and local authorities more directly concerned with efficiency in resource use and quality of service. Moreover, the contractor is responsible for delivering the service as specified in the contract and will be judged on that basis by the client, the public sector agency.

In addition to compulsory competitive tendering, a further manifestation of contractualism has emerged in the public sector which directly affects the nature of service provided to the public. This type of contract relationship is that within the National Health Service which holds together the internal market in health care. This is an important development in public sector reform in that it significantly expands the cultural shift toward a business-oriented approach in health care provision. Through the purchaser-provider split, one half of the new National Health Service receives funding for the services it provides, while the other is financed in order to purchase health care on behalf of patients. As such, the provider half of the service competes in the internal market for the "business" of the purchasing half. The basis of the relationship between purchasers and providers, as stated earlier, is the nature of contracts which determine the degree and type of health care provided to patients.

ACCOUNTABILITY FOR PERFORMANCE

Both the above reform themes represent an attempt to enhance the accountability of public sector institutions to the public they serve through a greater concern with performance measurement. Through the shift toward service on the basis of contract, public service providers are forced to engage directly with the question of service standard and service quality. This links directly to a central issue which lies at the heart of the consumerist ethos and the Citizen's Charter, namely the establishment of performance indicators and performance targets in the public sector.

Concern with the improvement of public services has focused on the pursuit of greater efficiency and effectiveness. Indeed, the quest for improvement in these areas has dominated government thinking toward public sector management since the early 1980s. However, while it is not difficult to subject private sector enterprises to performance measurement, a similar exercise in the public sector is more problematic. There are a number of reasons for this difficulty (Lawton and Rose, 1991: 151). First, many public sector organizations are monopoly suppliers of services. For example, there is only one Department of Social Security. Consequently, a member of the public dissatisfied with the quality of service received at his or her local benefits office cannot go elsewhere. In a competitive environment, the producer has a clear incentive to maintain a high level of performance in relation to the service provided to the customer. Monopolists lack that incentive. In order to counter this situation, as will be discussed, the Citizen's Charter embodies strong complaints mechanisms whereby the public sector consumer can claim redress should he or she be unhappy with the standard of service provided. Second, the public sector does not always provide a clearly identifiable product. What, for example, does a university produce? What is the "product" rendered by the prison service? Such ambiguities make performance measurement more difficult in the public sector. Third, the public sector often lacks a clearly identifiable customer. In the private sector, the customer is the individual to whom the provider wishes to sell his or her goods. In the public sector, however, the situation is not so straightforward. For example, a civil servant working in an executive agency established under the Next Steps programme could view several people as customers: the member of the public with whom he or she is dealing; the minister with responsibility for the service; Parliament which is elected by, and accountable to, the electorate and which approves the level of funding for agencies; or the taxpayer who might not use the service in question but who contributes through taxation.

These problems render the pursuit of efficiency and effectiveness in the public sector more difficult. Nevertheless, a great deal of effort has gone into subjecting the public sector to strict performance measurement. Indeed, this lies at the core of the Citizen's Charter which has enshrined within its pages a clear commitment to service quality on the part of the public sector; clear and agreed criteria of assessment for public service providers; increased visibility of people working in the public sector to provide a more tangible and accountable posture for the customers; a strong commitment to the public sector and to continued improvement in service provision; and a requirement that those delivering services be directly answerable to the public.

Through the establishment of performance targets within the Citizen's Charter, public sector managers are responsible for, and accountable to the public for, their particular agency's use of resources. For example, schools are individually responsible for the performance targets enshrined within the National Curriculum, while contractors in the National Health Service or local government are responsible for fulfilling the requirements of their contract. Moreover, the Citizen's Charter places a strong emphasis on the publication of standards which public service providers are expected to achieve:

> explicit standards (should be) prominently displayed at the point of delivery. These standards should invariably include courtesy and helpful-ness from staff, accuracy in accordance with statutory entitlements, and a commitment to prompt action which might be expressed in terms of a target response or waiting time. There should be a clear presumption that standards will be progressively improved as services become more efficient.
> (Citizen's Charter, 1991: 5).

THE ESTABLISHMENT OF MARKETS OR QUASI-MARKETS
"Traditionally, the public services have been monolithic organisations with overall management, finance control and budgetary control all held in the centre" (Major, 1989: 4). A key element of reform has been the replacement of this centralist organizational structure with a decentralist, market-oriented structure in which the different parts of the public sector are subjected to competitive forces. In this way, attempts were made to create multiple service providers in as many individual public services as possible, for example, through compulsory competitive tendering. Furthermore, as Stewart and Walsh (1992: 506) assert,

> in the government's proposals on community care, local authorities are to be encouraged to use many alternative sources of provision. In health and education, the emphasis is placed on the independence of the separate institutions through opting out, or on greater control over their own

management by the institutions through devolved control. The "monolithic" institutions of the health service and of the education service is being broken down into its component parts.

As such, the possibility arises for competition between alternative providers in the different sectors of public service. Of course, not all these markets which have been established are consumer-led. For example, in the National Health Service, markets are still largely dominated by healthcare providers, with health authorities, clinicians or general practitioners making choices on behalf of their patients. Even where the consumer does have a degree of choice, as in education where parents have some discretion over the choice of school for their children, we still have not moved to a fully market-oriented environment.

> Because there is no question of direct payment, and because of the limitation on the number of places available, what are being created are quasi-markets rather than markets. There is limited freedom on the demand side, with very little change as yet on the supply side. (Stewart and Walsh, 1992: 507).

A further element in the effort to subject the public sector to market forces has been the increased use of fees and charges for public services (Bailey, Falconer and McChlery, 1993; Walsh, 1995: 83–109). Across a wide range of public services, including health care, education and a wide range of local authority services, charges are used in different ways and for different purposes. Charges for prescription, dental and ophthalmic treatment in health care, for school meals, school trips and music lessons in schools, and for admittance to museums, recreational facilities and care for the elderly in local authorities; all these charges serve as signals of demand to service providers as to what consumers are willing to pay for a service. Charging is thus deemed to be fair in the sense that an individual who makes use of a particular service is paying directly for the benefit he or she receives. As such, charges serve not only as a way of introducing market mechanisms into the delivery of public services, but also as a means of reducing public expenditure since people are paying for a service which otherwise would require to be funded publicly (Bailey, Falconer and McChlery, 1993: 29).

THE SEPARATION OF POLITICAL AND MANAGERIAL PROCESSES

Traditionally, as we saw in Chapter 2, public service delivery was subject to political control exercised through departments of state, their ministers and thereby the government of the day and the elected House of

Commons. An important element of reform has been the attempt to separate the process of policy making from the operational management of the public services. For example, in the National Health Service, responsibility at the national level is exercised through both a Policy Board and a Management Executive. Basically, the role of government lies in setting the broad policy goals for the service, funding the service, and being accountable to Parliament for these policy decisions. Operationally, however, government has removed itself from the day-to-day management of the service, responsibility for which lies with the Management Executive.

We see a similar pattern emerging across the public services. As will be discussed later in this chapter in relation to the Citizen's Charter, this change has clear implications for the nature of accountability in the public sector, as more traditional forms of political accountability are being replaced with a more direct form of managerial accountability which forges a linear relationship between public service providers and the consumers of these services. Of course, this attempted shift from political to managerial accountability has not been accompanied by a commensurate alteration in constitutional convention governing the relationship between elected politicians and the citizenry (see Chapter 2). Consequently, while government ministers might wish to "pass the buck" on to public sector managers for the delivery and quality of public services, these same ministers cannot escape the fact that they are still constitutionally accountable for public services by virtue of their status as elected representatives of the people. Public service deliveries may indeed be directly responsible in managerial term to the public as consumers, but ministers remain equally accountable politically for that service to the public as citizens.

Having briefly outlined the character of the different elements of the public sector reform agenda, we can now move to the issue which underlies these themes, namely the concern with the status of the user of public services. In the attempt to foster an individualist, market-oriented culture in the delivery of public services, an important question considered by successive Conservative Governments since 1979 has been how to establish a consumerist ethos in which members of the public come to view themselves as customers in the public sector marketplace with similar rights and powers to those enjoyed in their relationship with the private sector. Efforts to subject public sector agencies to the competitive disciplines of market forces depend largely on the recipients of public services exercising their rights as consumers to hold public service providers directly accountable for their performance and maintenance of high standards in the provision of services. The policy embodiment of the shift to consumerism is the Citizen's Charter. However, before considering the Charter in detail, it is necessary to give some attention to the notion of consumerism in the public sector.

There is little doubt that the language of consumerism now dominates the public sector, from government policy documents, through public sector agency publications, to the academic literature on public sector management. Although the terms "consumer" and "customer" are often not defined and used interchangeably, their application has encouraged the growth of a more intense service ethos in the public sector.

However, when we consider the question of consumerism in regard to the public sector and the more specific issue of exactly who those consumers are, the picture is far more complicated. As part of their public sector reform agenda, the Thatcher and Major Governments have viewed the private sector experience as "the way forward" for the public sector. Consequently, a private sector conceptualization of the consumer was imported into the public sector. In this way, the public sector consumer is perceived in much the same way as a private sector consumer, active in the public sector marketplace, holding public service delivery agencies to the same sort of accountability for service to which private firms are subjected. In this way, the most important determinant of the nature of service provision is customer demand and customer satisfaction. However, viewing consumerism in this way, as a lever for the imposition of "consumer sovereignty" in public service delivery is to misread the private sector to some extent. In the private sector, it is often only the latest and most important customers who are held to be "sovereign" by private companies. Moreover, in the public sector, consumers are not sovereign and do not determine the nature of service which is provided by the public sector. Nor do they set the standards under which public sector bodies are assessed. Under the Citizen's Charter initiative, it is the public service delivery agencies themselves which set the standards of performance against which they are assessed, not the members of the public who use the service. In this way, there is often a shortfall between the level of service provided and that expected on the part of the public. In the National Health Service, for example, members of the public have been led to expect, as a product of reform, increased choice in healthcare delivery through the operation of the internal market. In reality, however, choice is limited due to the fact that health authorities are required to operate within budgetary constraints which necessitate the setting of priorities and a rationing of health care under which the scope for patient choice is limited (see Chapter 4).

Furthermore, whereas it is not a complex task to identify the consumer in the private sector, in the public sector he or she is less easy to distinguish. In the public sector, we can recognize a number of service "consumers", such as customers, clients, claimants, recipients, users and residents. Each of these categories entails very different connotations. For example, clients and claimants assume a dependency relationship with the public sector agencies whose services they "consume", whereas customers pay directly for services. Table 6.1 below provides a basic categorization of the relationship between the public and the public sector.

Table 6.1: *Consumer categorization and Management Responsiveness in the Public Sector*

Managerial Responsiveness	Consumer Categorization	Example	Managerial Rationale
Less responsive	Claimant/ Dependent	Prisoner	Rule based
		Long-term unemployed	Some discretion
	Client	Involuntary homeless	Entitled service
		Hospital patient	With discretion opportunity
	Consumer	Library user	Market orientation
More responsive		Leisure service user	

Source:
J. Harrow and M. Shaw, "The Manager Faces the Consumer", in L. Willcocks and J. Harrow eds., *Rediscovering Public Services Management*, McGraw Hill, 1992: 116.

The diagram emphasises the way in which different categorise of consumer in the public sector are viewed in terms of the nature of responsiveness on the part of public sector managers to their wishes. This, of course, has significant implications for public sector accountability, given that the rise of consumerism is tied up with an effort to make public service deliverers more accountable and more responsive to the demands of the public. Admittedly, the categorizations in Table 6.1 are of a general nature, but they raise the important question of whether public sector consumers are successful in having their demands met, or even acknowledged, by public sector agencies. As the table shows, where the nature of a service is delivered on the basis of set rules and procedures with little discretion in the way in which the service is provided, as in the case of social security, jobseekers' allowance or the prison service, public sector managers are under little pressure to "bow to the wishes" of consumers. However, where a service is more market-oriented and where consumer demand does have some impact, managers are required to be more responsive to consumer opinion.

A further element in the customer-public sector manager relationship concerns the nature of the service itself. In those services where members of the public are more positive about, and interested in, the level of attention received, such as education and health care, public service providers tend to be more "user friendly". Yet, even here, problems arise as to who the consumer actually is. For example, in education, is the consumer the parent or the pupil? In the prison service, is the consumer the prisoner, the general public who are kept safe through the incarceration of offenders, or the police and the criminal justice system which sends the guilty offender to jail? The nature of the service relationship is varied and complex. In the current example of the prison service, for example, the principal "users", to quote Flynn (1993,: 146) are "convicted people who are being held captive unwillingly. There is no value in treating them as if they have any choice about whether to use the service". The problem is that, in attempting to satisfy one group of consumers, the public sector agency might offend another. Again using the example of the prison service, the goal of punishing the criminal for his misdeeds is often viewed as detrimental to the role of the prison service in rehabilitating the prisoner (Flynn, 1993).

Nevertheless, despite these conceptual difficulties, the language of consumerism and its emphasis on customer service does have the merit of encouraging public service providers to consider more directly the quality of service offered to those who use and receive it. The principal policy mechanism through which this "encouragement" is enforced is the Citizen's Charter to which we now turn.

The Citizen's Charter: Raising the Standard?

As the centrepiece of the Conservative Government's public sector agenda for the 1990s, the central importance of the Citizen's Charter is clear, both as something of a "bill of rights and redress" for citizens and as a statement of standards to be maintained for deliverers of public service. Although the Citizen's Charter appealed to the interests and values of the "citizen", it is the citizen as consumer whose interests and values are being addressed. As stated earlier in this chapter, the dynamic for change in public service delivery under the Conservative reform agenda is the creation of market relationships between the providers of public services and their customers. The role of government within this relationship lies in two central responsibilities. First, government sets the broad policy framework for public management, deciding what services will be provided by the public sector and subjecting public service delivery agencies to certain standards of performance. Second, members of the public are empowered as consumers through rights to be provided with a particular standard of service; rights to receive information on the nature of services and the performance of the public sector agencies delivering these services; rights to articulate choices and preferences over public services; and rights to redress should they be unhappy with the standard of services received.

The empowerment of the citizen under the Citizen's Charter was to be achieved through a programme of public sector reform directed toward the *quality* of public services. The relationship between government and its citizens was to be determined through changes in the way in which service delivery was managed, with the emphasis placed firmly on the concept of customer satisfaction. The Citizen's Charter was characterised by an optimistic view of the role of the public sector and a predominant concern with "raising the standard" of service delivery across the range of public sector activities (Prior, 1995). This improvement in the standard of public service provision was viewed as deriving primarily from managerial reform, with its emphasis on a direct relationship between the service provider and the customer, the main indicator of quality of service being determined by measures of "customer satisfaction".

The importance of the Citizen's Charter as a central feature of public sector reform lies in its intention to locate the goal of quality and value for money at the heart of public service. Moreover, the first Charter was to serve as a proforma for the development of further charters covering a range of specific services, including education, the National Health

Service, British Rail, public housing and local authority services. As a document, it centres around sets of objectives, themes, principles of public service and a range of mechanisms by which the aims of the Charter are to be achieved. Table 6.2 sets out the different elements of the original Citizen's Charter under these four main headings.

Within the Charter, objectives, themes and principles were advanced as a coherent package though, as will be discussed, the links between them are sometimes less than clear. The main themes of the original document were defined as follows:

- *Standards*: "The citizen must be told what service standards are and be able to act where service is unacceptable".
- *Quality*: The Charter represents "a sustained new programme for improving the quality of public services".
- *Choice*: "Choice, wherever possible, between competing providers, is the best spur to quality improvement".
- *Value for Money*: "The citizen is also a taxpayer; public services must give value for money within a tax bill the nation can afford" (Prime Minister, 1991: 4).

Built on to these central themes are six principles:

Standards: explicit standards, published and prominently displayed at the point of (service) delivery. These standards should invariably include courtesy and helpfulness from staff, accuracy in accordance with statutory entitlements, and a commitment to prompt action, which might be expressed in terms of a target response or waiting time. There should be a clear presumption that standards will be progressively improved as services become more efficient.

Openness: there should be no secrecy about how public services are run, how much they cost, who is in charge, and whether or not they are meeting their standards. Public servants should not be anonymous.

Information: full, accurate information should be readily available, in plain language about what services are being provided. Targets should be published, together with full and audited information about the results achieved. Wherever possible, information should be in comparable form, so that there is a pressure to emulate the best.

Table 6.2: *The Central Elements of the Original Citizen's Charter (Cm 1599)*

OBJECTIVES	THEMES	PRINCIPLES	MECHANISMS
Raising the standard of public services.	Standards.	Standards.	More privitization.
			Wider competition.
Increasing the choice available to citizens.	Choice.	Choice.	Further contracting-out.
Securing better value for money in public service provision.	Value for Money.	Openness.	More performance-related pay.
Extending accountability.	Quality.	Information.	Published performance targets – local and national.
		Non-Discrimination.	Comprehensive publication of information and standards achieved.
		Accessibility.	More effective complaints complaints procedures.
			Tougher and more independent inspectorates.
			Better redress for the citizen when services go badly wrong.

Choice: the public sector should provide choice wherever practicable. The people affected by services should be consulted. Their views about the services should be sought regularly and systematically to inform decisions about what services should be provided.

Non-discrimination: services should be available regardless of race or sex.

Accessibility: services should be run to suit the convenience of customers, not staff. This means flexible opening hours, and telephone inquiry points that direct callers quickly to someone who can help them.
(Prime Minister, 1991: 5).

In addition, the Charter embodies a complaints procedure by which the customer, dissatisfied with the standard or quality of the service received, has a meaningful form of redress. It is a fundamental tenet of charterism that all public services and local authorities have clear and well-publicised complaints procedures which should be accessible, providing the customer with clear information concerning complaint procedures.

These central themes and principles of charterism contained within the original Citizen's Charter were, it must be noted, not "set in stone". They were not intended to be a blueprint for the imposition of a uniform approach to service standards and quality across the public sector. Rather, they were advanced as a framework of ideas around which further charters particular to specific public services could be tailored. Indeed, following the publication of the original Charter in 1991, each public service was required to produce its own charter, setting out details of the rights, quality of service and standards of performance which the customers of that agency could expect. Today, there are 38 charters, each covering a distinct area of public sector activity (Prime Minister, 1994: 1). Among the most notable are the Patient's Charter, covering the National Health Service; the Parent's Charter, covering schools; the Passenger's Charter, covering British Rail; and the Tenant's Charter covering public housing. Each charter is tailored to the specific nature of the public service in question and, in some cases, to specific geographical areas. For example, each of the Patient's, Parent's and Tenant's Charters have separate versions for England, Wales and Scotland, while the Tenant's Charter also has a Northern Ireland version.

THE PATIENT'S CHARTER
The Patient's Charter (Prime Minister, 1991: 10–12) lies at the heart of reform in the National Health Service. As part of the attempt to introduce consumer rights and market disciplines into healthcare

delivery, the Charter sets out for the public what they should expect from the National Health Service. Reductions in waiting times; personal out-patient appointments and a maximum waiting time which patients should have to endure; reduced waiting lists for treatment; greater choice for people in their choice of general practitioner; all these promises embodied within the Patient's Charter set out clearly the rights of patients and the standards of performance for which healthcare deliverers must strive (see Prime Minister, 1994: 5–12).

THE PARENT'S CHARTER

In a similar way, the Parent's Charter (Prime Minister, 1991: 13–14) sets out those rights which parents have in relation to their children's education and the standards which are expected to be met by schools in the delivery of education. The Parent's Charter built upon a number of reforms that were already in place. For example, prior to the Charter, parents enjoyed fuller representation on the governing bodies of schools and greater choice, through open enrolment, as to which school their children could attend. Moreover, through the Local Management of Schools (LMS) initiative in England and Wales, under which principal control of a school's budget is transferred from the local education authority to the head teacher of the school, the accountability of schools to parents was potentially enhanced. Prior to LMS, local education authorities were perceived by many parents to be remote, bureaucratic and not acting in the interests of parents or pupils. With LMS, budgetary decision making was devolved to the school level, with the establishment of clearly defined guidelines as to standards of achievement expected and value for money provided. The Parent's Charter, introduced in 1991, reinforces these developments through the following mechanisms:

- the production, at least annually, of reports on the performance of individual pupils;
- the publishing of clear details of examination results achieved in schools, thereby facilitating easier comparison of performance between schools and giving parents more information on which to base choices on school selection;
- regular and independent inspection of schools, to be conducted by a new agency, the Office for Standards in Education (OFSTED), with results being transmitted to parents (Prime Minister, 1991: 13; see also Prime Minister, 1994: 13–17).

THE PASSENGER'S CHARTER

The Passenger's Charter (Prime Minister, 1991: 17–19; British Rail, 1991), published in the autumn of 1991, is quite straightforward. Under the Charter, passengers are given the right to expect both punctuality and reliability from the service. Within the Passenger's Charter, clear performance standards are set out. For long-distance journeys, 90 percent of trains should arrive at their destination within ten minutes of the scheduled time, and 99 percent of all trains should run. For shorter journeys, 90 percent of trains should arrive within five minutes of their scheduled time and, again, 99 percent of trains should run. Moreover, the Passenger's Charter embodies a strong service ethos, aimed at providing a more personal and friendly service to its travelling public (see Prime Minister, 1994: 22–26).

THE TENANT'S CHARTER

The original Citizen's Charter (Prime Minister, 1991: 15–16) promised "those who prefer to remain as tenants, or cannot yet afford ownership" that a Council Tenant's Charter would be issued with the aim of strengthening their rights in regard to their relationship with local authorities. This Charter was published in February 1992, guaranteeing a number of rights to tenants. Among them, tenants could expect:

- to be provided with information about their local authority's policy on the allocation of properties;
- a written tenancy agreement;
- security of tenure, the right of succession and the right to buy their home following two years of "secure tenancy";
- the right to repair and to carry out improvements;
- the right to exchange homes; and
- the right to receive information on the performance of the local authority in regard to housing management.

Moreover, with specific regard to the maintenance of property, the Tenant's Charter engages with a long-held complaint, namely the delays involved in repairing damages on the part of local authorities. Under the Charter, residents can arrange to have repairs conducted privately and be reimbursed by their local authority up to a maximum of £250.

However, in the case of council housing, the principle of choice enjoyed by parents and patients in education and health care is less applicable. Local authority tenants do have the right to buy their own home, but choice is limited for those who remain in public sector housing. In the words of Flynn (1993: 65), "the public sector has become a residual for people unwilling or unable to buy their own home", and, as such, the power of council house tenants to exercise any significant degree of choice in a housing market is limited.

With the development of "charterism", it is interesting to note how the principles enshrined within the original document were altered in subsequent reports on the Citizen's Charter. In both the first and second reports on the Charter (Prime Minister, 1992, 1994), the "Principles of Public Service" are set out as follows: standards; information and openness; choice and consultation; courtesy and helpfulness; putting things right; and value for money. Thus, commitments to "courtesy and helpfulness" and to "putting things right" have replaced "non-discrimination" and "accessibility" as Charter principles. This is a clear indication of the attempt to place consumer satisfaction at the forefront of public service.

Charterism: Themes and Issues
Underlying all the various charters is a rigorous complaints procedure which provides the dissatisfied customer with direct avenues of redress. After all, in order for a consumerist ethos to operate in the public sector, it is essential that the service user is able to register his or her displeasure if that service fails to meet expectations. As stated in the original Citizen's Charter (Prime Minister, 1991: 42), "it is fundamental that all public services, including local authorities, should have clear and well-publicised complaints procedures". These mechanisms, according to the Charter should:

- be open and accessible, and supported by clearly displayed standards at the point of service;
- provide readily available information about how to complain, and a clearly identified point of contact for doing so;
- provide a code of practice for the handling of complaints. This should include specific targets for dealing with complaints and clear information as to what the customer can do if he or she is dissatisfied with the response of a public sector agency to a complaint.

Within the National Health Service, for example, every hospital and other unit engaged in the provision of health care must publicise the name, address and telephone number of a senior official responsible for dealing with patient complaints. This officer is required to fully investigate the complaint and report the findings of the inquiry to the complainant. In cases where complainants are still not satisfied, they may refer the matter to the Health Service Commissioner (Ombudsman), who is empowered to investigate all complaints of a non-clinical nature and reports directly to Parliament.

When we consider the central components of charterism as a whole, it is difficult, to quote Pollitt (1994: 9), to "get a handle" on the Citizen's Charter. An interesting analysis of the different elements enshrined within the Charter is provided by Pollitt (1994) and Prior (1995). The central arguments advanced by these studies are worth considering in some detail. Prior (1995: 88) views the Citizen's Charter as something of a "curious document. The framework it offers is complex and confusing, with a number of internal ambiguities and inconsistencies". Within the Charter,

> *accountability* appears as one of the four objectives in the introduction, but is not explicitly referred to again; *quality* and *value* are listed in both the objectives and the themes, but do not appear in the principles and do not clearly relate to any of the mechanisms; *choice* is an objective, a theme and a principle, but varies widely in its meaning; and *non-discrimination* is stated as a principle but no mechanisms are identified to realise it.
> (Prior, 1995: 88).

There is no indication within the document as to the interactive relationship purported to exist between these different central components. Indeed, many of these supposedly vital foundations on which charterism is built are implicit within the charter documents. For example, the terms of the Citizen's Charter do establish a relationship between the service provider and the service user, with the provider accountable to the user for service standards. However, the importance of accountability is not clearly stated. When we consider together the objectives enshrined within the Charter, we are provided with no indication as to why these particular aims are regarded to be the most important. As Prior (1995: 89) states,

> if they were intended to relate to fundamental concerns of citizens, it might be expected that they would be grounded in an explicit understanding of citizenship. Instead, the starting point seems to be an assumption that quality, choice, accountability and value are obviously desirable and

compatible aims which do not require justification. . . . Similarly, the implications of such objectives for public policy are not addressed: is choice an appropriate goal in all circumstances?

Furthermore, the existence of so many charters covering a variety of different services gives rise, perhaps understandably, to a complex web of charter forms. In practice, as Pollitt (1994: 12) points out, we have

> a collection of over thirty widely varying documents, some applying only to portions of the UK, and lacking any single definitive list of rights, entitlements and commitments. A further source of complexity is the thorough mixing up – in many of the charters – of pre-existing and new provisions, and of legal rights, administrative regulations and more management promises.

To pursue Pollitt's analysis, the very concept of "charter" is unclear. On a basic level, it is incorrect to speak of "the Charter" given that there are so many in existence. Moreover, it is difficult to glean from these various documents a common set of citizen's rights, duties, entitlements or government commitments in regard to public service provision. Even in regard to the centrepiece of charterism – standards – we find a degree of ambivalence. For Pollitt,

> while the concept itself is as unopposable as virtue, its main value is realised only if the precise status of each standard is defined, and if the consequences of breaching that standard are indicated (1994: 12).

In an interesting assessment of the concept, Pollitt (1994: 12) categorises standards into *minimum, average* and *best practice*. A minimum standard is one which requires to be maintained at all times. An average standard serves as a norm, a level which a public service should seek to attain on average. Best practice standards are aspired to in that they are standards for which public service providers will strive but which will not normally be maintained. The important point is that the performance of agencies in respect of these categorisations may differ significantly. For instance, minimum standards might be rising in a particular service area while average standards are falling. This situation is identified by some in relation to the recent performance of the National Health Service (O'Sullivan, 1992). In a similar fashion, minimum and average standards might both be increasing while the number of service units providing best practice is declining. In terms of the rights of consumers, such information is rarely available, since the charters often fail to identify which category of standard is being addressed in the document. To follow Pollitt's analysis to its conclusion,

> it is reasonably clear that all these types make their appearance in one place or another, but if there is any overall pattern or logic to their distribution it is not apparent from the face of the charter documents. (Pollitt, 1994; 12).

Finally, within the charters, the concept of "citizen" is given insufficient attention. Indeed, we can gather no general notion of the citizen from any of the charters currently in force. There are various references to users, customers or consumers, jobseekers, patients, passengers and parents. However, these are not citizens. The role of consumer entails a particular position within a network of market relationships. To be a citizen is to be a member of a political community. This embraces a wider role, comprising a range of political relationships which link the individual with government and the state.

In addition to these specific anomalies, the Citizen's Charter has been the subject of some political criticism. It has been attacked as little more than a public relations exercise or as something which does little more than "paper over the cracks" of the public sector. Nevertheless, notwithstanding these various anomalies and criticisms, the Citizen's Charter and its "children" remain the centrepiece of the Conservative Government's public service agenda for the 1990s and beyond.

In its implementation, charterism represents a more substantive political development than its critics appear to realise. In placing the responsibility for service delivery squarely in the hands of public sector managers, it establishes a direct relationship between the providers of public services and their customers, with the balance of power deemed to lie primarily with the customer. As such, though not stated explicitly, the Charter embodies an approach to accountability quite different in form and application to the more traditional forms of political accountability which bind governments to the public they serve, namely a managerial accountability which renders the providers of public services directly accountable to their customers through the mechanisms of quality assurance and redress enshrined within the Charter. This developing direct accountability of officials to customers may be viewed as a complement to the *de facto* accountability of civil servants to Parliament, as observed in Chapter 2.

Moreover, prior to the advent of charters, there were in many cases no public statements of what standards of service the public had a right to expect from public sector agencies. For example, before the publication of the Passenger's Charter, British Rail did not make public its punctuality and reliability targets. The very fact that it is now taken for granted that there should be published targets is perhaps an indication that the charter concept is beginning to take hold in the public sector. A further positive aspect of charterism lies in the original charters' status as a "baseline". The first charters established initial performance targets with the expectation that each subsequent year would see those targets improved. Each individual charter has or will be updated and reissued, containing a commitment to higher standards of service. In the area of public complaint and redress, the Citizen's Charter Unit, located in Downing Street, launched in 1993 a Citizen's Charter Complaints Task Force, charged with conducting a two-year review of the public service complaints system. This task force is scheduled to report its findings and recommendations in Summer 1995.

Alongside the question of complaints is the question of communication. In 1993, a telephone information helpline – "Charterline" – was established as a pilot scheme in the East Midlands. The role of Charterline was not to solve individual problems. rather, it was to provide members of the public with information regarding exactly who they should contact in respect of particular problems they were experiencing with public service delivery. In addition, Charterline provided basic information concerning services, service standards, and details of the Citizen's Charter. However, this service did not proceed beyond the pilot scheme. It was cancelled on ministerial advice due to its failure to contribute significantly to increasing public awareness of the Charters. Indeed, the experience of the pilot scheme gave little encouragement for a national charterline. To quote Pyper (1995: 134–5),

> it dealt with only 25 calls per day, at a cost to the taxpayer of £68 for each enquiry. To make matters worse, some of the callers seemed to have misunderstood the purpose of the exercise. One man rang to find out how he could take a sperm test. Another, who had apparently been pestered by his mother to the point of distraction, wanted to know how he could become a monk! The under-worked telephone operator obliged by providing the number of a local monastery.

A more significant element of charterism is that of the "Chartermark", launched in 1992. Each year, the Prime Minister's Citizen Charter Advisory Panel awards Chartermarks to those public sector agencies which demonstrate, in competition with other agencies, a measurable improvement is service quality. Chartermarks are given to those public sector agencies which successfully achieve a number of specific standards:

- publication of the standards of service that the customers can reasonably expect, and of performance against those standards;
- evidence that the views of those who use the service have been taken into account when standards are set;
- clear information about the range of services provided;
- courteous and efficient customer service from staff who are required normally to identify themselves by name;
- well-signposted avenues for complaint should the customer be dissatisfied, with some procedure for independent review wherever possible; and
- and an independent validation of performance against standards and a clear commitment to value for money.

In the first year, 1992, 36 Chartermarks were awarded in a field of 296 applicants. In 1993, 93 were awarded out of a field of 411 competitors, and in 1994 the figures were 98 and 520 respectively. The Citizen's Charter Unit is inundated with queries from public sector bodies pursuing the Chartermark. In 1994, for example, over 20,000 "expressions of interest" were received. In response to these requests, the Citizen's Charter Unit issues documentary material indicating what standards and level of performance are sought from a potential Chartermark winner. In addition, seminars are held, again to advise interested parties of the standards expected and of the "entry requirements". This process causes a number of potential entrants to rethink their grounds for application. For instance, in 1994, as stated, more than 20,000 expressions of interest resulted in 520 formal applications. For the first time in 1995, members of the public were given the opportunity to nominate public sector agencies for the Chartermark. Public nominations closed on 31st May, at which time more than 4,000 nominations had been received. It is important to note that Chartermarks can be withdrawn if, having been granted a Chartermark, an agency fails to maintain its level of service. In 1995, for example, British Gas was threatened with the loss of its Chartermark.

216 Charterism and Consumerism

Conclusion: Charterism – an Early Assessment

Although we are still in the early stages of a developing ten-year programme, we can report some early observations on the progress of charterism in the public sector. A 1993 ICM market research survey on public opinion (ICM, 1993), funded by the Major Government, painted an optimistic picture of the early progress of the charters (Pollitt, 1994: 13; Beale and Pollitt, 1994: 215). This survey, based on a sample of 3,097 adults drawn from 630 randomly-chosen areas, found that, while a majority of people are aware of the Citizen's Charter, few have any significant knowledge of its contents or purpose. Moreover, with the exception of the Patient's Charter and the Passenger's Charter, a majority of those surveyed possessed no detailed knowledge of other charters in existence. Beale and Pollitt's (1994) own research supports these findings. However, with regard to the question of service quality, the findings of the ICM survey and those of Beale and Pollitt differ. The ICM survey found that, in each of the 28 public services investigated, "a majority of users thought that the service had improved or maintained standards over the previous year" (quoted, Beale and Pollitt, 1994: 215). Beale and Pollitt's research criticised the nature of the questions posed by the ICM survey, arguing that they were more geared toward what citizens would like to see happen in the future rather than with their views on the present standards of public service. Beale and Pollitt detected no perception on the part of their respondents of any significant change in the quality of public service delivery.

A survey conducted in May and June 1994 by the Scottish Office (Scottish Office, 1994) into the performance of the Patient's Charter in Scotland found, like the ICM survey, that patients were highly satisfied with the standards of service received under the Charter. For example, eight out of ten people were satisfied with waiting times, while nine out of ten were pleased with the information they were given. In a similar vein, eight out of ten were happy with the amount of involvement and choice they enjoyed in relation to their health care (Scottish Office, 1994: 6). However, in the crucial area of complaints procedures, the survey showed that people are still highly unsure about how to register complaints, and that those who do complain are still far from satisfied with the way in which their complaint is dealt.

For Pollitt (1994: 13), a disturbing fact facing "charter enthusiasts" is the finding that "many of the quality improvements that *have* been achieved have little to do with the charter". A large number of these improvements had resulted from legislative requirements, financial pressures or local initiatives which had been implemented before the Citizen's Charter was born (see Beale and Pollitt, 1993; Vittles, 1993). Indeed, the introduction of charters was perceived, in some cases, as having a detrimental effect on service provision. The Charter

> sought bureaucrats where there were no longer any to find. Those organisations which were already embarking upon cultural change and well down the road to citizen-orientation found themselves being preached at by people who knew far less about serving local residents . . . In some organisations like the new Trust hospitals (for example), Charters were being "forced" upon the staff and public alike.
> (Vittles, 1993: 2).

Pollitt does lend a qualification to such a conclusion. After all, charterism cannot be said to have brought about no positive changes. The wearing of name badges identifying public servants, for instance, and the improvements in complaints procedures have been welcome additions to the process of service delivery in the public sector. Moreover, local managers have been able to employ charters as mechanisms by which improvements already in place could be enhanced.

At the time of writing, charterism is in its fourth year and remains at the centre of the Conservative Government's public sector reform agenda for the 1990s and beyond. Consequently, it is promoted expensively by the Government and its existence is now well-known to the vast majority of the general public. Moreover, even in the event of a change of government in 1996 or 1997, there is no indication in the policy statements of either the Labour Party or the Liberal Democrats towards the public sector to suggest that charterism would be abandoned. Yet, despite its perceived importance, it is still a complex phenomenon in its application, embodying elements and procedures with which the average citizen is far from conversant. Furthermore, as discussed above, the Charter is, in many respects, conceptually confused, with "many of its proclaimed standards lack[ing] either legal standing or clear penalties for failure, or both" (Pollitt, 1994: 13). At this stage, empirical evidence on the performance of the charters is far from conclusive, though the indication is that charterism has to date enjoyed only a limited success.

In conclusion, charterism has significant implications for accountability. With its development, the relationship between citizens and those responsible for providing public services has become more complex. Today, traditional forms of political accountability have been complemented by a more direct form of accountability which is more managerial than political. In this sense, it is public sector managers who are accountable for the standards of public services, not government ministers who view themselves as responsible only for setting the broad policy guidelines for public sector activity. However, it is important that this new managerial accountability develops alongside, and not as a replacement for, political accountability. Public sector agencies may be directly accountable, through the Citizen's Charter, to consumers and, as such, serve as "buffers" between consumers and government ministers. However, these government ministers must still accept ultimate responsibility to consumers as citizens.

References

Audit Commission (1994), *Read All About It: Guidance on the Publication by Local Authorities of the Citizen's Charter Indicators*, London: HMSO.

Audit Commission (1995), *Local Authority Performance Indicators*, Vols. 1, 2 and 3, London: HMSO.

Bailey, Stephen, Falconer, Peter and McChlery, Stuart (1993), *Local Government Charges: Policy and Practice*, London: Longman.

Beale, Valerie and Pollitt, Christopher (1994), "Charters at the Grass Roots: a First Report", *Local Government Studies*, 20, 2. Common, Richard, Flynn, Norman and Elizabeth Mellon (1993), *Managing Public Services: Competition and Decentralization*, Oxford: Butterworth Heinemann.

British Rail (1991), *The Passenger's Charter*, London: British Rail.

Doern, G. Bruce (1993), "The U. K. Citizen's Charter: Origins and Implementation in Three Agencies", *Policy and Politics*, 21, 1.

Farnham, David (1991) "The Citizen's Charter: Improving the Quality of the Public Services or Furthering Market Values?", *Talking Politics*, Winter.

Flynn, Norman (1993), *Public Sector Management*, London: Harvester Wheatsheaf.

Gaster, Lucy (1995), *Quality in Public Services: Managers' Choice*, Buckingham: Open University Press.

Gyford, John (1994), "Consumerism and Citizenship", in Tam, Henry (ed), *Marketing, Competition and the Public Sector*, Harlow: Longman.

Hinton, Peter. and Wilson, Elizabeth. (1993), "Accountability", in Wilson, John and Hinton, Peter (eds), *Public Services in the 1990s*, Sevenoaks: Tudor Press.

Holliday, Ian (1992), *The NHS Transformed*, Manchester: Baseline Books.

ICM (1993), *Citizen's Charter Customer Survey*, ICM Research.

Isaac-Henry, Kester, Painter, Christopher and Barnes, Christopher (1993), *Management in the Public Sector: Challenge and Change*, London: Chapman and Hall.

Lawton, Alan and Rose, Aidan (1991), *Organisation and Management in the Public Sector*, London: Pitman.

Mather, Graeme (1989), "Thatcherism and Local Government: an Evaluation", in Stewart, John D. and Stoker, Gerry (eds), *The Future of Local Government*, London: Macmillan.

Major, John (1989), *Public Sector Management: the Revolution in Progress*, London: Audit Commission.

Milne, Robin G. (1987), "Compulsory Competitive Tendering in the National Health Service", *Public Administration*, 65, 2.

Murray, Ian (1995), "How Your Council Rates in Efficiency League", *The Times*, 30th March.

National Audit Office (1987), *Competitive Tendering for Support Services in the National Health Service*, London: HMSO.

O'Sullivan, Jack (1992), "NHS Operations Delayed by Charter", *The Independent*, 5th March 1992.

Pollitt, Christopher (1988), "Bringing Consumers Into Performance Measurement", *Policy and Politics*, 16, 2.

Pollitt, Christopher (1993), *Managerialism and the Public Services*, Oxford: Basil Blackwell.

Pollitt, Christopher (1994), "The Citizen's Charter: a Preliminary Analysis", *Public Money and Management*, April-June.

Prime Minister (1991), *The Citizen's Charter: Raising the Standard?*, Cm 1599, London: HMSO.

Prime Minister (1992), *The Citizen's Charter: First Report*, Cm 1730, London: HMSO.

Prime Minister (1994), *The Citizen's Charter: Second Report*, Cm 2540, London: HMSO.

Prior, David (1995), "Citizen's Charters", in Stewart, John D. and Stoker, Gerry, *Local Government in the 1990s*, Basingstoke: Macmillan.

Pyper, Robert (1995), *The British Civil Service*, Hemel Hempstead: Prentice Hall/Harvester Wheatsheaf.

Scottish Office (1994), *The National Health Service in Scotland: the Patient's Charter – What Users Think*, Scottish Office.

Stewart, John D. and Walsh, Keiron. (1992), "Change in the Management of Public Services", *Public Administration*, 70, 4.

Tam, Henry (1994), "Exposing the Public Sector to Market Forces", in *Marketing, Competition and the Public Sector*, Harlow: Longman.

Timmons, Nicholas (1995), "Council Performance Figures: League Tables Aim to Spur Local Debate", *The Independent*, 30th March.

Vittles, Paul (1993), "Beyond the Rhetoric of the Citizen's Charter", paper presented at the annual conference of the Public Administration Committee of the Joint University Council, University of York.

Walsh, Kieron (1991), "Quality and Public Services", *Public Administration*, 69, 4.

Walsh, Kieron (1994), "Citizens, Markets and Contracts", in Keat, Russell, Whitely, N. and Abercrombie, Nicholas. (eds), *The Authority of the Consumer*, London: Routledge.

Walsh, Kieron (1995), *Public Services and Market mechanisms: Competition, Contracting Out and the New Public Management*, Basingstoke: Macmillan.

Walsh, Kieron and Davis, Howard (1993), *Competition and Service: the Impact of the Local Government Act 1988*, London, HMSO.

Willcocks, Leslie and Harrow, Jenny (1992), *Rediscovering Public Services Management*, London: Chapman and Hall.

Conclusion

THE LIMITS OF ACCOUNTABILITY

Robert Pyper

In the course of this book it has become clear that accountability, in the real world of British government, can be defined in part by the limits which are placed upon it. Although it occupies a prominent place in political rhetoric and practice, true accountability often seems to be an aspiration which lacks fulfilment. This is not to say that British government at all levels and in every form is "unaccountable": such a conclusion would be at odds with the evidence presented in the foregoing chapters. Nonetheless, as in any system of government, what we find in Britain is a form of bounded, or delimited accountability. It is possible for us to classify the limits of accountability in the British system with reference to four interlinked factors:

- inadequate or dysfunctional mechanisms of accountability.
- developmental trends in the executive, which effectively outstrip the evolution of mechanisms of accountability.
- some forms of accountability may be deemed to be more important than others.
- the supersession of accountability by another imperative.
  Let us comment upon these factors in turn.

Inadequate or Dysfunctional Mechanisms of Accountability
In Chapter 1, Allan McConnell argued that "popular" mechanisms of accountability (elections, parties, pressure groups and the media) can hinder as well as promote accountability. To some extent, this inherent duality lies at the heart of all mechanisms of accountability. This is due, in part, to the imperatives of *Realpolitik*, which will be mentioned again in due course, but it can also be ascribed to failings in the mechanisms themselves. Such failings may be caused either by fundamental inadequacies in the mechanisms, or by dysfunction.

Inadequate mechanisms are handicapped by their limited scope or jurisdiction and/or by the limited nature of the powers allocated to them. For example, as we saw in Chapters 2 and 3, early critics of the Parliamentary Commissioner for Administration scheme drew attention to the exclusions from his remit and the lack of enforcement powers in relation to his proposed remedies. While we might conclude that, in practice, the PCA functioned effectively and often overcame these inherent inadequacies, the general point we are seeking to establish should be clear.

In the case of dysfunctional mechanisms, the jurisdiction and powers *per se* are not the problem, but the practical operation of the mechanism is flawed to such an extent that accountability is diluted to some degree. There may be evidence of a lack of preparedness to use the mechanism's powers to full effect, or weaknesses in personnel. An appropriate example here would be a House of Commons select committee which is blighted by high membership turnover, bitter partisanship amongst the members and poor chairmanship. Consequently, the ministers and civil servants in the department of state (and its agencies) being monitored may be given an easier ride than would otherwise be the case. Similarly, as we saw in Chapter 5, the idiosyncrasies of a Director General of one of the utility regulatory agencies can result in a limited or slanted construction being placed upon the agency's remit, with the consequence that the utility is exposed to a less rigorous form of accountability.

Developmental Trends in the Executive
If systems of accountability are to function effectively, they must be able to keep up with the pace of development set by the executive. Occasionally, in some spheres, the form and responsibilities of government may change (either incrementally or radically) in such a manner that an accountability "gap" is created, due to the failure of mechanisms of scrutiny to develop (or to be developed) in an appropriate fashion.

One illustration of this relates to the increasing utilisation of quangos in the early 1990s. There is considerable debate about the nature and form of these bodies, and, indeed, about the extent to which their numbers are increasing (Hogwood, 1995; Wilson, 1995). Nonetheless, most analysts seem to agree that there has been a marked tendency over recent years on the part of central government to assign advisory and executive functions to unelected boards comprised of ministerial appointees. Housing Action Trusts, the Funding Agency for Schools, Training and Enterprise Councils, Local Enterprise Companies, and NHS Trusts can be located in this category. The capacity of local government and Parliament to keep up with these developments, and to enforce effective accountability, has been severely tested. Considerable variations exist between quangos in terms of appointment procedures, rights of access to meetings and the publication of policy statements and financial accounts, and these have served to make the task of enforcing accountability even more complex (Hirst, 1995; Local Government Chronicle, 1994; Weir, 1995). Greatest concern has arisen in cases where a function or service was formerly provided in whole or in part by an elected authority, but has been handed over to an unelected quango. Critics argue that this replaces a form of local accountability (albeit one which may have been attenuated and incomplete) with a vague accountability to the centre and a vacuum at the locality.

The development of the executive in another sense, through membership of the European Union, has also created an accountability gap. Largely due to the fact that it is a supra-national entity, which was created and moulded by governments, not parliaments, the European Union does not readily lend itself to parliamentary modes of accountability. Thus, although the policies emanating from the Council of Ministers and the Commission have had a steadily increasing impact on Britain (and all the member states), Parliament has failed to keep up with the pace of executive development. The mechanisms of scrutiny available to MPs have been subject to remarkably little change since Britain's accession to the Community in 1973.

It is true to say that Parliament exercises ultimate control over major constitutional change, in the sense that any amendments to the founding treaties of the Union must be approved at Westminster (examples of this would be the ratification of the Single European Act in 1986 and the Treaty on European Union in 1993). However, Parliament's role in scrutinising the more routine products of the Brussels machinery is rather limited. The European Communities Act of 1972 established the supremacy of European law, and made clear the fact that the assent of Parliament was not required for specific European measures. The mechanisms utilized by Parliament in its attempt to monitor burgeoning executive activity in this sphere are: debates, select committees and standing committees.

Until 1991, nearly all European documents were debated on the floor of the House of Commons (Norton, 1993:120). These debates were usually scheduled late at night, and were very poorly attended (Adonis, 1990: 180; Grantham and Hodgson, 1985: 124). Since then, due to the increased utilization of standing committees, less time has been spent debating documents, and debates have tended to focus on the general issues likely to arise at the six-monthly meetings of the heads of government in the European Council (Norton, 1993: 121). Inevitably, these sessions are dominated by broad-brush political debate rather than detailed scrutiny.

The departmental select committees of the House of Commons can examine any European issues related to the functioning of "their" departments. However, given the range of departmental work they are charged with scrutinising, the committees devote relatively little time and resources specifically to EU work (Norton, 1993: 121).

Parliament attempts to enforce detailed accountability for European business through two heavily pressurised select committees, the House of Commons Select Committee on European Legislation and the House of Lords European Communities Committee. The Commons' committee considers draft proposals emanating from the Commission, and seeks to identify those which require further consideration by one of the two European Standing Committees of the House of Commons. (In 1989 the Procedure Committee recommended the appointment of five standing committees, the government agreed to allow three, but by 1991 enough members could only be found for two committees). The 16 members of the Select Committee on European Legislation face a mountainous task: the committee examines between 600 and 900 highly technical documents each year (Norton, 1993: 118).

The House of Lords' European Communities Committee has a wider remit than its Commons' equivalent. This select committee operates through a range of subject-based sub-committees (involving a total of about 70 peers), which not only examine EU documents, but discuss the merits of Union legislation, conduct inquiries and produce reports containing specific recommendations (Adonis, 1990: 150–51; Grantham and Hodgson, 1985: 118–129; Norton, 1993: 122–24). Nonetheless, despite producing widely-respected work of high quality, the Lords' committee cannot possibly do justice to the increasing waves of law and policy emanating from the EU institutions.

In sum, therefore, the conclusion reached by informed analysts is inevitably the same: Parliament's attempts to enforce accountability in the sphere of EU matters are worthy, but beset with fundamental difficulties related to the executive-dominated characteristics of the Brussels machine. Philip Norton encapsulates the accountability deficit: "the role of the UK Parliament is the same as that of other national

Parliaments: sporadic and operating largely at the margins." (Norton, 1983: 128).

Some Forms of Accountability Deemed More Important Than Others

In Chapter 4, Allan Bruce and Allan McConnell offered an interpretation of the changes which have taken place in accountability within local government and the National Health Service over recent years. A close reading of their argument leads one to the conclusion that a specific strand of accountability in these spheres, political accountability downwards to "the public" and service users, has come to be given considerably less emphasis than managerial accountability upwards, to central government. Thus, the roles played by the Audit and Accounts Commissions have loomed ever larger, and the centrally-devised mantra of economy, efficiency and effectiveness has come to ring out with increased volume. At the same time, the scope for locally-elected representatives to vary service provision in accordance with locally-determined priorities (and to be held accountable for such variations locally) has diminished.

As Peter Falconer demonstrated in Chapter 6, new forms of managerial accountability have emerged via "charterism and consumerism". He made an important point when arguing that the new managerial accountability should be allowed to develop alongside, and not as a replacement for, more traditional political accountability.

One is led to the conclusion that accountability may be limited, by accident or design, by placing greater emphasis on the need for parts of the system of government to account to the centre, rather than to the locality, or by attaching more importance to one strand of accountability than to others. Of course, we are not saying that accountability to the centre and to the locality are necessarily incompatible: one might argue that the process of strengthening the accountability of local government and the NHS to central government has positive merits and might even expand rather than limit accountability. Nonetheless, the manner in which the new regimes of managerial accountability to the centre have been introduced in these spheres is such that accountability to the centre has a clear pre-eminence over all other forms. More generally, the emphasis given to managerial accountability in the new wave of charterism and consumerism ought to ring some alarm bells unless it can be clearly demonstrated that accountability in this form is not being enhanced at the expense of accountability in other forms.

Supersession of Accountability by Another Imperative

The principles embodied in the concept of accountable government can become irksome to politicians faced with the strongly competing demands of other imperatives. In particular, official secrecy and *Realpolitik* have a marked tendency to squeeze out accountability. This can be illustrated with brief reference to a small number of indicative cases.

The demands of power politics have occasionally ensured that mechanisms of accountability are effectively neutered, or even abolished. One of the clearest examples of this came in the wake of the 1987 General Election, when the Scottish Affairs Select Committee of the House of Commons fell victim to a prolonged argument between the parties over the matter of composition. As a result of the continuing political manoeuvres of the parties, the Committee was not established for that Parliament, with the consequence that the Scottish Office escaped the type of detailed scrutiny to which virtually every other government department was subjected, until the Committee was revived following the 1992 General Election (McConnell and Pyper, 1994;, McConnell and Pyper, 1994a).

It is more common for the penchant of central government ministers for secrecy and *Realpolitik* to produce a limitation of accountability through an effective refusal to answer or explain a particular event in sufficient detail (a substantial dilution of Marshall's "explanatory accountability"), or through an avoidance of sanctions (that is, a refusal to resign).

In the introductory chapter, it was argued that the concept of accountability could be differentiated from that of answerability by virtue of the fact that the former connotes the possibility of sanctions being invoked when answers are unsatisfactory or problematic, and a preparedness to deliver redress of grievances in cases of proven error. At the ministerial level of British government, studies of particular cases and patterns of ministerial resignations (Finer, 1956; Pyper, 1983; 1987; 1991; 1992; 1993, 1994; Woodhouse 1993; 1994) have revealed that sanctions are imposed in a fashion which owes much to political factors (including the standing of the minister concerned with his or her party at local level, in Parliament, and with the ministerial colleagues in general and the prime minister in particular). The imperative of *Realpolitik* has a tendency to override the theoretical requirements of accountability.

In a similar vein, redress of grievances is not always forthcoming when political factors intervene. Although the remedies prescribed by Commissioners for Local Administration, the Health Service Commissioner and the Parliamentary Commissioner for Administration are usually accepted and speedily implemented by the relevant government bodies, this is not invariably the case.

Even the weaker, diluted form of accountability, mere answerability or "explanatory accountability", can be circumscribed by the demands of official secrecy and *Realpolitik*. In this context, we can cite the case of Clive Ponting, the Westland affair, and the Matrix Churchill "Arms for Iraq" affair. A recurring theme here is the apparent willingness of ministers (occasionally aided by senior officials) to mislead individual MPs, select committees, and the House of Commons as a whole. False trails were laid in an attempt to confuse MPs seeking the truth about the sinking of the *General Belgrano* during the Falklands War (Ponting, 1985). Parliament was denied access to key witnesses during the investigation into the Westland affair, which had culminated in the resignation of two Cabinet ministers (Linklater and Leigh, 1986; Madgwick and Woodhouse, 1989; Pyper, 1987a). At the time of writing, the denouement of the Matrix Churchill "Arms for Iraq" affair is not known. However, even at this stage, there is already enough evidence in the public domain for us to draw the conclusion that offering accurate explanations of policy changes and the course of events to Parliament did not figure very highly in the priorities of ministers and senior civil servants (Adams and Pyper, 1994–5; Leigh, 1993; Norton-Taylor, 1995).

Remedies?
Would it be possible to overcome these limitations to effective accountability? As we saw at the end of Chapter 2, when discussing the deficiencies in the system of Parliamentary accountability, there is a fundamental distinction to be drawn between those who believe that meaningful improvements can only come about through substantive and broadly-based constitutional change, and those who believe that continuous fine-tuning of existing mechanisms, coupled with further structural reforms and behavioural change, can lead to improvement. What was true of Parliamentary accountability is also true more generally.

There are times when it seems that the proponents of root and branch constitutional reform envisage an apolitical polity (if this is not a contradiction in terms!) In their ideal world, where the systems are flawless and government is invariably held fully accountable for its every thought and deed, there could be no serious limitations on accountability. Yet, as we have argued here, *Realpolitik*, and crude political manoeuvring can act as limits on accountability. No one would argue that this is entirely acceptable, but the British system of government which forms the major target for these constitutional reformers, is not unique amongst liberal democracies in facilitating the interplay of power politicians. This is an inherent part of practical government and politics. In the same vein, is clear that all executives have a propensity to develop in ways which outstrip (in some cases temporarily) the capacity of systems of accountability to cope: this is as true in states with written constitutions as it is anywhere else! The blueprints for perfect systems of accountability all too often seem to be characterized by a combination of idealism and naivety, which envisages government without the politics. In addition, the new constitutionalists have a tendency to confuse the failings they associate with an extended period of single-party government, with perceived systemic deficiencies.

It is less "exciting" and "dramatic" (and increasingly unfashionable to boot!) to put the argument in favour of the evolutionary approach to enhanced accountability. Nonetheless, it is probably more realistic to work for improvements within the existing system than to place one's faith in the unpredictable outcomes of fundamental constitutional reform. After all, for all the failings and limitations of the extant arrangements for accountability in the British system of government, we already have sufficient evidence of the capacity of organs of scrutiny to evolve quite effectively, while exhibiting the potential for still further improvement. (Examine the development of House of Commons select committees over the period since 1966, or the steady expansion of the system of ombudsmen since 1967, for proof of this).

There are no simple and easy remedies for the limitations upon effective accountability. The task is to constantly expand, modernise and improve the mechanisms of scrutiny at all levels, while engendering attitudes of serious inquiry and vigilance in those who are charged with the task of operating these mechanisms.

References

Adams, Juliet and Pyper, Robert (1994–5), "A Guide to the Scott Inquiry: An Exposition of Truths, Half-Truths and Nothing Like the Truth", *Talking Politics*, Volume 7, Number 2, Winter.

Adonis, Andrew (1990), *Parliament Today*, Manchester: Manchester University Press.

Finer, S. E. (1956), "The Individual Responsibility of Ministers", *Public Administration*, Volume 34, Winter.

Grantham, Cliff and Hodgson, Caroline Moore (1985), "Structural Changes", in Norton, Philip (ed), *Parliament in the 1980s*, Oxford: Basil Blackwell.

Hirst, Paul (1995), "Quangos and Democratic Government", *Parliamentary Affairs*, Volume 48, Number 2, April.

Hogwood, Brian (1995), "The 'Growth' of Quangos: Evidence and Experience", *Parliamentary Affairs*, Volume 48, Number 2, April.

Leigh, David (1993), *Betrayed. The Real Story of the Matrix Churchill Trial*, London: Bloomsbury.

Linklater, Magnus and Leigh, David (1987), *Not With Honour. The Inside Story of the Westland Scandal*, London: Sphere.

Local Government Chronicle, (1994) *The Governance Gap: Quangos and Accountability*, London: Local Government Chronicle and the Joseph Rowntree Foundation.

Madgwick, Peter and Woodhouse, Diana (1989) "The Westland Affair: Helicopter Crashes into British Constitution", *Social Studies Review*, March.

McConnell, Allan and Pyper, Robert (1994), "A Committee Again: The First Year of the Revived Select Committee on Scottish Affairs", *Scottish Affairs*, Number 7, Spring.

McConnell, Allan and Pyper, Robert (1994a), "The Revived Select Committee on Scottish Affairs: A Case Study of Parliamentary Contradictions", *Strathclyde Papers on Government and Politics Number 98*, Glasgow: University of Strathclyde.

Norton, Philip (1993), *Does Parliament Matter?*, Hemel Hempstead: Harvester Wheatsheaf.

Norton-Taylor, Richard (1995), *Truth is a Difficult Concept: Inside the Scott Inquiry*, London: Fourth Estate.

Ponting, Clive (1985), *The Right To Know. The Inside Story of the Belgrano Affair*, London: Sphere.

Pyper, Robert (1983), "The Foreign Office Resignations: Individual Ministerial Responsibility Revived?", *Teaching Politics*, Volume 12, Number 2, May.

Pyper, Robert (1987), *The Doctrine of Individual Ministerial Responsibility in British Government: Theory and Practice in a New Regime of Parliamentary Accountability*, Unpublished PhD. Thesis, University of Leicester.

Pyper, Robert (1987a), "The Westland Affair", *Teaching Politics*, Volume 16, Number 3, September.

Pyper, Robert (1991), "Ministerial Departures from British Governments, 1964–90: A Survey", *Contemporary Record*, Volume 5, Number 2, Autumn.

Pyper, Robert (1992), "Apportioning Responsibility or Passing the Buck?: The Strange Cases of Mr Baker, Mr Prior and the Disappearing Prisoners", *Teaching Public Administration*, Volume 12, Number 2, Autumn.

Pyper, Robert (1993), "When They Have to Go . . . Why Ministers Resign", *Talking Politics*, Volume 5, Number 2, Winter.

Pyper, Robert (1994), "Passing the Buck to Officials", *Parliamentary Brief*, Volume 3, Number 1, October.

Weir, Stuart (1995), "Quangos: Questions of Democratic Accountability", *Parliamentary Affairs*, Volume 48, Number 2, April.

Wilson, David (1995), "Quangos in the Skeletal State", *Parliamentary Affairs*, Volume 48, Number 2, April.

Woodhouse, Diana (1993), "Ministerial Responsibility in the 1990s: When Do Ministers Resign?", *Parliamentary Affairs*, Volume 46, Number 3, July 1993.

Woodhouse, Diana (1994), *Ministers and Parliament: Accountability in Theory and Practice* , Oxford: Oxford University Press.

Index